AFTERLIFE

Other books by Morton Kelsey

Tongue Speaking

God, Dreams and Revelation

Encounter with God

Healing and Christianity

Myth, History and Faith

The Christian and the Supernatural

The Other Side of Silence: A Guide to Christian Meditation

Can Christians Be Educated?: A Proposal for Effective Communication of Our Christian Religion

The Hinge: Meditations on the Cross

The Age of Miracles

Dreams: A Way To Listen to God

Tales To Tell: Legends of the Senecas

Booklets by Morton Kelsey

The Art of Christian Love

The Reality of the Spiritual World

Finding Meaning: Guidelines For Counselors

AFTERLIFE

The Other Side of Dying

Morton Kelsey

PAULIST PRESS
New York/Ramsey/Toronto

To my friends
Peter and Margie
and their family

BT902

K37

Library of Congress
Catalog Card Number: 79-90224

ISBN: 0-8091-0296-X

Published by Paulist Press
Editorial Office: 1865 Broadway, New York, N. Y. 10023
Business Office: 545 Island Road, Ramsey, N. J. 07446

Printed and bound in the
United States of America

Contents

Introduction

Everyone dies. Everyone meets death. There are few statements which apply to every human being, but these do. Death is one of the greatest crises in the life of each of us. Indeed the conscious knowledge that we die is one of the crucial factors which separate us from the animals who share so much of our biology and our psychology.

From the earliest times mankind has reacted to death with awe and fear. Edgar Herzog has traced clearly the meaning of death among primitive people in his book *Psyche and Death*. Death represents the unknown, the vast world of darkness, the world of spirit. Death stands before emerging human beings as *the* great problem. One of the reasons they make an incredible struggle to survive is to avoid the frightening prospect which death represents.

Most of the religions of humankind have offered some solution to the problem of death. Christianity is no exception. One of the key beliefs of the early Church was the conviction that the followers of Jesus shared in his victory over death, shared in some significant way in his resurrection. The early Christians outlived, outfought and outdied the ancient world because of a conviction that their lives went on into greater meaning. They even believed that they had tasted something of the reality of the future kingdom of heaven in their experiences of their risen Lord.

Recent Christian theology has not shared very deeply in this hope. Some theologians who consider themselves Christian have expressly denied that belief in life after death is an essential part of the Christian world-view. Gordon Kaufman writes the following

statement about life after death in his *Systematic Theology*, a book used
in many liberal seminaries: "For individuals die in a matter of a few
years!—and we have no reason to suppose that their life continues
beyond the grave."[1] In his book *The Reality of God* Schubert Ogden
comes to the same conclusion. He writes that "what I must refuse to
accept, precisely as a Christian theologian, is that belief in our
subjective existence after death is in some way a necessary article of
Christian belief."[2] Even the more conservative theologians like John
Macquarrie in his *Principles of Christian Theology* fail to show much
conviction about a life after death. Dr. Paul Badham of St. David's
University College has summarized much of the recent thinking
concerning life after death in an article in the April 1977 issue of *The
Expository Times*. He concludes that, on the whole, Christian theology
has avoided the subject of life after death or else it has come out on
the side of Kaufman and Ogden.

Does it make any difference what we believe about what
happens to us after death? It makes a great deal of difference. How
we look at death determines a great deal of how we live in this
world. Jung has stated that meaninglessness is really a disease. Belief
that our existence terminates with this physical body throws many
people into meaninglessness and so into a state similar to illness.
Dag Hammarskjöld states well the significance of humankind's
view concerning death and the life beyond: "No choice is uninflu-
enced by the way in which the personality regards its destiny, and
the body its death. In the last analysis, it is our conception of death
which decides our answers to all the questions that life puts to
us. . . . Hence, too, the necessity of preparing for it."[3]

How we view death determines to a large extent how we live
our lives. And paradoxically how we live determines how we view
death. Death and life seem to be two poles of the same reality.

The purpose of this book is to examine the Christian hope of an
afterlife and to trace how this belief has been lost. It is my conviction that the present denial of belief springs out of an inadequate
view of the world and rests upon a pre-modern view of science. I
shall reaffirm the reasonableness of this central idea of historical
Christianity, and then present the evidence that has been accumulating about life after death. This recent data has not been integrated
into theological thought. In conclusion I shall try to portray as
clearly as possible what human beings can expect on the other side
of death.

Someone has stated that theology deals with three questions:

From what? To what? And how? In the following pages we shall examine these questions in depth and come up with some answers to these ultimate questions.

Those who have experienced the love of God in the here and now usually have confidence that this experience of love is not confined' to this life. They even believe that the full realization of the experience of the love of God will only be known in the life which continues after death. Our purpose is to consider the reasonableness of this conviction and hope.

I am deeply grateful to many who have shared with me as I have struggled with this writing over several years. John Sanford and I have talked over many of these ideas, and he has given me permission to use some of his writing on the kingdom of heaven.

It was my Jungian friends who opened the door to the belief in life after death by showing the reality of the non-physical world. One has to have some kind of existence into which we move after death. These friends led me into that reality through the unconscious. Max Zeller, Hilde and James Kirsch, and Barbara Hannah presented an understanding of a spiritual dimension of life which was not dependent upon physical reality. It was then easy to see the truth of the Christian hope in immortality and resurrection and to realize it as a part of my Christian heritage.

For eight years at Notre Dame I have conducted seminars on death, dying and suffering. With eight or nine different groups of students we have wrestled through the problems facing doctors and others as they deal with death and the dying. We have looked deeply at our own death and what it means. These students have taught me a great deal about how human beings react to death.

I am indebted to my friends who keep me posted with the latest books and articles, especially Dr. J. Andrew Canale and Dr. Francis Whiting. Dr. Leo Froke gave me the book which first opened my eyes to the research done recently among doctors and psychologists on the subject of life beyond death.

My wife Barbara has been of great help in research, in reading manuscripts, in talking over ideas and in giving encouragement. She also has had experiences which give her a strong belief in life after death.

Paisley Roach has helped with this manuscript as with many others. She has again gone through this manuscript, editing and helping in many ways. The book would not have received its present form without her devoted and skillful help.

Richard Payne has encouraged me to continue with this project through two and a half busy years at Notre Dame.

I am grateful to Carmela Rulli and the typing pool at Notre Dame for typing the final typescript.

Guadala, California

PART ONE

The Problem of Our Beliefs

I. Whatever Happened to Heaven and Hell?

Not long ago I attended a service at a Lutheran church and heard the pastor remark that in the last ten years he had not preached a single sermon on life after death or the subject of heaven and hell. It was not a problem of belief, he explained; he had been reviewing his sermons over that period and was surprised to realize that he had felt no call to speak on the subject. Later that same month I happened to overhear another discussion between two Catholic priests who were expressing strong feelings on the subject. While they obviously considered themselves good priests and had no intention of leaving the priesthood, they felt that it would be hypocritical for them to teach or preach about life after death. They simply did not believe that there is anything in store for human beings after this present life.

As I thought about these two instances, I realized that they represent an attitude that has been developing for a long time. Christians do not often speak with confidence today about life after death. Most of us avoid examining our doubts, and we scarcely seem aware of how little discussion there is in the ordinary church about heaven and hell or what may happen to human beings after they die. Only at funerals is the topic mentioned, and then often in a half-hearted way. This is an amazing change from the attitude of earlier Christians, particularly in the early Church and the Middle Ages when clergy and lay people seemed to know as much about the next life as they did about this present one.

In polite society the subject of death was simply indecent. Then

7

Elisabeth Kübler-Ross opened the door to discussion of death with her ground-breaking book *On Death and Dying*. It is difficult for human beings to face death if there is nothing certain beyond it. About this we shall have more to say in a moment.

Earlier Christians believed that there was a life awaiting the individual after death whether one wanted it or not, and they seemed to have quite a clear idea of the nature and even the geography of that world which everyone would enter. There were always a few unbelievers and agnostics, of course, but until the last century most of our Christian forefathers, Catholic and Protestant alike, spoke with conviction about the life to come.

One of the greatest Christian poems was written by Dante in the fourteenth century to describe his visionary journey into the world beyond our present existence. For most people today the name Dante stands for hell or the "Inferno" because most of them do not read any farther in *The Divine Comedy*. Yet this work, which Dante called simply the *Comedy*, tells a fascinating story of the way out of hell, up Mount Purgatory, and out through the heavens finally to meet God face to face.[1]

Artists from earliest Christian times until at least the seventeenth century in the West have created pictures of heaven, purgatory and hell, and in Eastern Christianity these visual representations still have a special place. The religious paintings known as icons are understood as windows into heaven that give a glimpse into the world beyond, while the Eastern churches themselves are seen as symbolic representations of heaven. The Church Fathers spoke with confidence about life after death, and they took care to see that this belief was represented in both the Communion service and the creeds which we still use today.

What has happened to the Christian conviction about life after death? Why have we apparently lost any vision of heaven and hell? There seem to be a number of reasons, some of them quite complex. Probably one of the biggest of them is that there are difficulties, even dangers, in believing that there is a life to come after this one is finished. Since there has been no effort in modern times to examine the reasons either for or against believing in a future life, we have to start from scratch and consider some of the sources of our ideas about life after death. Let us look first at the difficulties and the dangers in believing, as well as in *not* believing in a world to come. We shall next examine the kinds of beliefs which human beings have held about such a world of the future. Then I shall outline the personal history which has led me to try to express my limited, mortal thoughts on the subject of life after death. With this background we shall go on to explore our view of the world, and then the subject of heaven and hell and the evidence that can be found to support the idea of life after death. We shall then try to describe as best we can the nature of that reality.

The Case Against Belief

For two of the most earth-shaking thinkers of modern times the idea of life after death held little attraction. According to Karl Marx, religion is the opiate of the people, while Sigmund Freud held that religion represents a return to the womb. If one stops to analyze what these men were saying, it appears that they were not so much against religion as against ideas that lead to neglect of this present life. They were both concerned with transforming human beings and society so that all people might share more equally in the material goods and the joys of this life. They were convinced that belief in a future life, which is more valuable than this present one, keeps individuals from working to achieve this goal. Both of these thinkers were very concerned about morals and human beings and both had religious fervor. In fact their attitude sometimes reminds one of the Hebrew prophets of old. But the followers, particularly of Marx, did not understand this and heard only a warning about religion in general, rather than a warning about certain dangers.

There are several dangers which modern reformers see in people's concern with heaven and hell. In the first place there is the problem of how people can know anything that might be true about life after death. With the development of materialistic thought any existence not connected with the physical body became unthinkable. This is equally true for those who follow the meaningful materialism of Marx, and for those behavioral psychologists who adopt the meaningless materialism of Watson and B. F. Skinner. Materialism and behaviorism do not really gain meaning from Skinner's attempt to provide it in his book *Walden Two*.

If there is no existence other than physical, material existence, then it is futile to talk about heaven and hell. If this is so, any effort to convince people of the reality of life after death is based on illusion and untruth and may be dictated by base motives or by an effort to exploit human beings through fear. Since it is believed that people should try to be honest and value truth, ideas that are untrue are considered dangerous if not vicious. Since any idea about non-physical life is a meaningless and false illusion, therefore it is deceptive and dangerous in itself to discuss life after death. If one believes that there is a possibility of an existence beyond the material and physical one, then in order to counter this argument one must offer some alternative to materialism. This is a big job, but it is one that we shall try to tackle.

The second argument of many reformers is simply that men and women whose eyes are always turned toward heaven tend to forget this life. They tend to deny life rather than supporting and enhancing it. The worst form of this denial of the world is found in the Gnosticism with which the early Church contended. Not only was heaven seen as available and the only ultimate good, but earth and material reality were evil and pulled people away from heaven. It was believed that only as people turned to asceticism and away from earth and human pleasure did they find their way to eternal bliss in heaven. Hell was thus experienced on this earth, and an evil deity was the god of this earth. Sex and procreation were considered highly evil because these acts brought more soul-material into matter and thus more of this heavenly substance was contaminated.

This view of matter, sexuality and the physical body was not the one officially adopted by the Church. The Christian creeds state emphatically that God is the creator of heaven *and earth*, but the problem is that Christians have not always acted as if this were true. The original effort of monasticism to break away from the corruption of this world often became a denial of the world and of any value in this world. A Gnostic view of sex and matter crept in through the writings of Augustine who had followed for a long time the world-denying Gnostic sect of Manicheism. In the deserts of Egypt monks tried to live on cabbage leaves for the whole of Lent and others sat immobile on pillars for years.

Many Christians came to feel that death was a blessed relief from this vale of toil and sin. Chastity was often considered more valuable than charity or love. In popular devotion, particularly among those who faced the disintegration of civilization and culture in Western Europe, the world seemed impossible and hopeless. *The Imitation of Christ* by Thomas à Kempis, as fine as it is, has more than a trace of this world-denying attitude. Of course the greatest Christian mystics and devotional writers like Suso and Tauler do not fall into such misunderstanding of essential Christianity. *The Classics of Western Spirituality* which are now being published by Paulist Press show the balance, depth and wisdom of Western devotional life. Unfortunately many of these great classics have not been available to the average reader until recently.

One of the great contributions of Aquinas was his insistence on the value, goodness and importance of the physical world and the domain of sense experience. He counteracted the world-denying, popular Platonism of the Middle Ages. Almost no one in the West in Aquinas' time was able to read Plato in the original Greek. He was known through popularizers like Macrobius and Isidore of Seville who emphasized the otherworldly and spiritual side of Plato. They also saw Plato as denying the value of the physical world. Against this popular misconception of Plato, Aquinas provided a philosophical and theological basis for the value and permanence of the physical world. This was clearly the attitude of much of the Old Testament.

The tragedy is that Aquinas gave no easily understandable means by which people could have access to the spiritual world. Thus sense experience and the physical world were emphasized so much that later Scholastic thought was caught in a world-view which greatly undervalued human experiences of the divine.

The otherworldly attitude did not die out after Aquinas, however. It continued to develop and was finally incorporated in Adolphe Tanquerey's unfortunate description of the Christian way, *The Spiritual Life*. This handbook was used during over half of the twentieth century as a basic guide for nearly all Catholic priests and religious orders in this country, indoctrinating them with the idea that almost anything to do with emotion or the body is considered evil. It is no wonder that otherworldliness has been so thoroughly rejected by many of the individuals who were brought up on this point of view. They later discovered that they had often thrown the baby out with the bath water.

It is true that many Christians have found the only possibility of joy and hope in anticipating life after death. They have used belief in another world like an opiate, or a womb, to retreat from reality. There is no support for this attitude in the prophetic message of the Old Testament, in the teachings of Jesus, or the views carefully expressed by the early Church. In all of this heritage,

wherever the attitude of Christ is most clearly found, there is emphasis both on this life and on life beyond death. It is a matter of
both/and, not *either/or*. The idea that the future life is the only meaningful one is certainly dangerous. Both the individual and religion
suffer when people find life in this physical world of ours simply a
misery to be endured as long as necessary.

Other Difficulties

There are other difficulties created by our ways of imagining
heaven or hell. Most of us have trouble picturing heaven except in
terms of this life. When most of this world's pleasures are considered dangerous and destructive, if not downright evil, then the
pictures we paint of heaven are limited and tend to be insipid and
dull. The result is a view of a heaven which no warm-blooded,
lively human being would want to visit for more than a brief rest.
Sitting on a cloud dressed in an ample nightshirt and strumming a
harp hardly appeals to my ideas of growth and development, particularly since I am a musical moron. It is easy to understand the
medieval tales of red-blooded lords and ladies who complained that
if only the beggars, cripples and ascetics get into heaven, then
deliver them to hell where they would at least find ladies and
gentlemen. The limitations of our outlook on heaven have created
problems for many sincere Christians who are simply turned off by
visions of being stuck in static, unchanging "bliss."

The traditional view of hell, on the other hand, has not always
been so limited. In Puritan times there was often more emphasis on
the torments awaiting human beings in the afterlife than on the
possibilities of heaven. The problem for most Calvinists and Catholic Jansenists alike was not so much to achieve heaven as to avoid
going to hell. Jonathan Edwards, for instance, helped to incite the
civil and religious disturbances that such preaching caused in this
country with his blood-curdling description of a fiery hell in his
famous sermon *Sinners in the Hands of an Angry God*.

Even fifteen or twenty years ago sermons like this were sometimes heard in Catholic evangelical meetings. In my first seminar on
death and dying at Notre Dame all but one of the Catholic pre-
medical students said flatly that they did not believe in life after
death. As our discussions went on, the problem began to come out.
These students had been so frightened by the preaching about hell

in some of the evangelical missions they had attended in the 1950's and early 1960's that they had rejected the whole idea of an afterlife. It seemed better to them to get rid of any hope for a future life than to face the possibility of such a hell.

This kind of preaching uses people's fear as a club to bring them to "conversion" and force them into right thinking and acting. This may seem the easiest way to influence human beings and their behavior, but if we will take a longer and clearer look, there is not much question that through love and concern we can accomplish results that are more certain and likely to last longer. Whenever we use fear as a persuader there is a danger that we are letting loose hostilities and unresolved angers hidden within us.

While Jesus, of course, did speak of hell, his warnings were limited almost entirely to those who had power to influence the lives of other people, and in most cases he emphasized love rather than fear. He dealt with the difficult problem of offering people a vision of the kingdom of heaven without making it unsuitable or robbing the individual of the birthright of choosing the way of wholeness freely. If we wish to follow Jesus of Nazareth—as teachers, preachers, or parents—we had better examine our motives and see whether we are trying to lead individuals to make their own choices, and, if not, why we find it necessary to restrict them through any kind of frightening vision of the future.

Another problem in believing in an afterlife arises from seeing it only in a materialistic way. The idea that heaven is only a replica of this physical world which the individual enters with a reconstituted body is considered patently silly by most people. I remember how my agnostic father ridiculed such a belief. We had a woman working for us who was very concerned because her husband, who had died, had lost a leg in the First World War. As she chattered away about things, we discovered that she was really worried for fear this good man had been consigned to all eternity with only one leg. My father remarked that her ideas showed how naive and childish it was to believe in a future life.

We Christians certainly need to be as sophisticated as the rest of the world. It does no one any good to present the deepest truths of our religion in a way that makes them appear silly or preposterous to thoughtful people. This is particularly true of ideas about life after death. In earlier times there were Christian thinkers who presented their understanding of heaven and hell as part of a view of the world which made sense. There is a need for the Church and religious people to provide an understanding of life beyond death within a similar world-view today.

The idea of a heaven and hell which reward or punish the individual for life in this world also creates difficulties for Christian belief. Belief in another world after death then becomes mainly a support for one's present morality. There was obviously something wrong with the Old Testament idea that the just and the wicked are always compensated in this present life. The Book of Job blasted this idea on all counts. But later it reappeared in the form of a Christian belief about heaven and hell. The virtuous and those who were evil (those who suffered for others in this life and the wicked masters who ground their servants to the ground) might not get what they deserved in this world, but they would be paid back in heaven or hell. The belief in reincarnation expresses practically the same idea. Those who live the best lives go around again at a happier and higher level, while the wicked person is reincarnated into a lower caste or comes back as a lower animal. This idea of the world may be a comforting belief to some self-satisfied people, but nice beliefs are not necessarily true. To convince the modern world of a belief in life after death, it will take more than this approach of moral wish-fulfillment.

In addition, this approach, which provides future compensation for present misery, takes the edge off the Christian goals of relieving human needs and transforming society. This is seen most clearly in certain Eastern religions, as one member of a Hare Krishna group brought out under questioning by one of my classes at Notre Dame. He suggested that it was even dangerous to reach out to people in need because it might interfere with their *karma*, keeping them from paying the full price for the sins of their former life, and thus keeping them from progressing. They might then have to come through this world again at the same level. While Christians generally avoid such a clear-cut stand, they have sometimes played out very similar ideas of salvation and of the value of the world to come.

There are problems and difficulties, even dangers in really believing that there is a life beyond this one, particularly if one is convinced that the next life is better than this one, or that it will compensate us for the way we have lived this one. It is clear that belief in a future life must be balanced by a rounded and sane view of the nature and value of the physical world. While even then there may be dangers in believing in life after death, still I wonder if it is not more dangerous not to believe in it.

The Case for Life Beyond Death

One problem in having no belief in an existence after this physical one is that death then becomes a terrifying prospect. Until the work of Dr. Elisabeth Kübler-Ross and those who have followed her lead, the subject of death was even more taboo than sex. There were places, however shabby they might be, where sex could be discussed, but there was no place where death—that experience which comes to every individual—was confronted or honestly discussed. Doctors, nurses, family, friends (and even enemies) tried to look the other way. The reaction of the family and friends in Tolstoy's *The Death of Ivan Ilych* is chilling just because it is so real and accurate. Hospitals separate us from the dying person, and we then bring in a mortician to take death out of our hands and relieve us of having to deal with it. A dead person is not very attractive at best, and the "cocktail parlors of death," as one Episcopal bishop used to call mortuaries, do their best to make the corpse look natural, as if sleeping. They keep us, as far as possible, from having to confront the ugly finality and horror of death.

Dying itself is often unpleasant, and if that process leads only to total extinction, to utter nothingness, a person must be brave beyond measure to confront it without being gripped by the most devastating fear. In the seminar groups with which I have worked trying to come to terms with the problems of suffering and dying, the students have all come to essentially the same conclusion: the person who is totally caught in a materialistic world-view, with no glimmer of hope beyond this world, had better not try to work with individuals who are dying. If one can see only disintegration and annihilation as the ultimate end of all life, this provides little basis for the support which dying people need.

None of us, truly believing that there is nothing beyond this physical body, can escape either becoming insensitive to the problems of the dying, or sharing the uncertainty and dread and horror that so many people feel about death. It is no wonder that our society, which has swallowed nineteenth-century materialism hook,

line and sinker, has made the subject of death taboo. How else could
we deal with something that has only terrifying aspects, except to
avoid it?

If human beings are just the chance development of random
electrons and atoms, it is difficult to see life as having much meaning.[2] It is hard to find value in the lives of beings that originated by
pure accident, live for a brief time on this little planet and end in the
sod of some cemetery. Perhaps in the atmosphere of the nineteenth
century, with its belief that humankind was on an escalator to
utopia, it was possible to see enough value in human efforts to build
a better society and leave the world a better place for future genera-
tions. But few of us are that optimistic today as we face terrorism
and nuclear blasts, overpopulation, hostile destructiveness raging
between nations and races, and the violence and muggings that
make the streets of even our nation's capital unsafe after dark. Our
efforts to provide the material comforts of this life threaten to
destroy our physical environment, while the second law of thermo-
dynamics is always ready to remind us that the universe may be
gradually dying, thus robbing us of ultimate hope in that environment.

Sensitive individuals who look at these facts often come face to
face with meaninglessness which is one of the leading causes of
distress and illness today. The most common response is probably
simple depression, so widespread that it is sometimes called the
"common cold" of modern psychiatry. Yet these people are not
actually ill in the way that the psychotic or manic-depressive is sick,
and this kind of hopelessness does not often respond to ordinary
treatment. There are tricks to help a person look the other way and
try to forget that life seems meaningless. Or shock treatments can
make one fuzzy enough to ignore the problem of meaning and
value. But this does nothing to relieve the basic problem. Depression itself is at least an honest admission that the problem of
meaninglessness exists, as existential thinkers from Kierkegaard and
Heidegger to Camus, Sartre and Beckett bring out so clearly.

Our less conscious ways of avoiding the problem of meaning
are seldom very successful. Instead, these unconscious responses to
the fact that our lives often do seem meaningless can take the most
destructive routes. Sometimes people are plagued by anxiety without any visible or conscious reason, which turns life into a night-
mare and slowly and surely wrecks their bodies. Other people, more

irritable in temperament, may let loose anger and hatred on the meaningless world, fighting it every inch of the way. This takes an incredible toll on heart, arteries, digestive and respiratory systems, as well as on personal relations. Then there is the response of egotism which may affect any of us who finds no God or meaning in this world. When we find ourselves alone in the driver's seat, there is no real choice but to become God and run things for ourselves, suffering the inevitable stress that can literally destroy our bodies and minds.[3]

I know of no help for these reactions, or the depression that comes from finding life meaningless, other than belief in a power that values individuals enough to give them continued life and growth within and beyond this present existence. The dangers of a religion which fails to provide this outlook are very real. There is not only the incalculable cost to individuals, but these people who come up against meaninglessness very often have a great effect upon the whole of society. They are frequently active and creative individuals whose talents are needed, and their attitudes often have widespread influence. Unless there is some way to offer a point of view which these people can accept, which will show them the evidence for life and continued development of the individual beyond the grave, our society and our religion both lose and each of us is the poorer.

The belief that there is no life after death, in fact, casts doubt upon nearly all the religious ideas and hopes of most of humankind. As we shall consider in the next chapter, until this century some idea of life after death has been central to the religions of most people around the world. When an essential aspect of any system is seriously questioned or rejected, the whole system is likely to go with it. This is a particular danger for Western Christianity. Ever since the Enlightenment we have been moving farther and farther away from belief in a non-physical or religious realm of reality which was once a principal ingredient of Christian faith. With our increasing emphasis on materialism the dilemma for Western Christians has become acute.

In his book *Honest to God* John Robinson revealed the concern of some of the great theologians of our time over this dilemma. He presented the thinking of men who faced this problem and struggled courageously to find an answer. Bultmann, Bonhoeffer and Tillich all worked desperately to offer a solution within the present materialistic framework. They concluded that there was only one possibility, the one presented in *Honest to God*. People must accept a religious view of life without relying on the non-physical or spiritual elements that were important to religion in the past. These men made a valiant and sincere effort to create a meaningful vision of religion that played down or rejected these elements. What they apparently failed to realize, however, was how difficult this would make it for sophisticated Christians to believe in a future life. Once the idea of a non-physical realm of reality no longer has validity for us, we are left with little possibility but a literal biblical interpretation of life after death. It is no wonder that some believers are distressed by the views expressed by Bishop Robinson and cling like drowning men to their literal view of the world beyond.

The efforts to provide ethical standards for people's behavior on a purely materialistic basis have not been notably successful. Perhaps such systems are convincing to those who author them, but with no way of appealing to a future life, no way to show any need to prepare for what may come, our own notions of self-interest usually win out over other human ideas of morality. In fact, if there is no ultimate meaning or value in human life, we are left with a more or less sophisticated law of the jungle. Power or might then creates right. The strongest and most ruthless decide what to do about the world's problems and determine what is right. Even tyrants like Hitler can be justified if they avoid making too many mistakes.

By denying life after death we make it almost impossible to see any final meaning in our lives, and it becomes difficult to be faithful to any system of ethics or morality. Confucian morality is sometimes held up as an example of a system that worked without being tied to spiritual beliefs or religious practices, but this is far from true. Confucius based his thought on the shamanism of ancient China, and his followers understood that his teachings were the "way to heaven." To follow an ethical way most of us apparently need to realize that there may be more to live for than this present life.

Few people feel that they have been treated justly by life. When one gets beneath the surface in people, misery and hurt are usually found within them. The sense of frustration and agony is sometimes so great that the person who has no outlook beyond this physical existence ends up in despair, or even suicide. It is not merely physical pain and outer misery, however, that drive human beings to suicide. Most often they come up against an agonizing fear that life offers nothing better, either here or hereafter. Without any hope for the future, they meet the "death wish" which Freud described so accurately in *Beyond the Pleasure Principle* and *Civilization and Its Discontents*. The results of this failure of hope have been analyzed even more fully by Karl Menninger in *Man Against Himself* and by Ernest Becker in *The Denial of Death*. These books tear away our facades and bring us face to face with death. My students have found them powerful in forcing confrontation with death.

There is no way to estimate the distress that has been caused by giving up hope of some kind of existence beyond the grave. The effects of believing that life begins and ends in this world of physical matter may be even more dangerous and destructive than the most far-out, ridiculous idea of a future existence. As a purely practical matter few people are able to make the most of life—or even to survive in many cases—without the kind of meaning that comes with believing in life beyond death.

Of course, if the materialistic thinking found in works like *Honest to God* is right, then there may be little choice but to suffer the distress and tension caused by our limitations in this world. But the outlook which has been growing among scientific thinkers in this century suggests that the thoroughgoing materialism of the past was simply a belief which does not hold water any longer. The door has been opened by scientists themselves to consider the evidence. Since we need no longer rely just on logic or on faith alone, let us lay some groundwork and then turn to study the experiences which can help us find answers to the most central problem of Christian belief: Are we humans imprisoned within these four walls of space, time, energy, and mass, or do our lives and our ways of knowing extend into that unknown world where God and elements of spirit may be encountered?

II. Varieties of Afterlife: The Visions of Final Things

Most Westerners are really aware of only one or two ideas of what may come at the termination of our physical existence. This is undoubtedly the cause of some of our problems in approaching the subject of life after death. There are literally dozens—perhaps even hundreds—of such views of the future which have come to people around the world. By studying and comparing them we can gain far greater insight into the reasons for holding one belief or another. Such a task would obviously be overwhelming if one had to start from scratch to learn about each of these various visions and beliefs. Sooner or later, however, those who are interested in this subject will discover the study of eschatology and find that some of the work has already been done for us.

Eschatology is the term theologians use for the study of people's beliefs about the final things that may happen to human beings and what may come after life in this physical world. The word itself comes from the Greek adjective *eschatos* meaning "final" or "last in time or place," and the basis for the study comes from passages in both the Old and New Testaments. Among the Hebrew prophets, for instance, there was a vision of the Day of Yahweh when God would appear and all things would be brought to their final state. Eschatology can refer either to the last things that may happen to a society or a world, or to the ultimate destiny of human beings.

Over the years I have studied these beliefs, tracing them in the history and sociology of religion. Again and again I have realized that, for various reasons, certain types or patterns of belief tend to recur, and I have found that they represent eight essentially different views of what happens to the individual at the end of what we know as "life." While each of these points of view is important enough to be dealt with at length, let us start by taking an overall look at them. We shall then consider certain of these views in more detail later on.

Death as Probable Extinction

In the last hundred years the one view which in the past was probably the least common of all has spread among various people in Western Europe and America as well as among orthodox Marxists wherever they are found. This is the idea that there is simply nothing left of a human being after death, and that when someone breathes his or her last and the brain waves die away, nothing more can happen. Thus, a purely physical organism has ceased to exist. There are some chemical elements that go back into the earth and might be put together again as a flower or a duck-billed platypus, or even as another human being. But whatever went to make up a "person" is gone and no one can find a trace except for the marks that individual left on other people or perhaps hewed into stone or traced out on bits of paper. Everything else is gone.

It is difficult to know how many people are influenced by this point of view today. Certainly it is held by many honest and thoughtful individuals. This basic idea has been carefully and precisely stated by B. F. Skinner in his scientific works as well as in his novel *Walden Two*. It was also expressed with greater sophistication by Sigmund Freud. Although Freud broke with the materialism of his time in trying to understand human beings in the here and now, he saw no more meaning or hope for the individual after this life than the strictest Darwinian materialist.[1] Over the ages many Chinese intellectuals, particularly those inclined toward Confucianism, have held a similar point of view in which the value of an afterlife was played down.[2] Certain sophisticated men and women have held this view all over the world.

There is a second, closely related point of view. This is the belief of many philosophical existentialists, starting with Kierkegaard, that human beings can find no evidence for life after death.

But as they confront the existential situation of *angst* or death and make the leap of faith, they may find meaning and thus a hope that there is something beyond the grave. For most of the careful thinkers of this school all of our knowledge must come from sense experience through ontological analysis. Since this cannot break into the world beyond, belief is a hope which lies on the other side of despair. The evidence for anything more is shut off from us.

The result is that not all existentialists grasp this hope and leap into the promised land. There are just as many who find that jumping into the void leads only to nothingness, to almost a certainty that the whole human enterprise is absurd. Sartre, Camus and Beckett belong to this group. Sartre's *Nausea* is a perfect example of this point of view.

Karl Jaspers, Gabriel Marcel, and perhaps Heidegger (whose ideas on this subject are more of an enigma) come out with a more optimistic view. These thinkers make a real effort to accept the materialism of the Enlightenment and still offer a hopeful view of life after death. In his influential work *The Denial of Death* Ernest Becker made much the same effort, and his death itself was a noble expression of his beliefs. The existential point of view apparently works for those who believe that something will be found on the other side of death, but it can give little idea of the nature of this reality and no experience which might support such a belief. It is interesting that this philosophy, which has little direct impact on rank and file Christians, is really *in* with the theologians.[3]

Archaic Views of the Life Beyond

It is hard for most of us to believe that the next view of an afterlife is actually the one found in most of the Old Testament. One of the few times I remember feeling really shocked in seminary was when we looked at how little meaning the early Hebrews saw in a future life for any individual. They believed that the dead went to Sheol, which was a place of gray half-existence where there was practically no joy or hope or meaning. People become nothing but spirits or wraiths, living a mere shadow of life in this world without either its joys or torments. As the psalmists kept reminding people, one could not even praise God in Sheol. While the modern commentaries have a great deal to say about this understanding in the Old Testament, it was not very different from the idea of Hades in classical Greek and Roman religion.[4] Hades was also a colorless place with little hope or joy, and with no particular pain. While that ancient world did look beyond this life, the only outlook for most people was the possibility of a simply grim, boring continuance. This point of view is found in hundreds of variations the world over.

Gradually, however, these ideas began to change. Jewish thought came into contact with the ideas of Persian religion, and the view of life after death became more developed. There were also dramatic changes in Greece and also in Egypt. The Egyptians had originally considered that any significant afterlife was the privilege of kings and their royal families only. Then the idea began to spread to nobles, then to merchants and artisans, and finally all people were admitted. The entrance requirements to another realm (probably seen as a realm of bliss) became more democratic, and so ordinary people could make it in. In Greece the same thing happened as a few heroes made it out of Sheol-Hades into the realm of the gods where a satisfactory afterlife seemed possible.

One important factor in this lowering of eschatological standards was undoubtedly the influence of the fourth point of view, that of the immortality of the soul found in shamanism. Where the ideas of shamanism first arose is difficult to discover, but four centuries before Christ the shaman's influence was already felt in Greece in Orphism and in Pythagorean and Platonic thinking. Shamanism is found all over the globe. As Mircea Eliade has shown in his monumental study *Shamanism*, this view of the soul is spread far and wide and goes back into pre-historic times. The basic idea is that man has a soul which is immortal and that it is not entirely confined to the body in this life. The shaman is one who has acquired the ability to leave the body in ecstasy or trance. He can either descend into the regions below the earth (usually viewed as non-physical in nature although represented by earthly symbols), or ascend into the regions above the earth and out into the seven, ten, or whatever number of heavens.

The shaman's journeys gave people a realization of the realms their souls may enter after death. The body is seen as only a temporary housing for the soul. The soul has a continued existence apart from the body. When someone's soul wanders away and leaves the person lost and sick, the shaman's task is to find the soul, bring it back and help the person become reunited. After a death he or she (for women are often shamans) is often asked to go with the person's soul on the journey through hell to heaven. In their initiation experiences shamans have known the dismemberment of death, the descent into hell and rising to heaven. Along the way they have met destructive demons and helpful, angelic spirits. Because of these original journeys they need not fear this inner world and they can help others in sickness and in making their final journey. What we call the Greek idea of immortality was apparently derived from this point of view. The Greeks transformed the shamanistic myth into a philosophical theory and system.

These archaic views of life after death are probably far older than most of us ever imagine. There are burial sites that may go back fifty thousand years, perhaps almost to Neanderthal times, in which archaeologists have found bones painted red and vessels laid out for the final journey. The preparations may have represented either one of the archaic beliefs. But we are certain that from the time agricultural settlements began, most people believed that something awaited them at the end of their physical lives and that such preparations were necessary. One of the worst things that could happen to people's souls was to remain flitting aimlessly around their former habitations and not make it to their destination, either to Sheol-Hades or through hell to heaven. Where primitive people have survived, such as the Australian aborigines, this view can be seen in highly developed form. It is quite similar to the idea in Dante's *Divine Comedy* that spirits who couldn't even make it into limbo or purgatory were worse off than those in hell.

Since earliest times many people have apparently seen reasons to believe that some kind of immortality is inherent in the soul whether one wants it or not, and that the soul longs to reach a destination. The burial practices of both primitive and highly civilized peoples—for instance, the Chinese—have reflected this understanding, trying to help souls on their way and keep them from having to come back again and again to search in familiar places. People performed the burial rites because they cared about the deceased and also because they feared their influence if they returned.

The Eastern Point of View

Another widely held view about continued existence is the idea of reincarnation or the transmigration of souls. According to this idea human personality has continued existence, but after death the individual belongs to a bank of souls in an intermediate state known as *bardo*. At the right time one's soul is given another go at this life. Those individuals who have done well in their former lives return to a higher caste and station. But if one has made a botch of things, he or she returns to a lower caste, or even to a lower form of life to try to do better. Of course, in this way the caste system is supported on the basis of justice. Everyone gets what is fair, exactly what the *karma* of each requires, and perfect justice is seen as fulfilled.

There are two quite different goals at the end of the process. In one case, that of classical Hinduism, the individual soul which has passed beyond reincarnation enters the realm of the immortals and continues on in the eternal realm of spirit which alone is real. In fact, one of the efforts of this religion is to recognize that the physical world is an illusion in order to enter more quickly into the realm that is real. This goal is well expressed by the Hindu scripture, the *Bhagavad Gita*, and both this goal and the next one are described with understanding and appreciation by Joseph Campbell in *Myths To Live By*.

The followers of Buddha go a step farther. These teachings have had an impact on Eastern life which is comparable to the influence of Christianity on the West and of Islam in the Middle East. To Buddha not only was the physical world evil and ensnaring, but the world of spiritual reality was also illusory. The goal of the Buddhist way is *Nirvana* which is not heaven in any traditional sense, but rather loss of individual consciousness by merging into cosmic consciousness and being absorbed by it. The idea of the ego and of any kind of separate continued existence is one of the illusions which must go if one is to have true enlightenment and enter the imageless state of total reunion with cosmic mind. In this state one experiences a final and abiding "peace."

On a recent trip across India in burning weather I found myself sympathizing with Buddha and his desire to get off the world. He had reason for despair if the India of his time was anything like that country today, a land overburdened with masses of people living at the edge of hunger, often in the filth of the streets next to the dead and dying. Where would one start to redeem a world like this? Faced with these odds, it is probably sensible to let go of all feelings and passions and, dying to all images, come to total unconscious absorption into cosmic mind. Some of the world's most deeply religious people, some who were the most sensitive and highly spiritual, have believed that this was the only satisfactory goal. In his later writing Joseph Campbell seems to be attracted to this conclusion although he is a Westerner born and bred.

The Christian Views of Life After Death

There are three more ideas about a future life which are all found in Christianity. The first of them was the official point of view of Western Christianity for a long time, and this understanding, or some variation of it, is the present position of most of the more literal and fundamentalistic churches. The basic idea is that the dead will sleep until the general resurrection at the end of the world. There will first be a final battle between the forces of God and Christ and those of the Anti-Christ. In the end Satan will be bound and those who followed him and were evil in their earthly lives will remain in hell. The dead who are worthy of life with Christ will then be raised to share in a new era, a new heaven here on earth in which all who are redeemed will be with Christ forever.

This point of view, which probably goes back to the Old Testament prophets and their understanding of the coming of the Messiah, is found in the New Testament Book of Revelation and in Paul's Epistles to the Thessalonians. Since there can be an equal emphasis on heaven and hell, it is attractive to many Christian churches. In his several books Hal Lindsey, for instance, stresses the second coming and a new heaven and earth in graphic descriptions. At the same time there is a note of urgency and fear because the end is close at hand.

In the thirteenth century when the Western Church was at the height of its power a different understanding was adopted as the official Christian view. This was the one presented by Dante in *The Divine Comedy*. In this view the nature of hell was spelled out in detail. Satan was frozen in a block of ice in the center of the earth and around him every kind of torment awaited people who were really wicked. For the good pagans or unbaptized Christians, there was a place called limbo which was much like Sheol, with no discomfort or joy.

Then there were most of the others, people who were neither bad enough for hell nor ready for heaven. They were ferried to the unknown regions at the foot of Mount Purgatory to begin a purifying climb and be transformed and enter the Garden of Eden at the top. From there each soul ascended to its proper sphere in the ten heavens stretching out in concentric circles around the earth. To the more sophisticated thinkers like Dante this whole picture was symbolic as well as actual, but the general public of that time took it as the literal geography of a heaven and hell that were located in physical time and space out there. There are some hints of this view to be found in the Old and New Testaments.

The first of these Christian views puts the kingdom of God off to a future age, and the second of them places it out in space. While it is obvious that we can no longer take the second view literally because of modern astronomy, the understanding that a new age and the new heaven are near at hand is still held by many modern people. This view developed among the earliest Christians, and people who want a blueprint of the future search Scripture, particularly the Book of Revelation, to compare present-day events and find hints of just when this present world may come to an end.

This is only one of the views found in the New Testament, however. There is also the last of these eight views, the understanding of eternal life which sees the resurrection of our personalities in a realm described by Jesus of Nazareth as the kingdom of heaven or the kingdom of God. As he suggested, there are experiences of such a realm which give hints about it. This view finds truth in several of the ideas we have sketched. It incorporates much that is found in the literal understanding of heaven and hell, and it also sees truth in the belief in immortality so common to humankind the world over. In this point of view, however, once-and-for-all resurrection or simple immortality is not enough. It sees that we humans need something more than just a perpetuation of our willful and earthly attitudes to find a meaningful eternal life.

What is suggested by this picture of the reality to come is a continued process of transformation and resurrection. As C. S. Lewis shows so well in *The Great Divorce*, the split between heaven and hell is found within each individual soul. With profound insight and with superb wit and imagination Lewis portrays the nature of these separated aspects of reality. And both here and in his children's story *The Last Battle* he suggests quite clearly the way of rebirth that may lie ahead for the human soul.

In approaching the realities beyond the present life this point of view respects the agnosticism of the rationalists, existentialists and materialists. Far from trying to bury these doubts, those who hold this view generally consider them a healthy check on our credulity and naiveté. There is also understanding of the views of the Hindus and Buddhists who speak of the need to lay aside most of our myths and images in order to find out what reality lies beyond this life and the world of matter. One of the great spokesmen for the point of view of eternal life as a continued process of transformation was Baron Friedrich von Hügel. His fascinating studies of the subject are found in his book *Eternal Life* and in the second volume of *The Mystical Element of Religion*.

In the chapters that follow we shall take a deeper look at these eight visions of the world to come, trying to see how each of them may contribute to our understanding of the total reality in which we live and toward which we are moving. By considering the experiences that come to us and the beliefs of the great religious systems of the world, hopefully we shall find a synthesis emerging that will place human life in a renewed framework of meaning and value.

III. A Personal Odyssey

For almost as long as I can remember the problems of death and what comes after it have seemed very close to me. First in my own life and then in my ministry and teaching I have had to struggle with these questions. I have often had to deal with the devastating effects that facing death usually has on human beings, and again and again I have seen how much we need some kind of answer to the erasing hand of death. Out of the depth of this struggle and this questioning have come insights and understanding that have given me hope. These are the things I hope to share out of my own experience.

One reason for writing about this subject is my need, as I grow older, to gather these thoughts and share them with others in order to see where they may strike a familiar note and whether others may have had experiences that were similar. I certainly have no privileged knowledge or experience other than sixty years of concern with the problem and some effort to learn about the reality that can be discovered on the other side of silence. In my book *The Other Side of Silence* I have described these experiences of a non-physical reality and how one can find and interact with the "Other" through such experiences.

My early life, however, seemed to be more involved in encounters with death. Looking back it appears that, beginning with a traumatic birth, my childhood was dominated by one sickness after another so that death never seemed very far away from me. Even in my twenties this body seemed to be a frail and utterly unreliable instrument, dependent on unpredictable resistance to disease and infection. By the time I was ten it was obvious to everyone that this was simply a fact I had to live with.

That summer I stumbled into a nest of yellow jackets and was stung by dozens of them. I started to run for help, but collapsed, unable to scream. There happened to be a doctor close by, and a prompt injection of a stimulant saved my life. Until then no one had realized that, besides everything else, I had some allergic reactions that could cause death within moments. One thing that no one seemed to understand was that I had not lost consciousness. While I lost contact with the world around me, I still remember the brilliant colors and images which surrounded me.

I also remember the deep impression made by a story my mother told about an incident that had happened to her as a girl. The importance my mother attached to the experience had a real impact because she was usually careful not to exaggerate or add color in telling her experiences. Years before when she was a teenager she had gone skating one evening with a young man, and after a pleasant evening had gone home and to bed. At 2 A.M. she was awakened suddenly by what seemed to be a cry for help and opened her eyes to see the young man standing at the foot of her bed pleading for help. As she came to herself the figure was gone and she realized that it had been a dream or vision. The experience left her shaken and frightened. The next morning she was told that the young man had taken his life. A day or two before he had learned that he had tuberculosis, and at that time the diagnosis was practically a death sentence. He had decided not to wait for the disease to do its work. At about the time my mother had glanced at the clock in her room he had picked up a gun and shot himself.

My personal struggle with death began when my mother was declared incurably ill and I transferred from the college I had been attending in the West to a university in Virginia to be nearer our family home in Pennsylvania. During the last four months of her life I drove the long miles home each weekend, fearing it would be the last. In these months there were few things which we did not share. I found myself one of her chief supports as she slipped closer and closer to death. This was one of the most painful and yet rewarding experiences of my life. By facing death honestly with another human being one comes to know that person in a new way. Then there was the shock of my mother's death and the incredible sense of loss which is even greater when this kind of relationship of mutual trust and honesty has been established.

The vacuum in which I found myself after my mother died was intensified by the studies I took as a graduate student at Princeton, particularly as I began to understand the ideas of Immanuel Kant. I became more and more convinced that life cannot be sustained without meaning, and yet the world around me gave no rational reason to expect that any ultimate meaning existed. I found myself in turmoil, all the worse because few people seemed to understand the possibility of the utter loss of meaning, or the effect on an individual of such despair and the sense of emptiness in life.

The existentialists made sense to me simply because they face life as it is, stripped of any sickly sentimentality. Three years in seminary scarcely made a dent in this basic problem, but on a foundation of essentially reason alone they showed me how to erect a superstructure of reasons for believing in meaning that are probably every bit as good as the reasons for not believing, and this logic appealed to me. Armed with this new conviction I went out into the parish ministry.

I found that the difficulties I had faced stood me in good stead as I visited the bedsides of the sick and the dying. I knew that I could stand by the dying and their families through the most agonizing experiences, and that I need not fear the worst of their questioning and doubts. I had met many of these experiences and I had survived. The gratitude of those who were dying gave me a real sense of service to others, a feeling of having tried to help other human beings without self-interest, expecting nothing in return. Some of my most cherished memories came from those visits with people when all their masks were torn away in the presence of death.

The demands of this kind of inter-relatedness with those facing death, added to the responsibility of running a large parish, soon forced me to seek a better solution to the problem of meaning than the inadequate one which I had jerrybuilt in seminary. There seemed to be only one way to find an answer, and that was to experience and know whatever central meaning there was in the universe. I realized that I needed knowledge as well as belief. A growing anxiety over giving out a message of which I had no real knowledge forced me to stare again into the abyss of death and meaninglessness. Either I had to find some meaning myself or the idea of ministering meaning to others was absurd. The task, as Tillich puts it so well in *The Courage To Be*, was to find the God who waits on the other side of meaninglessness, death and condemnation.

It became all too clear that there are things worse than physical death. Looking into the darkness within oneself, into one's own fears and doubts and destructiveness, may be far worse than facing the end of this life. I came to appreciate the wisdom of the early Church in speaking of *Death* with a capital "D" as a reality which is responsible not just for physical death, but for most of the destructiveness, sickness and evil in this world. One can know death either in its most tangible effect on our physical bodies, or as an entity which brings the fearful ravages of both mental and physical illness and sin.

I shall always be grateful to my Jungian friends, Dorothy Phillips, Max Zeller, and Hilde and James Kirsch, who had made their own encounters with this entity and were willing to walk with me as I confronted it. Dorothy Phillips had known years of being an invalid and she still worked with her own inner material. Max Zeller and Hilde and James Kirsch had known the destructiveness of Nazi Germany and had escaped by the grace of God. From these individuals, some of whom had studied directly with C. G. Jung and were working with his ideas, I learned truths which have proved some of the most important ones in my life. Later I had a chance to meet Jung and talk over some of these things with him myself.

First of all I found that the ideas of rationalism and materialism which I had accepted as incontrovertible truth were only hypotheses that did not account for nearly all the *facts* of human experience. These followers of Jung showed me that he offered a new hypothesis which has a place for another dimension of reality, and thus a place for the continuation of human life. As I followed up what Jung had to say about today's scientists, I realized that they are the first to admit that we do not know enough to insist that physical matter is *all* that exists. Only the facts of experience can tell us what is true and these facts cannot be overturned by any theory.

Besides giving me the courage to turn to the inner world and face the darkness that appeared, these students of Jung also showed me how to recognize the signs of light in the darkness and then how to do two things—first to allow them to develop, and second to help direct my own growth toward the light. In both ways the signs of meaning gradually became stronger. What I discovered was an entity which is a reality more powerful than the darkness. In the midst of the darkness any of us can find the reality of *Love* (the same reality of the One of whom Jesus Christ was the incarnation). He or Love can be met in the depths of one's own soul. In fact, he was there knocking, reaching out and waiting for me to respond. When I did respond, I discovered the meaning of the atonement. It was not a doctrine buried in theological history and discussion, but for me a present experience and reality. In this way I found an experience of light that outshone the darkness and gave meaning to the whole of life.

Gradually these insights started to take root in my life and began to grow. Human life is so deep and complex that it takes time for them to take root in the deep and rocky places and then spread out over the garden of our beings. There is still much growth needed in many areas of my life, but at a certain point I found that I could speak with the dying with a new conviction, with a certain sureness, and that the visits no longer drained me so completely. I was not trying to sustain them with my own strength but sharing a reality with them that I had experienced myself. This confidence was just as helpful to those who were left bereaved. The same hope could be shared with them and with others who met something Death-like in experiences of depression, anxiety, of inner lostness and darkness.

As I became open enough to listen and hear what people were saying—without first filtering it through my screen of personal opinions—I found more and more parishioners coming to share with me experiences they had had on the edges of life and death. There was one spring day which I remember vividly, when three of the various people who came to my office wanted to talk about experiences similar to those described by Dr. Raymond Moody in *Life After Life*. In lecturing to audiences whether in this country or Europe or farther places, I have discovered that there is nearly always someone who wants to tell me of such an experience. These people clearly show relief at finding another person who is interested in hearing what happened to them.

Soon after I came to Notre Dame I was introduced to the first group of pre-medical students, who wanted to talk about the dangers involved in entering the medical profession. They had been reading about the unusually high rate of suicide, mental breakdown, divorce, alcoholism, and hard drug use among physicians, and they wondered if the problem were related to the fact that medical education gives so little preparation for the burden of death and suffering which physicians must constantly bear. These were exceptionally bright students who recognized that neither rationalism nor materialism offered answers to the problem, and they were willing to struggle with their own doubts and meaninglessness and anxieties. Together we worked out the course I have mentioned which has been repeated year after year.

Nine groups of pre-med students and others have now wrestled with these problems in order to find hope and meaning. I have learned a great deal from these students and many of them have become my close friends. My experience with them has also helped me in working with theological students, nuns, priests, and ministers from various churches, who all respond to death and suffering with just as many doubts and fears as students preparing to go into medicine. In addition, it has shown me that others who will face the fear and darkness within themselves nearly always find experiences that open up new meaning in their lives, and sometimes even hint at the continuance of that meaning beyond this present life.

I have found two other things of equal importance in most of the groups I have worked with at Notre Dame. First, there are few of us who are able to make use of such experiences of meaning until we can accept a world-view which makes sense of these experiences and offers ways of putting them to work. And second, we seem to need the guidance and the directional signs that are provided by having some picture of the kind of world that might lie on the other side of this earthly, physical life. I have been amazed at how often this idea is brought up in groups who are trying to work with the problems of death and inner darkness. Again and again such groups have come to the conclusion that there can be no real answer to these problems until they have dealt with the question of what may come after this present life. Apparently since the dawn of time human beings have had experiences which gave them a basic belief in a future life. Generally the students have agreed that this belief deserves to be discussed along with a world-view which can outline the possibilities and a description of the most plausible ideas about the future.

Although a number of writers have tackled the subject of death since Dr. Kübler-Ross broke the taboo against discussing it, few of them have shown much interest in considering what may be in store for us after death or what view of the world is suggested by our experiences of death. These are questions which need to be dealt with so that we humans may see where to put our hope and in what ways we may prepare for whatever lies ahead. For these reasons I shall do my best to present the experiences, ideas and theories relating to life after death, and then show which view seems to me the most realistic and honest.

The Task—How To Go About It

Trying to make some sense of ideas about the life beyond is obviously not easy. In order to approach this complex material, we shall first of all look at the idea of heaven and hell which was the heritage of nearly every Christian, serf or prince, tradesman, professor or priest, in the thirteenth century. We need to know what we once believed and how much of that belief can be retained by sophisticated Christians today. It is even more important to see what happened to that world-view because of the impact of Columbus, Copernicus and Galileo. Almost the last traces of this world-view vanished under the spotlight of rationalistic materialism that was turned on by the Enlightenment.

There is no possible way for any of us to believe in life after death unless our world-view admits that it is possible. The trouble with materialism as a world-view is its single-mindedness. Materialism does not admit any possibility of life apart from physical matter. It even tends to deny any facts which do not fit into its preconceived system of ideas, as T. S. Kuhn shows so clearly in *The Structure of Scientific Revolutions*. Since there *are* facts which point beyond the limitations of physical matter (and these are facts the materialist cannot accept and remain true to materialism), it is necessary to provide an alternative view or hypothesis which can take these facts into account. There is clearly not much point in talking about evidence for a life beyond this one if no one is able to accept the evidence that is offered. And so the next step is to show a world-view which has room for both the facts of this material world and other evidence of quite a different nature.

We shall then look at several different kinds of facts and experiences which seem to point definitely to something beyond the physical world.

This will bring us to the subject of immortality and resurrection, and to see how the ideas differ and how they can be pulled together or synthesized. We shall thus be ready to formulate the idea of eternal life, considering this developmental view of life after death as, in my opinion, the most honest and careful theory that can be produced. In order to get a picture of the nature of the future world that is suggested by this view, we shall use the words of Jesus about the kingdom of heaven. We shall also draw upon Jesus' teachings for some suggestions about the best way to prepare for the fullest experience of this new life. I shall conclude by trying to answer some specific questions about our view of the afterlife.

First, I shall offer some practical thoughts about how to minister to the dying based on the material I have presented. Second, I shall discuss the evidence for reincarnation and try to evaluate it. And, last, I shall take up the subject of hell, including the many references to hell in the New Testament. I shall attempt to show how the idea of hell, which is so largely avoided by modern liberal Christians, can be reconciled with the Christian hope of eternal life.

Let us turn now to the vision of heaven which gave hope to people in the Middle Ages.

PART TWO

Our View of the World

IV. All Dressed Up
and No Place To Go:
The Vision of Heaven
and How It Was Lost

It is difficult for most of us today to imagine a time when the universe and the human being's place in it were clearly understood and offered a satisfying prospect. For at least three hundred years we humans have been struggling to find how we fit into the scheme of things. We no longer enjoy the security of the absolute certainty that was developed by Christians over a great many centuries because the scientific discoveries of Copernicus, Kepler and Galileo shook that world with the knowledge that the earth was not the center of the universe.

For people living at the end of the Middle Ages, however, the entire cosmos was a totally integrated system. In one of the most magnificent pieces of thinking of all times, Thomas Aquinas had taken the scientific and philosophical system of Aristotle, the astronomy of Ptolemy, and the moral and spiritual vision of the Old and New Testaments and compiled out of these somewhat unrelated elements a total, unified cosmology. The whole universe was seen as a physical reality, with the denser, less pure and less spiritual parts of it collected at the center. This center, of course, was the earth. Around it moved the heavenly bodies. The moon and sun, the fixed stars and the realms beyond the stars moved around the earth in perfect circles to the music of the spheres. The planets with their peculiar orbits (the word planet means "wanderer" in Greek) were seen to move in the carefully calculated Ptolemaic epicycles.

Heaven itself was a kind of purified and rarefied material reality. As one went further out from the earth the material became more ethereal, but heaven was of one piece with the grosser physical world and a continuation of it. When the findings of Copernicus became accepted the whole cosmology collapsed and there was no place for heaven at all. The Greek Orthodox ecclesiastical tradition never took this Aristotelian-medieval world-view seriously. Heaven and earth were understood in that tradition as being different kinds of realities. Human beings experienced these different realities by different kinds of knowing. The Greek Church continued to see heaven as a separate level of reality rather than as an extension of the physical world. These two levels of reality interacted and influenced each other, but they were clearly differentiated. This tradition used concrete physical imagery to tell of the nature and quality of heaven, but understood the symbolism as only an allegorical picture. The Greek icon was important just because it signified more than it pictured. It was a window into heaven.

Because of this different way of looking at the world, the cosmology of the Eastern Church was not tied to any one view of the physical world. The spiritual world was independent but interrelated to the physical world. For this reason the Western Christian conflict between science and religion has never greatly troubled the Orthodox Church. A more careful description of these two world-views is found in Appendix A.

The Medieval Vision of Heaven and Hell

In the Western vision of the world the whole of this universe had been created to bring forth human beings in the very center of it. This world-view made it easy, almost necessary to believe in a place set aside for the dead. This was what the heavens were for, and deep in the earth there was also the pit of hell created when Satan was thrown out of heaven. As he fell, of course, he fell toward the center of things, and struck the earth with such a force that he left a great cavity in the regions under the earth's surface. He came to rest at the bottom of this yawning and fiery pit at the very center of the earth. There Satan became frozen in a cake of ice, the perfect symbol of total separation and isolation. The angels who fell with him, however, still obeyed his will and tried to lure men and women into his realm in an effort somehow to soften the pain of separation from the rest of the universe.

According to this medieval idea, Jerusalem, the Holy City, was the actual center of the universe, and it was here that Jesus, the Son of God, came to rescue humanity from the domination of Satan. By meeting and finally conquering the Evil One on Golgotha, Jesus gave all people the chance to be liberated from death and hell. Then he ascended back to the highest level of heaven to sit at the right hand of the triune God and share his glory. Human beings still needed to live their earthly lives trying to follow the right way, and then strive toward heaven after death, but in the end the result was assured for all who would make the effort.

It is strange how we treat this medieval Christian vision of the world and death. Most of us, especially when we have no other view to take its place, treat it like a poor relative who comes visiting smelling strongly of alcohol. There are students who describe and even analyze the similar visions of other cultures and point out how interesting they are. But there seems to be a fear of this Christian view, as if learning about it might contaminate us unconsciously with superstition. For instance, nowhere in the new edition of the *Encyclopaedia Britannica* is there a full presentation of this point of view. Even more important, in all the literature about the various religions of the world I have found almost no effort to compare this vision of another life with the views from other cultures in order to see if, in some way, they might have meaning for people today. Yet there are dozens of these visions from people all over the world which show enough basic similarities to this one to suggest that they may have meaning for many people in the world today.[1]

The problem for us Christians today, however, is to try to understand the meaning of this description of heaven and hell which comes from the union of Aristotelian thinking with Christianity. First of all, it is important to realize that this view comes from the period of history when there was a growing interest in the physical world. This description is expressed in terms that represent the need for a greater interest in physical reality and tell of the growth of that interest. It also expresses the fact that to the people of that time heaven and hell were as real as the physical universe. They could not actually see heaven and hell but they were real to them nonetheless. (In the same way we cannot "see" X-rays or atomic particles although we believe they are a part of the structure of things.) To leave heaven and hell out of the total picture would have been as unthinkable as if a physical geographer simply ignored the tops of all mountains that were hidden by clouds or all land below sea level.

In addition there were other senses in which this view of the world beyond was real to at least a good many people of that time. When Dante Alighieri set down the most detailed description of these ideas in the *Comedia*, which we now call *The Divine Comedy*, he wrote to his patron, Can Grande della Scala, that his work was not simple, but had more than one level of meaning. Within the world-view of that time there was no question that the medieval picture of heaven and hell was understood literally. As Dante was quite aware, the picture he presented was also an allegory of human salvation and our journey toward our ultimate destiny. It had a third level of moral meaning and was understood as a revelation of the moral fiber and structure of the universe. In addition, it was clearly understood in a fourth way as offering a spiritual or mystical meaning, and in this spiritual and mystical sense the great medieval vision of another world may still be somewhat valid although the world-view which gave it literal meaning has long since been put on the curio shelf.

In the *Comedia* (which means simply a tale that has a happy ending) Dante combined the literal vision of his time with the more mystical, Platonic view of human beings and their destiny. In this way he produced a story which expressed the deepest kind of religious experience, first on a personal level, and then by expressing an eternal meaning which the people of his time could grasp. Dante warned more than once that his story should not be taken too literally, however, in regard to either the political figures he con-signed to various fates or the exact location of heaven and hell.

This man was not an isolated poet, dwelling secure by his fireside, but an important political figure of his beloved city of Florence. In 1302 he was exiled under sentence of death and for years knew "how salt is the taste of other men's bread, and how hard a path it is to go up and down upon another's stairs."[2] By using his imagination to picture what he might meet if he could visit hell, purgatory and heaven, Dante kept his deepest religious experiences alive and moving, and this enabled him to live creatively in the most difficult of times. In this way his creative contact with another realm helps to offer hope to all of us. Let us look at the way he pictured the afterlife.

The Geography of Heaven and Hell

Dante was well acquainted with the writings of the great synthesizer, Thomas Aquinas. He had studied philosophy, theology, science, particularly astronomy, and classical poetry. He was a universal scholar, and on top of that he was a true poet. There are people who have been caught by the music of his verse and learned Italian simply to experience it fully. Modern readers, however, seldom try to understand what he was saying. A few people read the Inferno, the description of hell, for its more lurid passages, and some may adventure up the slopes of Mount Purgatory with him. But it is the rare individual who goes on with Dante. It is so much easier for us humans to imagine hell than heaven. We are sure that hell is what we deserve, and we have trouble imagining a continued life as meaningful.

On every level, beginning with the dark wood in which he found himself on earth, Dante told an exciting and moving story, and he apparently knew what he hoped for in the end. He found what Agnes Sanford has called the "healing of the memories" in the earthly paradise on top of Mount Purgatory and was ready to soar into the ten levels of heaven. At last in the celestial white rose he came to the divine encounter. Of that meeting with the triune God he wrote:

> Power failed high fantasy here; yet, swift to move
>> Even as a wheel moves equal, free from jars,
>> Already my heart and will were wheeled by love,
> The Love that moves the sun and the other stars.[3]

Dante's story begins when he realizes that he is lost in a dark wood. Hoping to escape by climbing a beautiful mountain, he finds his way blocked by fierce animals. He is stumbling headlong in despair when suddenly Virgil appears. The ancient poet—whom Dante has loved through his works—tells him that he cannot escape by going that way. The only way out of his dark wood is to pass through hell and purgatory and finally ascend to heaven. In ordinary language Virgil is saying that the inner way is not easy and

In order to see Dante's picture of the afterlife without going into too much detail, it is necessary to use some diagrams. Let's first of all look at a general view of paradise[4] which also gives an over-all picture of this vision of the cosmos.

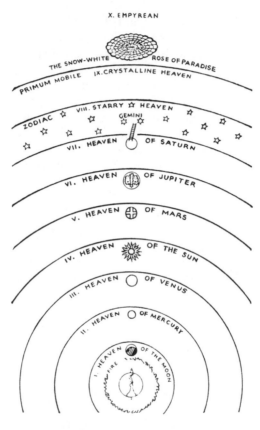

GENERAL VIEW OF PARADISE

At the bottom of the diagram is the central sphere of the earth, a dense physical reality surrounded first by a ring of fire and then by the heavens in concentric circles—the heavens of the moon, the planets and sun, the stars, and finally the two that belong to God himself.

The following diagrams show first the location of hell and purgatory in the earthly sphere and then the detail of these two regions through which Dante passed to reach the heavens.

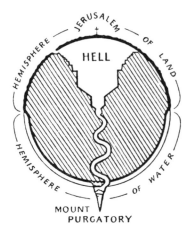

Just below the Holy City lies hell, extending to the center of the earth, and exactly opposite is Mount Purgatory which was pushed up when Satan fell into the depths of the earth.

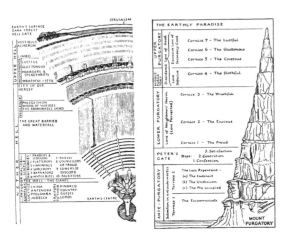

The details of hell and purgatory are shown. Dante's path led down from the surface of the earth through each area of the sinful who chose not to be redeemed, and then up the steep ascent of Mount Purgatory past all those souls who were struggling to be free of their sins. Together these diagrams suggest the journey from the earth's surface to the heights of heaven.

that one must go through hell to achieve a true vision and an experience of reality. Dante is dismayed, but he sees no other way but to ask Virgil to lead him, and together they approach the gates of hell and read the inscription: LAY DOWN ALL HOPE, YOU THAT GO IN BY ME.

When Dante hesitates, Virgil asks him to lay down all his distrust, and Dante, at least half-consciously, decides to abandon his own hopes and rely on Virgil, thus accepting the way of faith, hope, and of course love. The two go on, first into the vestibule of hell where they meet crowds of people flitting back and forth and running futilely from wasps. These are the shades of people who were never able to decide for or against anything on earth. Across the river Acheron lies hell itself, and when the ferryman comes to take them across, Dante falls into a trance, as so often happens when he passes from one stage to another.

When he comes to, they are on the edge of the pit of darkness. Level after level encircle the pit to its very bottom, separated into three divisions. The poets enter the first five levels with little trouble, finding first in limbo the good pagans and unbaptized Christians, including many of the great philosophers and heroes of ancient times; then people who have let sexual desire run away with them; third those who have indulged other appetites to excess; fourth the misers and the spendthrifts; and last those who have either nursed their anger or vented it on others. In each level Dante talks with souls, often recognizing someone he has known on earth. He also meets demons and furies and strange monsters.

A little farther down the river Styx encircles the red-hot walls of Satan's City of Dis which guards those who have let violence rule their lives. Again the poets are ferried across and come to the barred gates. Finally they are allowed to go on when a messenger of God demands it. There are two circles here. They find first, entombed, those who have done violence against their own beliefs, and down a precipice the people who have done violence to their neighbors, themselves, and against God and nature. The two then are carried down the great barrier and enter the last two circles of hell.

There are first those who have committed all kinds of fraud on other people, as listed on the diagram of hell. This is a level of fire and boiling mud and pitch, very different from the ninth and last circle. Here all who have betrayed love, the traitors against family or friends, those like Judas, Brutus, and Cassius, are frozen in a lake of ice. And at the very bottom stands Satan encased in ice breast high, his generative organs at the exact center of the earth. He is a frightening sight, and Virgil takes care to prepare Dante who is cold with fear. Then he tells Dante to hold fast to him and, grasping the hair on Satan's body, begins to climb down it. As he reaches the legs, Virgil makes a great effort, turns them completely over and begins climbing up, so that Dante is sure they are heading back into hell. But they come into a little cavern with a passage leading up toward Mount Purgatory. They sit for a moment looking at the great legs sticking up. As Helen Luke has explained:

> Once past the generative organs of evil the down becomes up and up becomes down. The poets are climbing towards the antipodes. (They have passed the center of the earth and gravity is reversed.)[5]

The two waste no time starting the long climb up. They emerge into the breathtaking beauty of starlight and fresh air at the foot of Mount Purgatory.

Purgatory and the heavens are also divided into three sections with nine levels and a tenth which is the culmination rather than the entryway. The same kinds of forces and appetites and impulses are found in purgatory and heaven as in hell, but the difference is that they are being redeemed and transformed by love, while the people in hell want and are given only more of their evil. Before the poets can set foot on the mountain, Dante must be interrogated by the old moralist Cato who tells him to wash the grime of hell from his face and cut a reed from nearby to gird his robe. These acts symbolize his readiness and desire to be free of his sins and his acceptance of humility.

Virgil and Dante move quickly past those who have been excommunicated or were too lazy or preoccupied to keep up their religious practice and so must spend time on the lower slopes. When these souls are ready to begin working toward redemption, an escort will take them to Peter's Gate. But Dante has a dream of being carried by an eagle, and while he sleeps Saint Lucia, who has had special meaning for him, carries him to the gate. The angel who is the keeper of St. Peter's keys is doubtful about admitting this pair without an escort, but when he hears how Dante reached this level, he is convinced and the heavy gate creaks open.

They join the souls who are learning to contemplate the opposite images of indulging and redeeming their instincts. On each of the next seven levels (or cornices) each group also learns by doing the opposite of the way they acted on earth. For instance those who were proud are bent under the weight of heavy stones; people who were greedy and grasping must lie face down weeping and unable to look up toward the release and the heaven which is now their greatest desire. It is from Dante himself, however, that we learn the most about the process of redemption that goes on.

On the ledges of envy, sloth, greed, and gluttony he is merely an observer, but when it comes to pride, anger and lust he is an active participant. Virgil begins to give him careful instruction about love and free will, but at the same time stresses something quite different. On the top of the mountain Dante will meet Beatrice whom he loved from a distance while she was alive, and who then became the central image of love for him. Virgil instructs him that through Beatrice he will find the realities he seeks. Dante then has dreams which force him to deal with his most central problems. On the last cornice he passes through the fire that purifies every kind of love and immediately has another dream that brings him relation with the parts of his soul. Virgil, who is still a pagan and cannot go on to heaven, is no longer his guide, and Dante leads the way into Eden, the earthly paradise on top of Mount Purgatory.

There he meets Beatrice, his own particular image of love. He cannot hold up his head when she accuses him of having betrayed the deepest inspiration of his love. At that point he is literally dragged into the waters of Lethe which take away all memories of wrong-doing, and then he must drink of the stream of Eunoë so that his memories are refreshed and blessed and his wits and consciousness are fully restored with new meaning. In this way he becomes light enough so that the soul's natural pull toward heaven lifts him beside Beatrice above the earth.

The compelling genius of Dante's vision of another life becomes very evident when it comes to the heavens. In heaven there is room for practically everyone[6] who loves and desires love. Each has a "place" and, as Beatrice explains after Dante has learned about the souls in the first circle of the Moon,

> . . . all share one sweet life, diversified
> As each feels more or less the eternal breath.

They're shown thee here, not that they here reside,
  Allotted to this sphere; their heavenly mansion,
  Being least exalted, is thus signified.

This way of speech best suits your apprehension,
  Which knows but to receive reports from sense
  And fit them for the intellect's attention.[7]

Thus each soul, remaining individual, finds the wholeness that is possible for all of us. They have access to all of heaven and at the same time a place where they particularly belong.

In each circle Dante meets and talks with individuals, among them some of the greatest men and women from Christian history, and throughout Beatrice continues to instruct him. At last his eyes and heart, instinct and intellect are prepared. His eyes are bathed in light that strengthens them, and he experiences the center of all reality and knows that he is moved by "the Love that moves the sun and the other stars." His poetic story presents a vision of total reality seldom equaled in human history.

The Copernican Revolution

In the Middle Ages, however, the full reality of Dante's vision was lost on many people because they understood it only as a statement of literal facts. Then in 1543 the discoveries of Nicolaus Copernicus fell like a cosmic explosion into the neatly ordered medieval cosmology. The theory which Copernicus supported with facts simply stated that the sun and not the earth was the center of our solar system. Rather than resting at the center of everything, our earth was just one of the planets which revolved around the sun and also turned daily on its axis.

The way was prepared for this momentous change by the discoveries of Columbus which robbed the earth of its mystery and gave a new understanding of the earth. It is difficult for us to realize the effect these voyages had upon the minds of men and women. A few years later the last of Magellan's ships completed the first voyage around the world, practically eliminating the possibility that there was any far, inaccessible place for Mount Purgatory. The medieval picture of earth was shattered. Now the whole idea of the physical-spiritual structure of heaven was blown asunder. The shock wave is still being felt. It has been only a few years since a Russian cosmonaut seriously remarked that he had not seen any sign of God out in space.

In the end heaven was not the only thing demolished by this new idea of the universe. Soon the importance of our very lives began to diminish as astronomers gave us an even clearer picture of the relation of our earth to the universe. In less than four hundred years we have seen human life on this earth removed from being the center of the universe to what seems like existence on a speck of dust circling a minor star on the remote edge of a small galaxy. From a purely physical point of view the former drama of salvation as Dante wrote about it has lost its centrality along with the earth. In addition the words of the Bible appear to have been contradicted. For instance, if the earth revolves around the sun, then Joshua must have been mistaken when he told the sun to stand still. By the twentieth century what had been the well-developed world-view of most Christians was in utter chaos.[8]

It is not easy for us today to understand how completely the theories of Copernicus shook the world of medieval Christianity. Few of us have ever been as secure about our place in the universe as the medieval people were and we can hardly imagine being as sure as they were about heaven and the ultimate importance of this earth in the scheme of things. There is one trouble with relying on the kind of logical certainty which medieval thinkers had achieved. Such perfect and coherent systems are vulnerable. If one element of such a system of thought is shown to be false, the whole system is likely to collapse like a house of cards. And if the system happens to be people's over-all view of the world, which necessarily involves their religious beliefs, then men and women are left struggling to find some belief or framework to which to cling.

This was the trouble with the security the Church had developed through this Dantean theory of the universe during the Middle Ages. This theory had a soft underbelly of fear, and Church authorities saw the implications of the Copernican theory and reacted to it with fear. Strangely enough, the theory itself was saved because those responsible for publishing it were afraid and inserted a preface explaining that the heliocentric hypothesis as the Copernicus theory was called was merely a convenient way of simplifying planetary computations.[9] But there were individuals who were not so lucky as these people who published the Copernican theory.

Giordano Bruno who supported the view of Copernicus was burned at the stake in 1600. Before he died, Bruno told his accusers, "You who pass judgment over me feel, perhaps, greater fear than I upon whom it is passed." In 1633 Galileo had to deny his belief that the earth moves around the sun in order to escape the same fate as Bruno.

It did not occur to Catholics—or to the new groups of Protestants, for that matter—that their great vision of another reality could be supported adequately on any other basis than the medieval system. They believed that the vision which Dante had portrayed so magnificently could still remain intact only if the orderly view of physical reality with the earth at the center could be maintained. By this time in history the ideas of Aristotle had been accepted so thoroughly among Christians that they apparently saw no way in which an actual heaven, hell and afterlife could be believed except as part of the physical reality found on this earth and in the heavens surrounding it.

It is very difficult for human beings to change their world-view even when there are facts that clearly show that it is necessary. The tremendous growth of interest in the physical world during the Renaissance did not give the Church any clearer insight into the problem of its world-view. Instead scientists were claiming a right to learn the truth about the physical world even if their findings conflicted with religious truths determined by the Church. Religious leaders saw no hope but to try to hold the former line. Any discoveries that did not agree with their established view of the world were called heretical. As a result the split between science and religion continued to deepen.

For over two hundred years the Catholic Church banned any book which taught that the sun, rather than the earth, was at the center of our system. Until at least 1822 no Catholic scientist could teach the Copernican heliocentric system (the view that the world revolves around the sun), without the risk of being tried for heresy.[10] The effect on science in the Catholic-dominated countries can be traced in the history of science. There were also determined efforts to hinder discoveries in such fields as medicine, particularly anatomy.

At the end of the nineteenth century the idea of using scientific methods finally began to ferment within the Catholic Church. This movement, known as "modernism," involved some of the leading

Catholic thinkers in Europe. They wanted to see the Church's doctrine and its world-view start to develop by using the tools of evolutionary theory and scientific understanding of the Bible and Church history. The movement was stopped dead in its tracks by the decree against modernism *(Pascendi Dominici Gregis)* issued by Pius X in 1907. By 1910 every cleric in the Catholic Church—including practically every professor at the beginning of each academic year— and each seminarian had to sign a statement agreeing to accept the faith as it was taught, as final, complete and not subject to growth or change in any of the ways suggested by the modernists.

The Catholic Church was thus cut off from using any of the critical tools that developed out of the Enlightenment, although these tools can help us understand our faith and help us understand what we really believe. This vow was required until 1967 when it was replaced by a new oath that is far less stringent and less hostile to human inquiry. During these years, however, the Catholic faith lost some of its finest minds, although others like Baron von Hügel remained within the Church and worked to bring about a view of religious realities which can be accepted today by the modern scientific world.

On the positive side the Catholic Church was preserved from the eroding effects of the Enlightenment by this action. Thus it maintained its organic unity and vitality until Vatican II. Now the Church has tools to stand against an atheistic science which it did not have in the first part of the twentieth century.

The scientists, of course, had their work cut out for them. They had more than enough to learn without undertaking to develop the religious meaning in the facts they discovered. Scientists struck out on their own, breaking away from the restrictions of what was considered the final religious truth and letting the facts lead them to whatever truth the physical world offered. So many different facts were convincingly demonstrated by scientific methods, and so many inaccuracies and inconsistencies were shown in the beliefs of the past, that, before the nineteenth century ended, many people were changing their way of understanding the world. There was no real effort by philosophers or theologians to help people come to an understanding based on Christian experiences as well as on the reasoning and findings of science. Although science was fast providing the tools that would make such a world-view possible, most of the leaders of philosophy and theology showed far more interest in a rational, scientific point of view than in Christian ideas.

The findings about the physical universe seemed to leave no place where heaven and hell could be located. If heaven was not up in the sky, and hell was not deep in the earth, where could they be? It never occurred to thinkers like Rudolf Bultmann that heaven and hell were real *in a non-physical sense* (as in another dimension of reality), and that the physical descriptions of them gave people ways of picturing these realities and sensing inwardly what might perhaps lie ahead. As late as the 1940's and 1950's Bultmann and his popularizer Bishop Robinson felt justified in debunking any picture of the universe with heaven and hell lying above and below the surface of the earth. They then left these ideas right there, in a void, without suggesting any new way of imagining their existence.[11]

In reality the medieval vision of heaven and hell did not stand a chance once the facts about the physical universe were becoming known. The Aristotelian point of view which we inherited from the Middle Ages made it impossible to separate people's images of the afterlife from physical matter. It was therefore inevitable that sooner or later the whole projection of heaven and hell onto physical realities would become absurd. There was no clear way to show that the descriptions refer to another area of reality. Consequently, most of us in the West have found ourselves all dressed up for a future life with no place to go.

For a while the soul still had reality in popular thought but gradually materialism overtook even the soul and people began to wonder if human beings had any destiny beyond this material world. Let us look now at the effects of materialism and how this world-view is beginning to change.

V. Is There a Soul
To Go Anywhere?
The Dogma of Materialism
and Beyond

Even after the nearby heavens were cleared of cobwebs by Copernicus and the Renaissance astronomers, it was still possible to believe that somewhere there was a realm partly spiritual in nature waiting for human beings. But scientists continued to take great bites of knowledge which kept suggesting nothing but physical qualities in things. Newton showed that there are physical laws that seem to govern matter wherever it exists in the universe. Things of every kind—large and small, far and near—appeared to follow the same impersonal laws that do not vary or change. Gradually the chemists learned about the ninety-two atoms which made up matter everywhere. They described them as similar to hard little billiard balls that had no choice but to react according to Newton's immutable laws. There apparently was no place in the universe that was not utterly material.

Even then, one could hang onto the idea of the human soul as something different from the rest of the material universe. But even the idea of the soul vanished after Darwin formulated his theory of the process of natural selection of the fittest so that human beings were seen as just one more result of a chance interaction of some meaningless atoms. Not only was there no place for human beings to go, but they now appeared to have no soul which could go anywhere either. Human beings apparently had no more meaning or future than leaves on a tree or any other thing created out of matter that lives for a time and then dies leaving hardly a trace.

The System of Materialistic Certainty

About the end of the nineteenth century these theories were developed into systems of materialism by some of the most influential thinkers of the time. The systems of Karl Marx in Germany and England, Auguste Comte in France, Herbert Spencer in England, and later of the behaviorists John Watson and B. F. Skinner in the United States all had one basic idea in common. They all considered that human beings had no importance or meaning in themselves. Each individual was merely an intricate combination of atoms that obviously would go back into air and soil after death and leave little else. Any notion of a soul was absurd. Everything about human beings could easily be explained by science without using metaphysical ideas.

The ideas of the soul and heaven and hell became useless baggage once thinkers recognized that there is a simpler, more rational explanation for the world as a whole. This left people with little choice. They could simply adjust to the new understanding that human life starts and ends as a meaningless, purely chance development, the result of random atoms directed toward complex structure by physical laws. Or they could see themselves caught up by the kind of purpose which Marx described as an inevitable process of rational, dialectical materialism. Konrad Lorenz even considers that the most basic cause of human aggression is people's failure to accept their hopeless fate of no eternal life with good humor. Lorenz develops this idea at length in his book *On Aggression*.

For a long time the Church continued to talk about life after death as if the Copernican revolution had never taken place. But as science became more sure of its own point of view, it seemed more and more foolish to talk about experiences that might give evidence of a life beyond this material universe. Any ideas of human capacities that did not come directly from sense experience began to appear as nonsense. Dreams seemed to be only playback as the human tape recorder rewound itself during the night. Visions, on the other hand, were completely illusory and showed that the machine itself was out of order. Extrasensory perception was simply absurd because it was considered an impossibility.

It is no wonder that Hermann Helmholtz, one of the famous

physicists of the last century, could declare to the world at a meeting of the Fellows of the Royal Society:

> Neither the testimony of all the Fellows of the Royal Society, nor even the evidence of my own senses, would lead me to believe in the transmission of thought from one person to another [telepathy] independently of the recognized channels of sense.[1]

Helmholtz was a very bright man, who recognized that the addition of any other way of knowing would upset the absolute certainty of nineteenth-century science in which he found such faith and security. It is ironic that the scientists were now falling into the same trap of certainty which had trapped the Church in the time of Copernicus. Scientific thinkers had begun to rely on faith in the established dogmas of science almost to the exclusion of new experience just as the Church had relied on faith in established dogmas in religion also to the exclusion of new experience.

Our perception of how we see or understand facts is a very delicate matter at best. When it comes to facts that do not fit into the accepted system of thought, there is a good chance that most people will not even notice such facts. The inability to recognize facts includes renowned scientists as well as officers of the Inquisition who may have denied facts because they actually did not see them. T. S. Kuhn has demonstrated this truth with a great deal of evidence in his important study of the development of modern science, *The Structure of Scientific Revolutions*.

For instance, in 1054, according to scientists and historians, there was a gigantic explosion in the Crab nebula far out in space. This explosion was recorded by the Chinese. Although this cosmic event was quite visible in Western Europe, it was simply not noticed there. In the West the belief in the cosmology of fixed stars had become a dogma of religious philosophy. The idea that no change could occur in the stars was so firmly entrenched in people's minds that they apparently did not even see the explosion.* Kuhn also

---

*Arnold Toynbee helps to explain why it was easier for Chinese observers to spot this phenomenon. Chinese science developed along practical rather than theoretical lines, and for this reason it did not come into conflict with either religious dogmas or the dogmas of established scientific theories. Thus the Chinese students remained more free to observe facts as they appeared, rather than looking only for established "truths." Chinese science originally developed faster than Western science, but because it did not develop a theoretical basis, particularly of mathematical theory, it could progress only to a certain point.[2]

discusses at length experiments with a deck of cards which has a red six of spades instead of a black one. Almost invariably the individuals who were asked to inspect the deck saw the red six of spades either as the expected black color, or else as an eight of hearts or diamonds.[3]

A trial attorney has discussed with me the problem of evidence in accident cases involving automobile-motorcycle collisions. He said that it is difficult to know whether the responsible driver is lying when he claims that he did not see the motorcycle. A person expecting to see another car may simply not see a motorcycle in front of him. Anyone who has had to proofread a manuscript knows how often an omission or other mistake is missed because one expects to see the right word in the right place. Our expectations can determine what data we are able to observe. Some of these expectations are based on our own view of the universe.

This problem of perception (seeing or taking in facts) has been discussed in some detail by Aldous Huxley. In *The Doors of Perception* he suggests that the function of the brain and nervous system is largely to eliminate too many perceptions rather than to produce them. These organs function so as to help us to concentrate and keep us from being overwhelmed and distracted by a mass of largely irrelevant and useless information. In *The Psychology of Consciousness*, Robert Ornstein, a research psychologist who teaches at the University of California Medical School, has developed practically an entire psychology of perception based on his efforts to understand this problem. His ideas are carefully supported by facts from his research and the research of others.

The nineteenth-century view of reality has left its mark on all of us who grew up in that school of materialistic thought. We learned almost from the start to believe the dogma that only physical matter is real by accepting only facts which could be seen and tested in the physical, material world. And therefore we go right on rejecting many experiences because they do not appear to have the tangible reality of physical matter. Often this view of the world keeps us from being able to see many of the facts and experiences which are most important to us in our religion.

In addition, most theologians are so completely caught in the dogma or world-view of materialism that they scarcely question the thinking on which it is based. Instead, theologians for the most part have done their best to rig Christianity to meet the specifications of this nineteenth-century science as they have not kept up with the twentieth-century scientific discoveries. The result is a Christianity which has little place for a real human soul and no place for a meaningful heaven. On the whole the subject of life after death is simply discreetly avoided.

Most of us who are Christian seem to be left facing an impossible dilemma. On one hand we can choose a way which is usually uncomfortable for Westerners. We can try to live with a divided mind, with religion in one compartment and science in another. If we can accept the claim of the more fundamentalist religious groups, it may even be possible to keep our heads in the sand, ignoring science and the world and hoping that these disturbing facts will go away. One then leaves one's intelligence outside the door as one goes to church or a religious meeting. On the other hand, we can dismiss religion—particularly the ideas of the soul, the afterlife, the breakthrough of God into the world—as so much illusion and nonsense, perhaps even becoming evangelists to reveal this truth to the world. There can be a third choice, however, which probably offers the only real solution to the dilemma. This is the possibility of changing our view of the world, of finding and accepting a new vision, of finding a new hypothesis about reality. This is what we hope to be able to do in the remainder of this book.

It takes time for us to change any of our views of reality. New scientific ideas often take fifty to seventy-five years to reach the general public, while the earth-shattering theory of Copernicus actually took centuries to become generally accepted. There appear to be some real signs of change beginning in our time, however. The works of Baron von Hügel are gradually becoming known. As I have mentioned, his *Eternal Life* is the only significant attempt that I know of today to offer thoughtful people in the modern world an approach to a theory of the possibility of life after death. While von Hügel did not have the scientific data to show exactly at what points the old materialistic world-view was open to serious doubt, his brilliant intuitions led him to the most essential conclusion. His study of the life of St. Catherine of Genoa and her mystical experiences convinced him that there must be another dimension of reality, besides the physical ones, with which we human beings can interact.

In the last decades many questions have been coming from the scientists themselves. We shall look now at the amazing results their investigations have revealed, and then outline briefly the view of the world to which they lead.

Disturbing Evidence

In his recent autobiography, *All the Strange Hours,* Loren Eiseley reveals the state of mind of many of the leaders of the present scientific community. After describing his struggle for an education, which he calls "Days of a Drifter," and the long period of growth within his profession, or "Days of a Thinker," the well-known anthropologist and essayist turns to his later years. He speaks of the "Days of a Doubter." Eiseley's doubt was not doubt concerning religion or religious ideas, but rather doubt in regard to the dogmatism of the scientific world. In describing it, he shows a new and increasing openness to the idea of meaning and purpose in the universe.

There has been a scientific revolution in our century. More and more evidence has accumulated that the materialistic view of the universe is not adequate. It simply does not take all the facts into account. Once this materialistic view is abandoned, then the way is open once again for serious discussion of another dimension of reality. The evidence for life after death and even for heaven and hell can thus be discussed intelligently. Within the materialistic framework asking about survival after death is to ask a non-question, as the researchers Richard Kalish and David Reynolds[4] discovered when they tried to find previous studies of people's attitudes toward possible contact with the dead. Their effort to find background material for their own study produced absolutely nothing. A question about survival was a non-question. One cannot ask sensible questions which have no place within one's paradigm or view of the universe.

If human beings, like other matter, are confined by walls of space and time, then questions about life after death appear to be pure nonsense. But how do we know that this space-time box does confine us entirely? In order to maintain seriously that we are totally contained within a purely physical universe, a person has to believe implicitly one of two things. One can decide that he or she knows *all* the facts of the universe and that there is no shred of evidence to the contrary and this is obviously an absurdity. Or else one must maintain that he or she knows the essential nature of the world itself. Since this cannot be demonstrated once and for all just by logic, one can maintain it only *by faith*. Yet it is this very *faith in materialism* which is being subjected to so much question, particularly among modern theoretical scientists. It seems humorous, but the questions come almost entirely from the scientists. Their facts come from such diverse fields of inquiry as physics, mathematics, medicine, anthropology, sociology, parapsychology, and clinical psychology. Let us now turn to these facts to see how they open the door to the possibility of a new view or a new vision of the universe.

Physics and Mathematics

In 1955 Robert Oppenheimer gave the keynote address to the annual meeting of the American Psychological Association. In it he pleaded with the psychologists (and this was directed particularly to the behaviorists who form a majority of the membership) not to base their psychological thinking and reflections on a model of the world that physics had abandoned. He went on to say that physicists are no longer convinced that they have clear knowledge of what matter is or how it acts. New methods had led to the discovery of so many new subatomic particles in each element of matter that scientists could no longer say for sure exactly what can or cannot happen within this matter.

The new discoveries did not even stop there. They have kept right on until there are well over two hundred subatomic particles known today. In *Space-Time and Beyond*, a recent book by Bob Toben, Jack Sarfatti and Fred Wolf, one gets a glimpse of the speculations which are opening up in modern physics and how interested the physicists are in all kinds of human experiences. This book, which grew out of conversations with two theoretical physicists, attempts to show how the new theories of physics can help to explain telepathy, precognition, psychokinesis, and religious healing. William Tiller, winner of a Nobel prize for his work in solid-state physics, also discusses the relation of radiation to consciousness and the developing sensory system. His fascinating article is found in *The Dimensions of Healing*. Many physicists at present are spending a great deal of time trying to see how physical theories relate to our experiences, our consciousness and our personalities.

In 1974 I was invited to address a group drawn from the three universities at Moorhead, Minnesota, and Fargo, North Dakota. I was asked to speak on several ways of opening individuals to spiritual reality. The meeting had been planned in part by clergy, but mainly by a group of physicists who felt that they needed to know more about this aspect of human life. They believed that this kind of insight might throw some light into the confusion existing in theoretical physics. As I presented ideas about encountering aspects of the inner, spiritual dimension of reality, it was the clergy who had been trained in nineteenth-century thinking who were the skeptical ones, not the physicists. I have had this experience time after time.

This revolution in physics began with Becquerel and Mme. Curie who started the collapse of the nineteenth-century scientific point of view by showing that one of the apparently indivisible or ultimate ninety-two elements was constantly breaking up and changing into "rays" and other substances. In this way they tilted one of the pillars of the supposedly "certain" and final system of scientific knowledge, and gradually the whole system began to collapse. In the end many scientists lost *faith* in the logically certain scientific system. A few years after that Einstein showed that the physical theories of Newton did not apply to the whole universe but only to a small part of it, and they did not even apply on the earth with perfect exactness. Therefore, these laws were not so omnipotent and perfect as people had generally thought. Einstein also discovered that there was relativity as far as space and matter are concerned and that time and space are interdependent and that mass or material can be converted into energy. Most of us are acutely aware of this last product of theoretical physics because of the atomic bomb and the electricity which keeps many of us warm and keeps our homes lighted.

Then Werner Heisenberg demonstrated that we can never know exactly what is happening to an electron, which is one part of each atom and thus is one of the basic building blocks of the universe. By observing an electron one disturbs its activity so that one can never be sure how the actual pattern of movement is developing. This discovery was called the principle of indeterminacy or uncertainty, and this brought Heisenberg into conflict with the Russian scientists who recognized the devastating effects of such an idea on the absolute certainty of their Marxist theory of dialectical materialism. Heisenberg commented on this in his important book, *Physics and Philosophy*. In this book he also remarked that physics has become so skeptical that it is now skeptical of its own skepticism. He went on to suggest that many words from the natural language of humankind like "God" and "spirit" and "soul" may be closer to the reality of things than many of the highly developed words of physics like "mass" and "energy" which physics has used to describe the developing field of modern science.

What these thinkers have shown, each in his or her own way, is that one can no longer assume that "physical" matter is all there is in the world. Although physics once provided reason enough to doubt whether there could be another realm of existence, this is not true today. Instead, many physicists themselves are investigating the kind of experiences that suggest, perhaps, *various* dimensions of reality. They would be the first to laugh at the idea that physics itself makes it impossible to believe in either a "place" or a life beyond this one.[5]

In mathematics there has been one basic discovery which is just as dramatic as those in physics. In 1931 a young mathematician, a twenty-five-year-old by the name of Kurt Gödel, published a paper "On Formally Undecidable Propositions of Principia Mathematica and Related Systems." Gödel has been termed by some the world's greatest mathematician, largely on the basis of this work. In it he proved the inadequacy of logic as a means of coming up with final, incontrovertible answers. He was able to get two totally different answers to the same problem, using the accepted principles of the mathematics of Russell and Whitehead. Gödel showed, by the methods of pure mathematical logic, that logic cannot supply absolutely certain proof of even the most basic propositions of simple arithmetic. What would seem in ordinary logic to be an unarguable answer turned out every time to be based on an assumption which could be proved only by making a further assumption. Each time the process started over . . . and over, without end.[6]

This proof has important implications for computers. They are based on human logic and occasionally spit out totally irrelevant answers to the problems posed to them. All long computer runs need to be checked by human beings with an understanding of what the answer ought to be.

The implications of this work are of tremendous importance for all fields of inquiry. Since logic is an indispensable tool, we must keep its use as close to experience as possible, testing the results by experience wherever possible, and being as sure as we can, through experience, that the right assumptions are fed into the process. It is easy to see the need for such care in computer work where, for instance, the lives of astronauts often depend upon instantaneous computer decisions based upon what human beings have fed into the machine and then checked by human understanding.

The same care is needed in religious thinking, including thinking about life after death, which can affect our lives deeply. Above all, we need to realize that logic can help us to find answers only when it is used as a tool to consider actual evidence and data and this evidence and data cannot come from anywhere but from human experiences. Metaphysical thinking which does not touch base with experience can become illusory speculation. If we are looking for answers that have meaning, there is no place to start but with the facts of people's experiences, past and present, using logical methods to compare them and understand them. Logic which contradicts and denies possible experience can be very deceptive and misleading.

Evidences from the Human Sciences—
Medicine, Anthropology and Sociology

There was a time within the memory of some of us when ailing human beings were treated like pieces of inert matter. The way medicine was still being practiced in the 1920's was ridiculed in a British medical journal with none too subtle humor. The physician remarked:

> I often wonder that some hardboiled and orthodox clinician does not describe emotional weeping as a "new disease," calling it paroxysmal lachrymation, and suggesting treatment by belladonna, astringent local applications, avoidance of sexual excess, tea, tobacco and alcohol, and a salt-free diet with restriction of fluid intake, proceeding in the event of failure to early removal of the tear-glands.[7]

People who were treated as just physical things could not be expected to have souls or any afterlife.

Things have been changing, however, in the medical profession, starting with the publication of the book *Emotions and Bodily Changes* by Dr. Flanders Dunbar. In the 1930's and 1940's Dr. Dunbar worked to uncover a mountain of evidence showing that human emotions have a direct effect on people's health. She had been deeply influenced by the discoveries of Sigmund Freud, and she was able to see the pieces of evidence that others had overlooked. Her studies influenced other physicians to become interested in psychosomatic medicine. Textbooks were written and two medical journals were started dealing with this subject.

In addition, the influence of religion and faith on bodily health began to be realized in many places. Two of the most impressive statements on this subject have come from two psychiatrists. The first, Dr. Jerome Frank, a professor of psychiatry at Johns Hopkins University wrote about it in his carefully documented study, *Persuasion and Healing*. Near the end of this book he noted:

> ... faith may be a specific antidote for certain emotions such as fear or discouragement, which may constitute the essence of a patient's illness. For such patients, the mobilization of expectant trust by whatever means may be as much an etiological remedy as penicillin is for pneumonia.[8]

He went on to emphasize that we need "faith" communities in order to mobilize the sick person's faith, concluding:

> "No man is an island," and the degree and permanence of change in any individual will depend in part on corresponding changes in those close to him and support from his wider milieu.[8]

The second psychiatrist, Dr. Alan McGlashan, a British psychiatrist practicing in London, has written a similar "praise of faith" in a book which shows how the scientific scene is changing. In *Gravity and Levity* he writes:

> It is in fact very difficult to cure anybody of anything by means of a remedy in which you yourself have no faith. The successful doctor, no less than the successful "quack," is the man who is really convinced he has got something.

> Every medical man has had experiences of achieving impressive results with a certain drug, *so long as he believed in it himself*. As soon as he has some failures and begins to doubt its remedial powers, the results on patients tail off, and in a few months the "wonder-drug" is, as far as that practitioner is concerned, discarded and forgotten.[9]

Dr. McGlashan adds that this applies to surgery as well as to drugs. He cites the nearly universal practice of removing tonsils and adenoids earlier in this century, concluding that "the procedure is no longer believed in; so it no longer works."[9]

Dr. James Lynch who teaches psychosomatic medicine at the University of Maryland Medical School has written a wise and important book on the effects of loneliness on human health. *The Broken Heart* is a study of neglected influences on heart disease, especially the effect of isolation and lack of human interaction. He wonders if this reality will ever be amenable to ordinary scientific study.

Some of the most interesting work dealing with life after death has come from doctors who have recognized that the dying were neglected in most hospitals. Dr. Elisabeth Kübler-Ross came up against intense resistance when she began the work which resulted in her book *On Death and Dying*. Dr. Kübler-Ross has had many experiences in dealing with the dying which defied the materialistic framework in which she was raised. At present she is preparing a book relating to these experiences, many of them involving contacts with the dead. She has also written an introduction to the book by Dr. Raymond Moody, *Life after Life*, which describes the experiences of persons who have recovered after being pronounced clinically dead.

Thus the medical profession itself is providing new evidence of other kinds of reality than just the physical kind by beginning to look at illness and death directly and without foregone conclusions. It also offers some evidence of life after death and support for some theories about it rather than denying the possibility. We shall look at this evidence in some detail in the next chapter.

One of the most damaging assumptions of materialism was the thoroughgoing denial of any meaning in the evolutionary process. This arose from Darwin's findings and theories. He maintained that evolution was a purely mechanical process which did not show any idea of purpose. Perhaps people needed to be confronted by Darwin's agnostic and critical thesis. Supernatural purpose and angels and God had been used from the Middle Ages to modern times indiscriminately to explain anything that seemed to need explaining. Now that the deficiencies of Darwin's approach are understood we can return to the idea of purpose with a new appreciation for the place of meaning and purpose (or God) in the developmental process. We are thus able to approach this idea with greater care and precision than we would have been able to at an earlier time.

It was the recognition that developments in any species came through mutations and not just through a step-by-step process which threw the first monkey-wrench into Darwinian evolutionary theory. Then Pierre Teilhard de Chardin provided a theory to show

the meaning of the evidence that was accumulating. In *The Phenomenon of Man* he suggests that even the smallest inorganic piece or
element of matter has associated with it some meaning or purpose or
spirit. He therefore sees evolution, not as a blind development of
chance, but rather as a directed purpose moving toward a definite
goal.

Loren Eiseley has proposed a somewhat similar theory in his
many delightful essays. His book *The Immense Journey* lays out the
evidence for a meaningful evolutionary process in a thoroughly
readable and less technical way than the approach that was used by
Teilhard de Chardin. In *All the Strange Hours* Eiseley has also described his studies of Charles Darwin, revealing that this great
genius was not even entirely candid about all the sources for his
theory of natural selection. This is a minor matter, but it is one that
helps us realize that Darwin was not infallible. He did not give
credit where it was due.

While there are still many who consider human beings the
chance product of a meaningless world, more and more thinkers are
taking a deeper look at the process of evolution. Teilhard de Chardin and Eiseley represent a growing group of anthropologists and
other thinkers who believe that humankind has a meaning and a
purpose and is moving toward a goal. Dr. Ilya Prigogine recently received a Nobel prize for an analysis which comes up with similar
conclusions about "dissipative structures." Therefore, there is reason to believe that human beings have a destiny and may well have
a life beyond the grave.

In anthropology much the same kind of shift is taking place. A
professor of anthropology, James Bellis, pointed up how the shift is
occurring when he spoke to one of my classes at Notre Dame on the
subject of ritual and liturgics. He introduced his remarks with a
most interesting illustration. He said that formerly when a group
of anthropologists observed a native going out to visit the grave
of a relative, they would say: "We watched the man go from
the village and come to the grave of his wife. There he poured his
libation upon the grave and *thought* that he talked with the spirit of
the deceased." Now an anthropologist would describe it quite differently, by stating: "The man went out to the grave, poured his
libation on the grave and *talked with the spirit of the deceased.*" The first
way introduces the assumption that the Western materialistic
world-view is the only possible approach, an idea which anthro-

pologists are beginning to realize is quite questionable. There are other world-views than ours, and the good anthropologist observes, describes, and does not pre-judge a situation like this one.

Two recent studies by sociologists show how they are beginning to deal with experiences and ideas which do not fit into the world-view of so much of Western civilization. One is the study I have mentioned by Drs. Kalish and Reynolds, who did a careful survey of four different ethnic groups in Los Angeles to learn what these people believed about life after death and the possibility of post-death contact with deceased individuals. As already noted, they became aware that they were breaking new ground in their field.

Dr. Andrew Greeley of the National Opinion Research Center in Chicago and his co-worker William McCready have recently published the results of a similar but more inclusive survey completed in 1973. Nearly 1,500 individuals were asked about mystical experiences, including déjà vu, extrasensory perception and also contact with the dead. Some of the findings are reported in an article "Are We a Nation of Mystics?" in *The New York Times* magazine section for January 26, 1975. A full report is found in Greeley's book *The Sociology of the Paranormal: A Reconnaissance.*

From the point of view of sociology the possibility of looking at the reports and evidence for survival after death is now gaining some acceptance, and we shall look at the evidence provided by these researchers and some others in the next chapter. The wall of ice has begun to melt.

Parapsychology and Clinical Psychology

The open acceptance of parapsychology among scientists has come fast in the last ten or fifteen years. It is probably doing more than anything else to open scientists to a new point of view. A recent survey of the attitude of scientists toward these experiences showed that only twenty-five percent of them had doubts about the reality of such phenomena, compared with seventy-five percent of them who did twenty-five years ago. In 1969 the American Parapsychological Association was accepted into the American Academy for the Advancement of Science, giving professional recognition to the study of these experiences. There has also been a rash of books about research into "psi" experiences in the past five years,[10] including my own book *The Christian and the Supernatural*, in which some of the recent researches are described.

There is a wide range of research going on in accredited scientific institutions around the country, as well as in other countries, especially in Russia. Various hospitals are working with telepathy, particularly as it occurs in dreams. In telepathy information or thoughts are transmitted directly from one mind to another without any known way of contact between them. At various universities and at the Stanford Research Institute in Menlo Park, California, healing, psychokinesis, and clairvoyance are among the phenomena on which research has been done.

Psychic healing is very likely a special form of psychokinesis. Psychokinesis is the manipulation of objects (for instance, moving an object, bending metal, separating the white and yolk of an egg, changing the temperature of something) by thought alone, again without any possible physical contact. In clairvoyance a person "sees" a hidden object without any way of touching or viewing it. Precognition, or receiving knowledge of an event before it happens, is also being studied by many scientists. In addition to the research in various institutions, there are also physicians and other scientists who are studying these experiences independently.

This research uses careful and highly inventive techniques which are producing convincing results in spite of the fact that the findings, which we shall touch on later, so often seem incredible. For those who are interested, my book *The Christian and the Supernatural* gives a sampling of the methods and the findings, while *Supersenses* by Charles Panati offers a complete picture of all the areas of parapsychology in one volume.

These phenomena have all been connected with religious practice, including that of Christianity, from the earliest times. In fact recent Christianity is one of the few religions of any era which has completely rejected these experiences. It sometimes appears that the present rejection may be largely an emotional reaction because the world-view which Church people have accepted for so long is being challenged by new data. Even a quick look at the research findings reveals that this present attitude on the part of many Christians is not dictated by an objective interest in the *facts*.

Probably one reason that many psychiatrists, clinical psychologists, and even physicians have become deeply interested in these experiences is because they are found in connection with a variety of out-of-the-ordinary states of consciousness. Besides occurring around religious leaders and sometimes as a result of religious rituals, these experiences can also occur because of the use of drugs or through hypnosis and trance (which is the kind of takeover or possession of a person's psyche which mediums encourage). They can result from falling in love (a somewhat milder but still similar possession) and from anger and hatred (which can also be a state of possession).

In addition, parapsychological events are quite often associated with both neurosis and psychosis. This has made it necessary for some of the leaders of psychological therapy to work toward developing a new understanding of human beings and the world in order to see the meaning of this kind of experience in the illnesses and healing of their patients. Quite a number of psychiatrists and psychologists have been forced to abandon a materialistic view of the world because of the very nature of their work. These therapists help people find healing by doing little more than encouraging them to deal with elements that appear in their dreams and in other ways from the unconscious. In the process they sometimes see surprising physical healings occur for no apparent physical reason. It is small wonder that this is the profession from which the basic outlines of a new world-view has come.

This, however, causes problems. When Sigmund Freud started writing in the last years of the nineteenth century, he had two strikes against him. First, he recognized the importance of sexuality, and, second, he had to create a theory of an unconscious mind and a psychic reality in order to see some meaning in the diverse materials his disturbed patients brought to talk about. His theories broke with the strict materialism of his time and so he was rejected and ridiculed by most of the medical and scientific world of that period.

Gradually his ideas took root and were found useful both in treating mental illness and in anthropology and social theory. In a letter written to a friend in July, 1921, Freud stated:

> I do not belong with those who reject in advance the study of so-called occult phenomena as being unscientific, or unworthy, or harmful. If I were at the beginning of my scientific career, instead of at the end of it as I am now, I might perhaps choose no other field of study—in spite of all its difficulties.[11]

When people get into the unconscious, at least to the extent that Freud had to become involved, they inevitably discover that there

are hidden ways of knowing and extraordinary results which the
materialistic world-view either ignores or rationalizes away.

A New View of Reality

One of Freud's colleagues and friends, C. G. Jung, picked up
where Freud left off and carried out the implications of depth
psychology for new ways of knowing. In 1921 Jung was just coming
to the full use of his talents. According to Jung it was an argument
with Freud on this very subject of occultism and its implications for
the reach of the human mind which caused the split between
them.[12] Jung developed a new and quite careful understanding of
the universe and human or psychic reality. A diagram will help to
clarify this new view of reality:

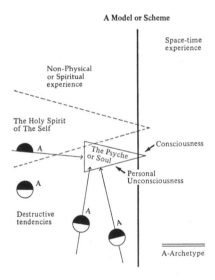

A Model or Scheme

Two kinds or realms of reality are suggested by the diagram. The world of space,
time, energy and mass (on the right) does not need to be detailed, since our
consciousness is turned in this direction most of the time. But our psyches are
surrounded by non-physical or spiritual realities of which we are scarcely aware.
"The Self" is used to depict the supreme or divine good, and the shadowed area of
"Destructive tendencies" represents the principle of evil at work in both realms of
reality. The term "Archetype," used centuries ago by Augustine, suggests various
kinds of beings which can touch and affect our psyches, which Christians have called
angels and spirits of various kinds.

For modern Westerners the Enlightenment wiped out much of the reality on the left side of the diagram and materialism finished off essentially all the rest. The only existing reality became the physical world of sense experience, reason and human consciousness, represented by the area on the right. The world of the unconscious, of non-physical or spiritual reality, on the left, became simply make-believe, created out of people's daydreaming. There could be no knowledge except that which came through sense experience and reason, as the physicist Helmholtz emphasized so strongly. Any knowledge of something that does not have material existence is non-sense.

To the Buddhist or the Hindu only the left side of the diagram tells of reality. According to the East, those things which we Westerners call physical reality and personality are only illusions created by the ego. They are *maya*. For followers of Eastern religion enlightenment occurs when people can get over believing that the physical world and the integral ego have any abiding reality. From this point of view, which Jung points out again and again is *not* for Western Christians, the events of the physical and historical world are not truly real or important.

The most basic understanding of Jung's view of reality is found in his statement that there are two kinds of reality in which human beings are immersed, two areas of which they have knowledge. Both are legitimate subjects for scientific inquiry. Jung has found that there are many kinds of experience which can be encountered on the non-physical side of reality. One can deal with archetypes and disembodied souls, with destructive and demonic forces, and sometimes people come into contact with the divine itself. One can also get a vision of the essential nature of this entire reality. The experiences that people have of this side of reality confront us with the existence of a very real non-physical world which has far-reaching effects on human life.

This world can be discovered and explored in several different ways. Probably the ways or methods that are the safest, the most direct, and the easiest to use are by listening to one's dreams and by using religious ritual and meditation. Since working with these inner experiences means that the psyche itself is investigating psychic reality, this kind of exploration is usually more difficult than investigating outer reality. There are no easy rules to know whether facts have been verified objectively or not. Like Columbus, we have only the test of whether the trip results in finding land. In this case the tangible results will show up in transformed human lives. Again like Columbus, the difficulty of being certain does not make this new world any less real or less valuable to discover.

The materialistic hypothesis has been questioned by so many thinkers and by so much data that it requires considerable faith to hang onto it. Although many people will find it easier and safer to do so, a more complete hypothesis has been suggested by Jung. This view is similar to the world-view of Jesus and his time and to the view of the early Church. Arguments are of no value in testing this hypothesis. It must be tried out to see if it accounts for most of the data, both old and new, including the facts that materialism explains as well as the newer data requiring a new point of view. Testing this new hypothesis is then a process of trying out various experiences. While this process may take a long time, my prediction is that in fifty years or so there will be only a few holdouts who opt for the partial view of rational materialism. By then the new understanding that human beings have direct contact with both psychic (or *psychoid**) reality and physical reality will very likely be the accepted framework of our Western world.

From the point of view of this hypothesis, the idea of contacts with people who have died and glimpses of the kind of reality one will encounter after death make perfectly good sense. This does not mean that one can accept any or all data that emerge from the non-physical world without critical evaluation, any more than one accepts experiences of the physical world without checking and comparing. But the important thing is that this view of the universe encourages discussion and evaluation of the data that can be gathered from our experiences. Facts can be brought out into the open rather than being kept in the shadow of old wives' tales or shoddy occult secrets. Our experiences can be examined and analyzed, and some basic picture of life after death can then be offered for critical evaluation. Without this kind of world-view the experiences and the data are either ignored or left in the hands of questionable practitioners.

*The word "psychoid" is used to speak of realities that are similar in nature to the human soul or psyche, but come principally from beyond the limits of any individual psyche. While it seems probable that these realities all originate in the beginning from the same source, our present understanding is so limited that we need to distinguish between *psychoid* realities that come, at least in part, from beyond any human being, and *psychic* realities that can be pinpointed as belonging to some human psyche or psyches.

There is a growing awareness, particularly among young people, that the old dogmas have lost their vitality. It is very difficult today to present a point of view to either young people or knowledgeable adults on the basis of authority alone. Modern human beings have lost their faith in dogmatic authority. They have also become more and more skeptical about the validity of conclusions reached by reason alone. Rational speculation simply seems irrelevant to many individuals, both old and young, who have absorbed the modern hypothetical way of thinking, and are no longer able to accept the closed, unvarying approaches to reality that reason and authority usually offer. As Dr. Alan McGlashan suggests:

> The current conflicts of youth against age and authority are in essence a revolt against *smugness*, against the closed, superior attitude of mind which assumes that somewhere there is always a final truth to be found, if only reason is followed patiently to its conclusion. Youth in some unconscious or intuitive way has tuned in to the physicists' discovery that there is no final truth to be found anywhere, that reality in the last resort is ambiguous, open-ended, a recurring balance of contraries.[13]

Modern minds have found that our experience is more real than any rational explanation of it. We must use authority and reason to sift and evaluate all the relevant data, but not to force decisions on potentially responsible people so that they can be led astray into false dogmatism again. No one has presented the implications of this data more clearly than V. S. Yanovsky in his recent book, *Medicine, Science and Life*.

We shall now turn to the data of experience which is available at this time. We shall look at the studies of a number of phenomena which have been mentioned and see how these occurrences give us confidence to take some vision or view of eternal life seriously. In the process we shall look at some "red sixes of spades," or pieces of experience which do not have a place in theology books today.

PART THREE

Opening the Doors to Eternal Life

VI. The Evidence for Survival After Death

It may seem that we have taken a long detour to get to the actual subject of life after death. There is no question that the evidence for some kind of survival after death is a very important matter. It is important if there are some facts, and it is equally important if there are none. But as I have tried to show in these first chapters, it is practically impossible to deal with this evidence so long as we remain within a framework or world-view which does not allow for non-physical reality.

Most of the researchers in this field have noted the lack of serious scientific study of this subject. Ordinary textbook science does not admit the existence of a spiritual reality. Because of this, within the world-view held by most people, any scientific question about a person's continued existence after death is considered a non-question. It is literally a meaningless question or, in the philosophical language of Wittgenstein, "non-sense." In most instances not even psychologists can conceive of any value in asking such a question as this.

Just a few days ago I received a letter from a professor in the department of religion of my alma mater, Washington and Lee University, asking me to speak on the subject of parapsychology and religion. He explained that someone had given a grant to the university to stimulate study in the field of parapsychology. When the proposal was discussed in faculty meetings, the psychology and science departments emphatically refused to have anything to do with it. The money was then offered to the department of religion which received the grant because the other departments were simply not interested in the subject. Stories like this turn up again and again. They show our rejection of non-physical experiences and of people's continued search to understand these experiences. Some of the most interesting published accounts of such rejection are found in the book *Song of the Siren*, in which Stanley Krippner tells of the problems that were met in the early research in this area.

Our culture still keeps its materialistic prejudice. In spite of the fact that this research continues and evidence keeps on accumulating, people find it difficult to consider the reality of parapsychological experiences, and so they automatically rule out any idea of life separate from material reality. Therefore the possibility of continued existence after death is denied. Once more (at the risk of being held repetitious): *Unless we can be open to the possibility of some kind of existence different from the life we experience in the material world, which perhaps is even immeasurable, it is useless even to consider or study the question of survival after death.*

Here and there some students have begun to gather evidence, however, and there are signs of many people's resistance to the view which would reject that evidence. But this is basically a "grass-roots" resistance which occurs at a deep level in some individuals. For the most part, it does not touch the theological community, which has been fairly well brainwashed by the world-view of rationalistic materialism. As a result we find many religious writers uncomfortable with any evidence for continued existence. They consider life after death a matter of revelation which should not and cannot be investigated by ordinary human experience. It must be accepted upon pure faith, and not because of any convincing evidence. Religious writers and theologians who are caught in the nineteenth-century world-view seem to be afraid of such facts. Apparently it does not occur to them that it is silly to rely on faith when there are both experiences and facts available. For instance, one very intelligent and usually broadminded theologian, hearing of my interest in Dr. Raymond Moody's evidence about life after death, remarked that I always seemed to be pursuing some kind of off-brand or odd interest.

Let us now turn to the actual evidence, keeping in mind that we must look beyond the current popular understanding of God and the world around us in order to be able to evaluate these facts. We shall look first of all at the experiences of people who were brought back from the actual point of death. Next we shall consider three different experiences of the dying, and then reports by various individuals telling of encounters with the dead. We shall find that some of the strange experiences and ideas of spiritualists and mediums offer understanding and support for the evidence, if scrutinized with real care. We shall then touch on the need for a better understanding of parapsychological and dream experiences in order to approach questions about life after death. Next we shall see what the evolution of our personalities or souls suggests about an afterlife, and then take a preliminary look at the subject of reincarnation. This will bring us to consider modern physical theory, especially Einstein's view of time, in order to see how present-day physics opens up the possibility of a continued existence. Finally we shall discuss mystical experiences, meditation and poetry and see what they express about another reality beyond the present world. We shall then see what conclusions can be drawn from all of this about the possibility of life after death and the beliefs in an afterlife which have been held by almost every culture from the beginning of recorded time.

Near-Death Experiences

In various kinds of literature we find stories of people coming to the edge of death, getting a taste of what it is like and then returning to describe their experience. Plato concluded *The Republic* with the story of Er, a warrior who apparently died in battle and found himself, with many other souls, met by judges who told him to observe and then go back to tell living people what he had seen. He regained consciousness as he was being laid on the funeral pyre, and he then told all that had happened to him.[1] Plato used this story to bring home his central message and to conclude his great dialogue *The Republic*. He provided a philosophy which makes room for life beyond the present existence. One of the best illustrations of his view is found in the famous allegory or myth of the cave in this same work.[2] He saw human beings chained in a shadowy cave and tried to show how different life would be when they were freed to come into the brilliant light of a wider existence.

As I have already indicated in an earlier chapter, there is a widespread belief that the human soul goes on a journey after the body dies, but there are few literary accounts of people coming to the edge of death and then returning. Probably experiences of this kind have contributed to the careful descriptions of what happens to the soul at the point of death described in shamanism and in *The Tibetan Book of the Dead*. It is interesting that the Bible, with so many suggestions that life continues beyond the grave, offers no clear, specific account of near-death experience. There are several returns from death, the most notable of them that of Jesus. There is the raising of Lazarus, Jairus' daughter, the son of the widow of Nain, Tabitha, and the young man who fell from a window while Paul was preaching. In each case the emphasis was more upon the raising from the dead rather than upon what the individual experienced on the other side. It should be remembered that people living in New Testament times needed little reaffirmation of their belief in life beyond death, but rather needed affirmation of the value of this physical life. The healing miracles usually are pointing in this direction. The Bible was never intended to be a source book of all human knowledge and experience.

Emmanuel Swedenborg, writing in the early eighteenth century, claimed to have been through the early events of death and to have had experiences out of the body. He described them in some detail. Carl Jung described carefully the experience of one of his patients and also gave a complete account of his own brush with death during a serious illness. The entire chapter entitled "Visions" in *Memories, Dreams, Reflections* is devoted to this experience which Jung described as appearing to be of a completely objective quality. A similar experience described by Arthur Ford is found in *The Life Beyond Death*, the book put together by Jerome Ellison after Ford actually did die. The complete text of these accounts from Jung's and Ford's writings is included in the appendix. Tolstoy appears to have known of the near-death experience, for his description of Ivan's death in *The Death of Ivan Ilych* is an accurate account of such an experience. Stanislav Grof and Joan Halifax give an excellent historical survey of such near-death experiences in their book *The Human Encounter with Death*.

Probably the most detailed and interesting story of such an encounter with death is that of George Ritchie in the book that he wrote with Elizabeth Sherrill, *Return from Tomorrow*. Dr. Ritchie tells of the clinical death he experienced when he was in the army in World War II. It was the most important experience of his life and provided direction and meaning for him throughout his professional career. Dr. Ritchie's experience is particularly significant as it comes from one who has examined his experience carefully and submitted it to the criticism of his supervisors in psychiatric training. The story, ably told with the help of Elizabeth Sherrill, is a very moving one, and I would heartily recommend it. This description is important, for it triggered one of the most important and best-known studies of near-death experiences.

In 1965 Raymond Moody, an undergraduate student in philosophy, learned of Dr. Ritchie's experience and went to talk with him. He was impressed by the story and the stature of the man who told it. He mentally filed away the account. Later, as he tells in the introduction to Dr. Ritchie's book, he heard of other quite similar experiences and began to investigate the subject in depth. Raymond Moody went on to receive a Ph.D. in philosophy from the University of Virginia and then on to teaching philosophy. Afterward he decided to become a medical doctor and a psychiatrist. Both Dr. Moody and Dr. Ritchie discovered that when they described the near-death experience, someone in the listening group would usually come forward to share a similar experience. By the time Dr. Moody began his residency in psychiatry he was writing his first book, *Life After Life*, describing these experiences of other people in detail. This study shows that experiences of something beyond this life happen far more often than most of us have imagined.

Because of his medical training, Dr. Moody has learned to be careful about his facts, and his background in philosophy has given the methods of analyzing and reporting the facts. He is well aware of the rules of evidence and logic. There is nothing sensational about his presentation. He makes no claims for final proof. He simply offers evidence. I have shared the lecture platform with Dr. Moody and I am impressed by his straightforward and honest handling of the material. He is a sincere and genuine person whom one enjoys knowing.

The material for *Life After Life* came from interviews in depth with about fifty people selected out of one hundred and fifty cases of near-death experiences. An over-all picture of what happened to them was given describing the fifteen typical elements in their accounts. The response to this book was almost overwhelming. Hundreds of letters poured in to contribute new examples. Out of this material Dr. Moody wrote a second book, *Reflections on Life After*

Life, in which he carefully analyzed further accounts, adding some other common elements. One of the most interesting things that he described is that this kind of experience can occur when clinical death has actually taken place, when the heart has stopped beating and respiration has ceased, or it can happen when there is simply a threat of death and the person suffers no apparent physical damage. He tells the story of a man in a truck accident who had a near-death experience without even getting a scratch.

In the two books we find nineteen elements in all which sometimes enter into these experiences. Only a few of these are common to all or most of the accounts, and so far there is none in which more than about half of these elements appear. There does not seem to be any rigidly pre-arranged order of occurrence. Most cases appear to differ in sequence, although some of the experiences are almost identical.

Almost everyone spoke of the first, most common element: their experience was inexpressible. There was something about it which was more than could be described. It was more than they had words for. This is not surprising. We Western men and women seem to limit ourselves to expressing common experiences. When it comes to unusual or mystical experiences like this one, our language is poverty-stricken. The Greeks used at least twelve words to describe encounters with the non-physical world, and students of Sanskrit tell me that they have over twenty words for various nuances of spiritual experience, while we blush to use more than one or two. Yet perhaps the important part of such an experience for us is its ineffable quality or the fact that something we cannot express makes us certain that it is a genuine encounter and not something we have thought up on our own.

The next characteristic is also found in practically every experience of individuals who return from clinical death. They report knowing or hearing themselves declared dead. Usually they hear the voice of a doctor or nurse, or perhaps a spectator at the scene. However, they do not feel dead. Like people who are "slain in the spirit," they feel perfectly conscious even though they are unable to move their bodies. To the outside observer they appear to be in a coma, both mentally and physically inert. For instance, if shock or an injection is given to bring them back, they show no reaction of pain. And apparently pain is not felt during a near-death experience. At the same time the person may hear every word that is said, sometimes with abnormal clarity. It is important for people who visit the dying to realize this fact. Dr. Alan McGlashan brings this out in his book *Gravity and Levity* in which he discusses several instances of patients in a coma who knew everything that was being said and done.

At this stage many people report a sense of incredible peace, and often comfort or pleasant quiet. Any pain they had suffered has suddenly disappeared and instead they are filled with a sense of well-being and comfort. Nurses and those in religious orders who work with the terminally ill report the same thing. At the point of death there often comes a time of peace and quiet acceptance, even contentment. The unpleasantness we fear so much does not seem to be connected with actual dying, but with the devastating suffering which often leads to death.

The accounts generally describe that other kinds of things then begin to happen almost immediately. Many people tell of hearing some kind of noise once they are cut off from direct awareness of their bodies. The noise can come in many different ways. Sometimes it is described as an unpleasant noise, a loud buzzing, roaring or banging which is absorbing and even grating. Some people hear a softer rush of wind, while others are drawn by a melodious ringing of bells or the sound of beautiful music. It is as if another realm of existence first breaks in upon dying people in a way that touches their senses and gets their attention.

Along with the experience of a noise, a great many descriptions tell of being drawn rapidly through a dark, tunnel-like space. To some people the area appears like a sewer or well, and there are other descriptions of a cylinder or funnel, a narrow valley or cave. However it is pictured, the experience seems to be that of being drawn through and out of one's body. These images all appear to imply separation from one kind of existence, from life in the physical body, and entrance into another realm and another kind of life.

At this point in the course of most near-death experiences people seem to be separated or disengaged from their bodies. They are apparently able to observe their bodies from the outside and watch what is being done to them. Some individuals have been able to describe in detail the efforts to revive them, even though their physical senses were in no condition to see or hear anything that was happening. They described "hovering" or "floating" above their unconscious bodies and watching the scurry of activity. Sometimes they described the backs of nurses and doctors bending over them. Later, to the amazement of their physicians who corroborated the details, they reported exactly what went on, including complicated medical procedures that they had never actually *seen*.

This aspect of the near-death experience seems to be similar to the psychic phenomenon of clairvoyance known as an "out-of-the-body-experience," in which the person seems to separate from his or her body and to get information about things that are completely out of range of sight, hearing, or other bodily senses. This kind of clairvoyance is discussed at some length by Charles Panati in his book *Supersenses* and also by Lyall Watson in *The Romeo Error*.

According to some of the reports, people in this state of disembodiedness find it difficult to believe that they are dead. They have what seems to be a body, but not a physical one. They can see and hear people in the physical world and feel baffled because they cannot make contact with them. Time does not seem to exist for them, at least in the sense of clock time. They have unimpeded thought and movement and perception. They seem to pick up thoughts of others in a telepathic way rather than through hearing in the ordinary way. Sometimes they mention how difficult and depressing it was to be separated in this way from the world one has known.

In most cases, however, the sense of isolation apparently does not last very long. Meetings with friends who had already died, and also with some other kind of being, are described in quite a few of the accounts given to Dr. Moody. Arthur Ford in his own near-death report told of being greeted by many of the dead whom he had known. There are also many deathbed reports of dying persons who appeared to speak with someone who was not present in the room with them. We shall discuss this later.

In addition there is another element of encounter described by the people whom Dr. Moody interviewed which is even more significant. This encounter, in fact, seems almost too good to be true.

The Most Significant Element

People who are brought back from actual death often speak about coming into the presence of "a being of light" who is experienced with the same intensity the disciples felt when Jesus was transfigured before their eyes. In spite of the intensity of the light and the fact that this being appears to ask probing questions about the direction of the person's life, there is seldom anything painful reported about this experience. Instead, what is described is a sense of direct, personal communication and a feeling that the being of light is expressing love and concern for the person, even in asking about the quality of his or her life.

As one would expect, this experience has a tremendous impact on the individuals who encounter it. This element is so important that an example is needed to help us define and understand it. In one account presented by Dr. Moody the person related:

> I floated . . . up into this pure crystal clear light, an illuminating white light. It was beautiful and so bright, so radiant, but it didn't hurt my eyes. It's not any kind of light you can describe on earth. I didn't actually see a person in this light, and yet it has a special identity, it definitely does. It is a light of perfect understanding and perfect love.
>
> The thought came to my mind, "Lovest thou me?" This was not exactly in the form of a question, but I guess the connotation of what the light said was, "If you do love me, go back and complete what you began in your life." And all during this time, I felt as though I were surrounded by an overwhelming love and compassion.[3]

There are so many descriptions of contact with the divine as an encounter with light that we can mention only a few. The Quakers speak of their experiencing God as an experience of the inner light. In Greek Orthodox thinking *the Light* is considered a central description of the invisible God. One of the main elements of Paul's experience of God on the road to Damascus was the appearance of a great light. This experience of light, which also occurs frequently in the depth of meditation, seems to be one of the most common and most significant aspects of the near-death experience.

This element of meeting the being of light seems to precipitate a review of the person's entire life. It appears from the accounts as if all the events and feelings and reactions of one's whole life are present, as in a rushing river flowing with incredible speed before the mind's eye. In some cases only the highlights seem to appear, while other people tell of feeling that they see everything that ever happened in their lives. Along with the review there seem to appear two standards for assessing the value of one's life, which are: Did one learn to love others, and did one acquire knowledge?

In addition to these most common elements of the experience

there are several other aspects that often appear. Some people tell of suddenly seeming to be in touch with all wisdom and knowledge. The possession of knowledge seems to be a quality of "the being of light," and these individuals, without any effort, suddenly seem to share in it. They express a sense of contact with a mind which understands everything and puts them in touch with all of that knowledge. It is like having an infinite computer at one's fingertips. This is an ecstatic or visionary experience which is greatly valued by these individuals.

Then there is the "city of light" or "heaven" which some people describe. Although Dr. Moody had few reports in his first book which could be thought of as describing a heaven, in his second book he included these accounts. They tell of seeing people in such a place, but in a form different from ordinary human existence. Apparently one does not see or hear them in the ordinary way but simply "knows" they are there. In the same way one "knows" that this is a place of vivid colors, flowers and fountains, beautiful scenery, with even the streets and buildings of a city. There is a sense of peace, of beauty, love and non-darkness. The same kind of detail was also told with fascinating clarity by Arthur Ford in his account, which is included in the appendix.

Another Kind of Element

In his first book Moody seemed to give a totally pleasant view of everything encountered in the near-death experience. But in his second book he tells of several persons who reported seeing other people who had evidently died and were caught in a rather unfortunate state of being. They seemed to be in a state similar to Sheol, a place of gray, dull, meaningless existence. They appeared bewildered. It is this kind of state which C. S. Lewis described in *The Great Divorce*. It is also found in *The Divine Comedy* in Dante's vision of aimless spirits flitting about the entrance to hell. Moody suggests that the descriptions given indicate individuals who could not see beyond their physical existence and remain attached to it. They are uncertain where they want to be and, compared with other descriptions, they seem dull and limited. As Arthur Ford suggests in the similar description in his account, these beings may be stuck in this condition until they make up their minds which way to go.

Dr. Ritchie, in his book *Return from Tomorrow*, also gives a vivid description of spirits who appear to be caught in their own desires and hates and fears. In the first stages of his near-death experience he found himself in this condition. Dr. Maurice Rawlings introduces his book *Beyond Death's Door* with the frightening experience of one of his patients who dropped dead during a stress test and apparently found himself tormented in hell. The man had to be revived more than once, and each time, in spite of his physical suffering, he begged to be kept alive and saved from the hell he was experiencing. Yet two days later when he was able to talk, the patient remembered almost everything that had happened *except* his terrifying experience of hell.

Dr. Rawlings, who is a heart specialist, discusses several other accounts of people who have "seen" or experienced something like hell and were able to recall the experience after they recovered. He believes that many more similar accounts would be reported if people undergoing near-death experiences could speak at the time about what was happening to them. His cases also show that people who are brought back from death more than once may, perhaps in many instances, go through an unpleasant experience the first time, followed by a pleasant or heavenly encounter later on.

Another aspect which Dr. Moody's later interviews revealed more fully is the experience of rescue from death. Some people who came to the brink of death reported that a voice or light appeared and protected them. Sometimes directions were given that brought them through. In other cases a presence was felt and assurance was given that the time for their death had not come and they would survive in spite of the odds. These people usually felt a sense of caring which all but erased their fear of death.

In some accounts of near-death experiences people tell of coming to a point of no return and finding the way blocked. They may see themselves at the edge of a body of water, or approaching a door or a fence across a field which they cannot pass. They are apparently not to go any further at this time. These experiences seem inconclusive, largely because the person comes just to the edge of the "realm" in which near-death voyagers seem to find themselves. For some reason the way is blocked at the boundary, and so the individual experiences only a fragment of the potential which appears to be available.

The very quality of the near-death experience makes it difficult for many people to want to return to ordinary existence, and the return is often resisted. In the first moments of apparent death there seems to be an intense desire to get back into the body. But as one experiences more of what is available on the "other side," there is evidently less and less desire to return. Some people say that they do not know why they return, while others realize a need to do so because they still have unfinished business to accomplish in this life. Whether people say that they were forced to return, or that they had a choice, their attitude toward the experience is usually the same. Again and again one finds reports that this was the most vivid and real experience of a person's life. People often speak of how this experience stays with them, and they value it as Jung did, as an experience of absolute objectivity.

There is no doubt about the frustration in returning to normal life after a near-death experience. One naturally wants to share what has happened, but most people cut off anyone who talks about this kind of experience. They are afraid of it because they share the current fear of death and the commonly held world-view which has no place for such experiences. Until Dr. Moody did his research almost no one would listen openly, with understanding, to accounts like these. Andrew Greeley says the same thing about the ordinary reaction to mystical experiences. It is difficult to listen to such experiences unless one has a view of reality which has a place for them. These experiences shake one's view of the world and one's confidence in it. Few things are more disturbing than having our view of the world questioned.

Many people report that their lives have been changed by this encounter with near-death and something beyond. They seem to have a deeper sense of human values, particularly love, and a new sense of purpose and meaning in their daily lives. They take life more seriously, and yet playfully, and their fear of death is diminished. They have been near the edge and have found that life did not cease and there is even more meaning beyond death than on this side. And so they no longer see death as either the cessation or diminution of life, but as an entrance into a larger and more complete form of existence.

Two questions have been raised as to whether it is wise to make studies like this at all. In the first place many people have wondered if such reporting may not be a dangerous incentive to suicide. The answer to this question, interestingly enough, is found in Dr. Moody's study. Certain of the accounts he received were reports of near-death experiences after attempted suicide. These, without exception, were unpleasant experiences which contrasted sharply with the bulk of the descriptions. These accounts all suggest that people who try to get out of a difficult situation in this world through suicide find themselves in similar difficulty after they leave their physical existence behind. Persons who are tormented here apparently cannot solve their problem by electing to leave this life. The torment seems to go on with them.

On the other hand, those who come to death naturally generally work through a series of stages. This process, which has been studied by Dr. Kübler-Ross, can bring a person to a real acceptance. And from all that we can learn from the experiences of near-death, this seems to be the best preparation for making the transition. Of course it is not always easy to distinguish between natural death and suicide. Some people kill themselves by stupid or careless living without resorting to violence, and there is need to ask what may happen to them. But in the case of violent termination of life, people apparently do not get rid of problems or find experiences which could offer them peace and growth. Understanding these near-death experiences may well deter suicide.

Second, Dr. Moody has been criticized because his reports have so little to say about judgment and punishment. These critics have been taught that an angry and critical God is waiting to judge them for every sin, and they question the reliability of accounts which tell a different story. Yet except for cases of suicide, very few people seem to experience anything resembling the fearful preaching of judgment to which many of us were subjected. In his second book Moody suggests that the real factor may be self-judgment. He finds that people sometimes feel severely judged during the review of their lives, particularly if they are faced with wasted talents and unwise decisions. The judgment, however, seems to come from themselves rather than from an "Other." One reason why solitary confinement is such drastic punishment is that the prisoner is forced inward into self-reflection. Few things are more painful than the self-castigation which often results.

Perhaps the difficulty and pain usually suffered in dying naturally are harsh enough so that human beings do not need more judgment than they find in examining their lives. If we see life itself as a constant process of dying to daily events and rising again, then we have already begun the separation which is finally completed in death. In this way we gain enough distance from this world to have some perspective on our lives. We will certainly not be upset to find that people's near-death experiences suggest that death is an initiation into a new stage of life and development rather than entry into a static place of reward or punishment. As St. Catherine of Genoa once said, hell may not be a place at all, but only the fire of the rejected love of God. As for judgment, in Jesus' words, "Here lies the test: the light has come into the world, but men preferred darkness to light because their deeds were evil" (Jn. 3:19).

This, then, is the kind of experience that Dr. Moody has found by listening to those who have come to the edge of death and returned. Let us also consider one more account which came to me several years ago, some time before the present studies had begun. It is the report of a woman who had been ill for quite a while. She did not seem to be recovering, but immediately after this experience at the point of death, she began to recover rapidly. She recalls:

On the morning of Friday, November 2 at 4:00 A.M. I was in bed in a hospital. . . . I was in such great pain that I called for the nurse to give me something for pain. She refused because I was reacting with an allergy to the medication that had been given before for pain. I begged for hours for something to relieve my paining body. After about seven hours of agony and begging they called the doctor who prescribed a medication for me. I remember being asked if I would eat dinner and saying, "No, I'm too tired and my body is too heavy to move." I also remember being asked to take muscle relaxers and replying that my tongue was too thick. After that I had no more pain and was not even conscious of having a body.

Then I went into a deep sleep. I felt that my body became heavier and heavier, and then lighter. There was so much pressure within me. My body seemed to get lighter and heavier, lighter and heavier, until I seemed to be two people or things. One was very heavy and one was practically weightless by now. The weightless part of me began ascending further from my heavy body. Everything around me was swirling and misty clouds—like fog, only very bright and beautiful.

A voice was calling to me. It said, "Connie, come. Connie, come." The fog left just as abruptly as it had appeared. There was God, the most beautiful being I had ever seen in my life. He was all white. His hair was white. His eyebrows, face, hands, feet, beard, and even his robe were white. I begged and pleaded with him, "No, not now, Lord. My husband and children need me. Please, not yet. Please, dear Lord, just a while longer. They need me. Please, dear Lord, please not yet." I was swirling round and round and going higher and higher.

Suddenly I stopped and said, "Lord, thy will be done. Please take me, dear Lord. I am ready. If it be thy will, I am yours. Take me home with you to the beautiful life you have let me see." I begged him to take me home with him, but he said, "No, go." I fell into the fog again and kept falling and falling. I saw my body below me getting nearer and nearer. I couldn't stand the falling and I begged God again to take me. And he answered softly, "No, go." The lighter part of me seemed to be slipping inside the heavier part. With every breath I took my body seemed to divide and become one, divide and become one. Over and over my body did this. Finally it seemed to be one, and I opened my eyes.

Nurses were bending over me. They asked me how I felt and I told them, "I have no pain. I think I died and went to heaven." Later they told me how worried they had been because they felt no heartbeat for a while, and then my heart began to beat so fast they couldn't count the pulse. My heart also seemed to jump from my chest. From this time on I became better. This is how I remember what happened one week later.

This woman speaks of the same quality of experience which Dr. Moody would later reveal from interview after interview. In addition there was apparently a remarkable effect upon her physical health.

Still, in these accounts there is always the question: Was the person truly dead? Before we conclude that these experiences come from beyond this present world and this life, some supporting evidence is needed. Can such evidence be found in the experiences of those who are known to have died? Let us see if reports about the dying show any similarity to the near-death accounts.

Evidence from Those Who Did Not Come Back

There has been one very thorough and interesting study of deathbed visions. In 1977 after nearly twenty years of research, Dr. Karlis Osis presented the results of his investigation of this phenomenon. He first became interested in it because of W. F. Barrett's book *Death-Bed Visions* which was published in the early 1920's.

Barrett had gathered all the examples he could find of the visions which some people appear to have at the moment of death. He and his wife, who was a physician, had been deeply touched by an experience of one of her patients at the time of death.[4]

Dr. Osis, a Latvian with a Ph.D. degree in psychology from the University of Munich, began this work in 1959 with a pilot study. A questionnaire was sent out to ten thousand doctors and nurses asking for information about any visionary experiences they had observed among dying patients. Six hundred and forty answers came back in which nearly three thousand deathbed visions and experiences of an unusual nature were reported. Dr. Osis was aware of how easy it is to manipulate such statistics, and so he next obtained another group of answers from the same professions, using careful methods to insure a random selection. This was followed by careful interviews with those who answered the questionnaire positively. He also wished to check the data in another culture, and in 1972 he and a colleague, Dr. Erlendur Haraldsson, did a similar survey in northern India. Dr. Haraldsson also holds a Ph.D. in psychology, and since he had worked on the same kind of data in Iceland, he was able to add another cross-cultural check.*

The results of three studies were presented by the two men in their book *At the Hour of Death*.[4] In each case the results bore out their carefully framed hypothesis about the kind of experiences which might be expected if death is a transition into another level of existence rather than simply the dissolution of personality.

Three experiences at the time of death were investigated: apparitions or experiences of other human beings or non-human beings, visions of places apparently not known to the physical senses, and elevations of mood or experiences of elation at death. Over a thousand reports of these experiences were investigated thoroughly and the results were subjected to statistical analysis. These were all reports by doctors and nurses, the group Dr. Osis had selected because they are in contact with so many dying people and are also trained in objective reporting. He discovered that the descriptions they gave tallied quite closely with the more personal accounts described by Dr. Moody in his two books.

*Osis and Haraldsson both earned their Ph.D. degrees on the basis of research in parapsychology, and both have worked at universities in this country. Osis is a noted research scientist, while Haraldsson is professor of psychology at the University of Iceland.

The most common experience reported was that of apparitions occurring shortly before death. Patients who were still clearly conscious and in touch with their surroundings would speak with someone not in the room, or they would tell of seeing someone as if from another realm. Very often the persons who appeared were recognized by patients as friends who had died and who seemed to welcome them and lead them away from this life into another dimension. Sometimes beings appeared that seemed to have a non-human quality and were described as angels or some kind of super-being, according to the cultural language for such realities. In either case the dying persons usually seemed to become aware of another level of reality. Fear of death usually ceased, the pain of illness abated or disappeared, and they seemed to have a sense of well-being and even joy. There were a few exceptions in which a patient fought the idea of death and seemed to turn away from the being who appeared. But most often observers noted a sense of joyous reunion with someone who had previously been very close to the dying person.

Long before I heard of Dr. Osis' work I had begun to realize that something like this might be true. I was given a fascinating account of a dying clergyman who lay for two or three days free of pain and, in joyous tones, talking alternately with his wife and apparently with deceased friends and angels. The letter describing this experience was published in a pamphlet entitled *The Reality of the Spiritual World*.[5] It recalled the experience of Stephen in Acts 7, who stood telling what he saw in the heavens and spoke to the Christ as he was stoned to death. I soon learned that such experiences are not uncommon, as Billy Graham points out in his book *Angels*, and that many Christians have had them.

The visions of some place unknown in this world were remarkably similar to the experiences of such a reality described in Moody's second book. These patients spoke of seeing gardens, green grass and great beauty and light. At the same time the words they used also stressed the supernatural quality of these things. They did not ramble on about places in this world in the manner of psychotic patients, but quite clearly, even precisely, described an "other-worldly" place. Much the same observations were made in India as by American physicians and nurses. In most cases they were not very different from the other accounts we have considered.

In a large number of cases mood elevation was reported in both

India and the United States. These experiences occurred close to the time of death, often when the patient was depressed and in great pain. Suddenly a dramatic change was observed. Pain disappeared or was no longer significant, depression lifted, and the dying person's actions and even words expressed peace and satisfaction. These changes made a real impression on observers, particularly the nurses. Patients often became more cooperative and less difficult to handle. Something of transcendent importance seemed to happen to them at the edge of death which was reflected in their mood and attitude and appearance. I have observed this experience of elation in a woman I was visiting who was dying of lung cancer. Her confidence and joy as she died made an impression on me which I shall never forget.

One of the most telling statements of such an experience is found in *The Nayler Sonnets* by Kenneth Boulding. Besides the twenty-six sonnets, Boulding reports the exquisite statement of James Nayler as he was dying. Nayler had just been released from prison and torture for being a Quaker, and almost immediately he was set upon by bandits and fatally injured. In his last words he confessed the nature of the Spirit that touched him at that moment, and then he died.

From their statistical analysis of the reports, Osis and Haraldsson find no evidence that these experiences might be hallucinations caused by brain damage, drugs, or psychosis. They give examples of hallucinations caused by these factors and then show how such illusory experiences differ from what often happens at the time of death. The experiences of the dying among the population in India showed as little hallucinatory quality as those of Americans. In fact the differences were surprisingly minor in view of the language and cultural differences.

Wishful thinking can also be eliminated as a possible cause of these experiences. Far from expecting a particular experience, people are nearly always surprised by what they actually find. As Dr. Elisabeth Kübler-Ross has shown, while wishing may open a person to such an experience, it does not determine what will happen. She has worked with children who were dying. If they wish for their mother or father to appear to them before they die, someone often does appear. But unless the mother or father has already died at that time it is someone else who appears. When all the data are analyzed, there seems to be very little evidence that either conscious or unconscious wish fulfillment is at work.

Osis and Haraldsson conclude from their research that these apparent ESP glimpses into the beyond provide evidence for some kind of survival after death. In addition these facts throw doubt upon the theory that our personalities disintegrate and dissolve with the death of our physical bodies, and also upon the world-view which gives birth to that theory. The two researchers make no claim of proof. They suggest rather that there is evidence which is real and needs to be taken into account. They would like to see further investigation done. They believe, along with Dag Hammarskjöld, Carl Jung and others, that the way we view death will affect the way we live life. The conclusions they offer are strikingly similar to the view presented by Moody. They also offer a wealth of illustrative material in addition to statistical analysis.

Experiences of Post-Death Contact

There is still another kind of evidence which has given a great many people reason to believe in life after death. This is the experience of contact with the deceased described by living individuals. Stories of these encounters have been told from time immemorial. One of the most vivid memories from my own childhood is of having my mother tell me about such an experience which I have described in Chapter 3.

Experiences like this are often described as occurring almost at the moment of death or soon after. Jung suggests the possibility that emotion may be responsible, because it seems to heighten the ability to send and receive extrasensory perceptions. He notes that ESP research generally depends upon the interest and emotional involvement of the researchers and that it is often impossible to repeat experiments once interest begins to flag. The time of death is often a time of peak emotion and so of ESP transmission.

In his book *Ring of Truth*, J. B. Phillips told of his own post-death encounter with C. S. Lewis a few days after Lewis had died. Phillips had not known Lewis very well. In his vision the dead man appeared vigorous and very much alive, bringing a message which was very important in a difficulty Phillips was facing. A week later, while he was reading in bed before going to sleep, Lewis appeared to him again with the same message and even more radiantly alive. When Phillips mentioned the experiences to a friend who is a bishop, he was told, "My dear J. . . . this sort of thing is happening all the time."[6]

So common and important has this experience been in the life of the Christian Church that it is included in the most basic of our creeds, the Apostles' Creed. This is what is meant by belief in the communion of saints, a belief that there is communion between those in Christ whether they are alive or dead. This kind of communion has been reported throughout the history of the Church. Two of the most interesting of these experiences were reported by St. Ambrose and by Sulpicius Severus.

Ambrose was deeply moved by the death of his brother Satyrus. The bond between them had grown even stronger after he was elected bishop, for Satyrus had resigned his official position to relieve his brother of managing the secular affairs of the diocese. After they were parted by death, Ambrose wrote his book *On the Decease of Satyrus*. In it he expressed his belief in the resurrection and described his encounters with his dead brother. He told of the reality of these contacts and how they came in dreams when the body had been quieted by sleep. He wrote: "So that, as I lay with my limbs bathed in sleep, while I was (in mind) awake for thee, thou wast alive to me, I could say, 'What is death, my brother?' "[7]

The experience described by Sulpicius Severus occurred just before dawn on the night in which St. Martin of Tours died. Severus wrote to the deacon Aurelius telling of his light and uncertain sleep and that it was the kind in which visions often appear. Suddenly he saw Martin standing there "in the character of a bishop, clothed in a white robe, with a countenance as of fire," and then, as he watched, the figure slowly rose toward the heavens.[8] Severus was still rejoicing at this vision of a glorious future for his friend when messengers arrived with the news that Martin had died. The letter, which is considered clearly authentic, speaks of his grief and also of wonder that God shares the numinous depth of reality and his deepest mysteries in this way.

There have been a number of surveys of such post-death encounters. Interesting and important material has been provided by people like Gardner Murphy, Rosalind Heywood, F. W. H. Myers, William James, C. D. Broad, Andrew McKenzie, and Ian Stevenson.* For the most part, however, the studies are inconclusive

---

*The literature on this subject is vast. The best bibliographies are found in Osis and Haraldsson's *At the Hour of Death* and in the article by Richard Kalish and David Reynolds, "Phenomenological Reality and Post-Death Contact," in the June 1973 issue of the *Journal for the Scientific Study of Religion*. Lyall Watson includes another excellent bibliography in *The Romeo Error: A Matter of Life and Death*.

because they are not based on a random sample and so have little statistical value. As far as I know there have been only two or three research studies of post-death contact which have tried to use sound statistical methods. One was part of a national survey done by Andrew Greeley working out of the National Opinion Research Center at the University of Chicago, and another main study was made in Los Angeles by Richard Kalish and David Reynolds.

In the 1974 poll conducted by Andrew Greeley,[9] 1,467 persons, selected at random as a sample of the population, were asked the following question: "Have you ever felt that you were really in touch with someone who had died?" Over twenty-five percent of those questioned replied that they had had such experience, almost half of them more than once or even several times. While thirty-one percent of the teenagers had had some post-death contact, few of them had had more than one experience. Among those over seventy years of age thirty-nine percent had had this experience, and nearly one-fourth of them reported several contacts. Translated into numbers of the total population, these figures are impressive. They suggest that about fifty million people in this country have felt or sensed the presence of a deceased individual, and perhaps six million have had frequent contacts.

The survey showed that Protestants are more likely to report this experience than Catholics, and that Catholics are more likely to have the experience than those of the Jewish faith. Eighteen percent of those with no religious affiliation at all reported the same kind of contacts. Among the denominational groups Episcopalians report the greatest number of experiences, with forty-four percent answering that they had had contact with someone after death. Having had some experience with Episcopalians over the past sixty years, I can assure you that although they are usually open to experience, they are far more likely to be hardheaded than superstitious.

Greeley's findings are borne out by a comparable study reported by Dr. Haraldsson in Iceland,[10] where thirty-one percent of a random sample of the population claimed some kind of contact with the dead. There is also support from England for Greeley's response from widows and widowers; fifty-one percent of them reported contact with the deceased spouse. In 1971 a study was reported in the *British Medical Journal* which showed much the same results.[11] The study was made by W. D. Rees in selected communities where he was able to question eighty-one percent of the widows and widowers. Rees found that forty-seven percent of them had had encounters with the dead in various ways. Thirty-nine percent reported feeling their presence, twenty-seven percent had either seen or heard them, while twelve percent had talked with the deceased, and three percent had been touched by them. It is interesting to note that none of these people had discussed the experience with their physicians, and hardly a fourth of them had even mentioned it to anyone else. The main reason given was fear of ridicule. British people seem to have been as thoroughly brainwashed by the materialistic culture as Americans.*

The most careful effort to date to learn about experiences of post-death contact was made recently by two men with backgrounds in sociology, Richard Kalish and David Reynolds. Dr. Reynold's work has been in suicide prevention, while Dr. Kalish has been associated with the Graduate Theological Union in Berkeley, California. Their study was financed by a grant from the National Institute of Mental Health.[12]

Each of these men had realized that encounters with the deceased seem to have a very positive effect on people's lives, and that this might be important in their work. Yet they could find no mention of such an effect in scientific literature. When medical or behavioral scientists mentioned these experiences at all, it was in terms of pathological symptoms and mental illness. There seemed to be no serious study of the subject by sociologists. Andrew Greeley has commented on meeting the similar problem of trying to get his scientific colleagues to take his data seriously. As I have suggested, the basic difficulty comes from our world-view which does not admit the reality of such experiences. Kalish and Reynolds, like Greeley, decided to bypass this difficulty and ask some things which most scientists considered "non-questions." They made every effort to approach their questions without jumping to conclusions or making assumptions, either way, about the "objective" reality of these encounters.

Their first step was to arrange for a representative sample for the survey with a mixture of people from different ethnic groups. Four sections from the census in the Los Angeles area were selected. From each section over a hundred names were obtained, scattered almost equally among persons with black, Japanese-American,

---

*Greeley calls attention to the extreme reluctance of Americans to reveal these experiences to a member of the clergy.

Mexican-American, and European backgrounds. Men and women were represented equally, and in order to keep the sample consistent the names were all chosen from those with an income of $10,000 a year or less. There were 434 individuals in the final sample, each of whom was questioned personally by an interviewer.

The interviewers were carefully prepared to ask questions of fact without making people feel that their experiences were being valued or judged either positively or negatively. They first of all asked if the person had ever experienced or felt someone present after that individual had died. Those who answered "yes" were then asked how this had been experienced—whether it was in a dream, an appearance, a visit, a séance, or by some other method. The positive or negative quality of the experience was next determined, and then there were questions about whether other people had been present, and if these others had experienced anything at the time themselves.

Forty-four percent of the sample responded that they had experienced contact with someone who had died, with over twenty-five percent of these persons indicating that the dead person actually visited or was seen by the respondent. Sixty percent stated that the contact was made through a dream. It is difficult to guess how these people who describe dream experiences view the dream. Do they believe that their experience gave them access to another realm of reality, or do they see it just as an ordinary dream, only more vivid? The other aspects of this study are covered by the authors in their interesting summary:

> Over half of the black and the Mexican-American respondents had felt the presence of at least one person who had previously died, and nearly half of these persons indicated two or more such encounters. When respondents cited more than one encounter, data analyses are based upon the first such encounter reported by each respondent. Japanese Americans and white Americans reported this experience considerably less often. Significantly more women than men mentioned the occurrence. Although there were no age-related differences, the trend for the less educated to report the encounter more often was significant. . . .
>
> Women did not differ from men in the quality of the experience, although more women reported either the psychological "feel" of the deceased or an actual physical touch, while relatively more men

claimed to have had an auditory or visual experience. Ethnicity also produced some nonsignificant differences in this regard. A slightly higher proportion of whites and of Mexican Americans who reported the encounter claimed to have had visual or auditory experiences, while a greater percentage of black and of Japanese Americans "felt" the presence of the dead person. Similarly the elderly were somewhat more likely to have had a direct encounter, rather than the psychological feeling of encounter.

Most respondents felt the experience to have been pleasant, with a smaller proportion describing it primarily as awe-inspiring and mystical. Slightly less than half as many persons reacted negatively to the experience as reacted positively, but the ratio of pleasant-to-unpleasant feelings was not equally distributed. Whites and women over sixty were more likely to find the experience rewarding; women 20 to 39 and Mexican Americans claimed the greatest relative dislike for the encounter.

Under 40 percent of the respondents who reported a post-death meeting stated that others were present at the time. A total of ten claimed that one or more others shared the experience with them, so that upwards of 85 percent of those whose meeting with the dead person was in the presence of others admitted that their individual reality was not shared. Using the entire study population as a base, slightly over 2 percent reported a post-death encounter that was a part of the reality of another person present at the time.[13]

In thirty years of pastoral calling I have known only one family for whom an apparent visit from the dead was decidedly unpleasant. In this case, one of the sons, a youth in his midteens, saw his grandfather appear not long after the older man had committed suicide. The two had been at swords' points for all the usual reasons ever since the boy began to mature, and he was frightened and overwhelmed by guilt to see his grandfather appear. Everyone in the house felt a sense of numinous and unpleasant darkness. It was like a terrifying ghost story. In his book *But Deliver Us from Evil*, John Richards gives several examples of this kind of experience.

An Experience at the Moment of Death

On the other hand, over the years I have listened to quite a few of these experiences which had deep meaning for the individuals involved, and which often brought a lasting sense of peace and even great joy. One of the best examples of such a joyous experience was given to me at a conference a few years ago by a woman who later wrote a detailed account for me so that it might be shared with others. She wrote:

At long last I am back at my desk and able to fulfill my promise to write you the experience I had at the time of the death of my husband's dear mother. . . .

Many states separated my husband and me from his mother and family during her prolonged and what proved to be her final illness. Throughout the years we had developed a lovely rapport and this illness gravely concerned me. When at length letters of encouragement relative to her recovery and insistence upon the certainty of it kept coming from members of the family, we began to plan and prepare for her to visit us during her recuperation. The almost daily letters I wrote her were filled with this pleasant anticipation to which she heartily responded. Later I was to learn that for her each day began with the delivery of my letter to her.

It was a pretty pre-dawn morning filled with the fragrance of spring when I was suddenly to find myself wide awake and sitting bolt upright in my bed. The room had taken on a rare atmosphere glistening with a white light tinged with gold. An air of expectancy permeated the room, so much that it made me turn my gaze questioningly to the window at my left, then to those directly across from me, and at that moment, just to the right, this scene appeared.

Two beings of stately yet gentle bearing, almost as tall as the room is high in that area, stood facing each other on either side of a large doorway. They were clothed, each one, in a soft, flowing, opaque garment with a radiance resembling sunshine on snow tinged with a faint pink. Their arms seemed wing-like, reaching from their shoulders almost to the floor.

They stood silent and motionless, and yet in a state of expectancy (I seemed to sense) until a feminine figure garbed in a darker hue came into view, with head bent slightly down and forward as if slowly ascending from a lower level. They then moved to enfold her, almost caressingly—and I distinctly saw the smiling face of our mother and heard her familiar voice laughingly say, as if a bit breathlessly, "I've finally made it!" She seemed happy. The smile remained on her face

as, still enfolded in their embrace, she and the two beings *glided* by me
. . . just inches from the foot of my bed. I reached out to touch her. My
heart cried, "Mother! Mother, don't you see me?" Taking no notice of
me they glided on by and out of sight.

The room was still scintillating. In fact my whole being seemed
charged with a force I had not before known. I fell back on my pillow
in wonderment. What did it all mean? After a time—how long I don't
remember—my reasoning mind found an answer. "She really *is* better—she really *is* going to be well." I was rejoicing. I felt electrified—
even the room seemed electrified. I don't know any other word to
describe it. I wanted to tell my husband. I *must* tell him the good news.
But, no—it was too early to awaken him. He needed his rest, and it
would keep.

The atmosphere in the room was changing now, becoming more
normal, although it still remained charged and my body still seemed all
aglow. As a matter of fact, this lasted to a degree for several days.
Presently the ringing of the telephone awakened my husband, and
from his response I sensed the message conveyed by his brother-in-
law: "Your mother has just passed away."

Mr. Kelsey, I do not feel I have done justice to the experience. Words
are so inadequate. It is an experience I do not forget. It did something
fine to my consciousness. I wish I might paint a picture of those
Angelic Beings! Even now, the mere thought of them stirs my soul. . . .

Whatever else we may conclude from such experiences, the
number of people who report them suggests that the dead do not
cease their influence upon the living at death. More research is
apparently needed in this interesting and significant area of experience. Greeley has made a careful study of the data available in
Western countries showing the belief in life after death. He concludes that this belief has not diminished significantly in the past
fifty years, in spite of the materialism and continued secularization
of Western society. One does not have to look far, he suggests, to
find the probable reason. It is the experiences so many people have
of contact with those who have died that keep the belief alive.

In addition many people find support for this belief farther
afield, in areas that often challenge our understanding in one way or
another. Let us turn now to see what these evidences can tell us
about life after death.

VII. Other Evidence
for Another Life

There is no question that it is difficult to approach subjects like spiritualism and the occult objectively. These speculations have sometimes been so surrounded by superstition and questionable practices that we have trouble realizing that they might offer actual glimpses of another reality. I can hardly help feeling embarrassed to suggest looking for valuable evidence in some of the fields we shall consider. But in recent years scientists have discovered certain techniques that go far to demonstrate the reality of various experiences described in areas like these. Our view of human personality, both in this life and beyond, has thus been greatly enlarged. Let us try to consider the varied evidence that follows for what it suggests about a life beyond this one, without deciding sight unseen whether it is acceptable or not.

The Non-Physical Double

One of the important ideas of occult speculation holds that human beings have etheric or astral bodies which can become visible as auras surrounding their physical bodies. Most of us have dismissed this idea as so much superstitious nonsense. But with the development of Kirlian photography* it has been shown that there

---

*This technique produces a photographic image by placing an object on top of the film or plate and shooting a low voltage electrical current from the back of the plate through to the object. Living objects are reproduced with an aura around them which varies with physical and/or psychic condition. For instance a freshly picked leaf shows a characteristic aura, but, photographed over several hours, this halo gradually disappears. Kirlian photographs have often been used to show the change in the auras around the hands of a healer and those of a sick person before and after laying-on-of-hands and prayer. In Charles Panati's book *Supersenses* there are excellent reproductions of actual photographs showing such changes.

actually seems to be an aura surrounding people's bodies which can be reproduced on photographic film. In his remarkable study of life and death, *The Romeo Error*, Lyall Watson suggests the idea that we live in an energy field and have a non-physical body. By this he means a body composed of particles of physical energy. This idea, he submits, makes sense of a lot of the unexplained data about us human beings and our ordinary existence.

The idea that each individual has a spiritual double, or a second, different kind of body which uses the physical body as a base of operations, has been known for a long time. It goes back to Egyptian thought and shamanism and seems to pop up all over the world in literature. The word *doppelgänger*, often found in German literature, means just this. Both T. S. Eliot and Charles Williams refer to this idea. In Eliot's play *The Cocktail Party* and in Williams' superb novel *Descent into Hell* it is used to show how meeting one's spiritual double gives a person knowledge of a spiritual world beyond the physical one. Both authors quote these lines from Shelley which reveal the deepest kind of poetic vision:

> Ere Babylon was dust
> The magus Zoroaster, my dead child,
> Met his own image walking in the garden.
> The apparition, sole of men, he saw.
> For know there are two worlds of life and death:
> One that which thou beholdest; but the other
> Is underneath the grave, where do inhabit
> The shadows of all forms that think and live
> Till death unite them and they part no more.

For most people, however, auras and spiritual doubles or etheric bodies have been strictly associated with occult speculation. This association began in the seventeenth and eighteenth centuries when most such phenomena became suspect among both Catholic and Protestant leaders. Ideas like these then went underground where they flourished in movements such as alchemy, astrology, theosophy, study of the Kabbalah, magic, divination, and witchcraft.[1] The understanding of our participation in a spiritual plane of being was soon almost hidden by superstitious and foolish imaginings. In this atmosphere it is no wonder that sensible people began to consider it silly to talk about experiencing an aura or having some ethereal or spiritual kind of body.

Even so, interest in occult phenomena went right on, and the discussions of an astral plane and astral bodies continued. Some people described experiencing another reality in out-of-the-body experiences, in which their souls seemed to leave their bodies without being in any danger of death. Many others maintained that they could see auras around individuals which gave evidence of our participation in the astral plane. Finally parapsychologists began to investigate these claims, and with the demonstration of auras provided by Kirlian photography, there have been more and more studies, including out-of-the-body experiences. The classic work in this area is *Journeys out of the Body*, written by Robert A. Monroe.

My own openness to the subject began when one of my sons, who was then ten years old, started having such experiences spontaneously. No one in our home had ever heard of such things. We were startled, almost shocked, on several mornings when he came down to breakfast and told us that he had "seen" or "heard" something happen in another place that he could not possibly have known about in any ordinary way. Almost immediately I ran across two or three passages in books I was reading discussing such experiences, and I began to read what I could find on the subject.* I came to realize that if one seriously entertains the idea of some non-physical dimension of reality, the possibility of experiencing a spiritual double is less hard to believe.

I also realized that Paul was talking about a deeper variety of the same experience when he wrote in 2 Corinthians:

> I know a Christian man who fourteen years ago (whether in the body or out of it, I do not know—God knows) was caught up as far as the third heaven. And I know that this same man (whether in the body or out of it, I do not know—God knows) was caught up into paradise, and heard words so secret that human lips may not repeat them (2 Cor. 12:3-4).

Followers of the occult often seek this kind of experience through ritual or various ways of meditating.

---

*In children and young people I believe it is important *not* to encourage this type of experience. Often their ego development is not mature enough and they should therefore be taught to keep their bodies together. There are techniques for doing this. Agnes Sanford taught our son to pray, each time he felt this happening, that he be surrounded by holy protection and that he be helped to keep physical and spiritual bodies joined together. This type of experience can be *very* dangerous to anyone with a weak ego development. It could lead to psychosis.

The halos or auras that appear on Kirlian photographs are apparently much the same as those described by followers of the occult. The Kirlian process has shown that these auras vary in width of the flares, as well as in color and intensity, according to the person's mental and physical condition. It is interesting that the places where the strongest flares are observed correspond directly to the points on Chinese acupuncture charts.

In addition, Dennis Milner at the University of Birmingham has discovered that a process similar to Kirlian photography can register patterns of force lines which apparently emanate from everything in nature. He was working with film sensitive to electrical charges and found that the pictures showed brilliant lines that connect glowing cores and spread out all over the objects he photographed. Another form of picture has been discovered that "is based on spheres and agglomerations of spheres in circular patterns, like a field of round-petaled flowers almost touching one another."[2] In this case the spheres seem to correspond to the *chakras* described in classical yoga theory. Lyall Watson also tells of meeting a child in Indonesia who knew nothing of *chakra* theory but was able to see and point to the same centers which she called "fires."

Added to all of this is the fact that we have no idea of where the gigantic memory computer could be hidden away within the human being. As Watson points out, our brains react to immediate experience, and memories seem to have little to do with the electrical stimulation that triggers mental processes. Huge sections of the brain can be destroyed or damaged, leaving early memories just as available as ever. When people's brains are damaged by loss of circulation, trauma, tumors, or old age, they may lose their ability to learn new things, to acquire new memories and to make judgments:

> ... they may lose physical sensation or become profoundly psychologically disturbed, but the memory of past experience usually remains intact.... There seems to be absolutely no evidence to suggest that memories are stored in any special part of the brain—or anywhere else in the body.[3]

For these reasons Watson believes that a second, "fellow traveler" personality might account for the human memory system and the ability to organize and direct one's life. He goes on:

> The assumption of a second system intimately associated with the normal body does provide answers for all kinds of problems that we

have left hanging without solution. The organizer that produces the directional patterns of life and death ... could be located here. Information acquired by the physical body or the somatic system could be stored as integral parts of this organizer and provide a base for memory and recall.[4]

He then suggests that such a "fellow traveler" must of necessity have some physical reality and "not be unlocated like some cosmic vapor."[4] It doesn't occur to him that there might be a level of reality different from the physical, as Jung and others have suggested, and that human beings themselves might be only partly physical.

He discusses the complexity of dream experience and the fact that dreams suggest "that the second system is capable of creating a personality complete with traces of experience, habits, and skills, organized in a way that is typical of that individual."[5] But he is convinced that every aspect of human personality depends upon having a physical body. His final suggestion is that the second personality may continue to exist for a while after the transmitter (the body) has been destroyed, but finally even that personality disintegrates and disappears. Watson does not try to explain why he believes as he does. He simply seems to accept the model of reality handed down to us which shows physical things and physical bodies as providing the only basic contact we have with anything in the universe. He cannot see any other possibility.

The facts that have shown up, however, appear to suggest that those who speak of experiencing auras and astral bodies are talking about some reality connected with the physical body but separate and different from it. I no longer consider these speculations sheer nonsense as I used to. There seems to be some kind of life force (*prana*, soul, spiritual double) which has form and can be detected, and which needs further investigation. It is probably related to the reality described by some people who have had post-death contacts and near-death experiences. The soul seems to have some observable effects.

Mediums and Spiritualism

One cannot help questioning what reality there might be in spiritualism. The idea of mediums as professional intermediaries between the physical world and the realm of the deceased is involved in such a morass of superstition, wishful thinking, self-

hypnosis and even downright fraud that many people doubt that
there is any reality in it. There has been a tendency for scientific
people in particular to reject the whole subject of spiritualism in
disgust and suggest that the only thing to investigate is the chica-
nery. Again, it has taken the efforts of the new science of parapsychology to discover that there is some fire behind all the smoke.
There appear to be quite real facts which need to be looked at. At
the same time there are reasons why it is generally better for people
not to become involved in spiritualism, and I shall include some
suggestions for helping people who are drawn to seek this experience.

Spiritualism as a religious movement is an American invention.
It began in the late 1840's when strange psychic events, supposedly
coming from the dead, occurred around the Fox sisters who lived in
rural upstate New York. The time was ripe. Most of the traditional
churches had been deeply influenced by the growing materialism
and rationalism which I have described in an earlier chapter. It
appeared that human beings were only physical things, probably
limited to what they could get out of this present life. The idea that
the dead could speak through certain elected people brought hope to
numbers of people who joined the new spiritualist churches. They
were convinced that there was a real possibility of a future life. The
movement spread to England and then around the world.

About the same time a French author by the name of Rivail,
writing under the pen name of Allan Kardec, started a slightly
different spiritualist movement that has also spread widely. It has
had a great impact in Brazil, and the spiritualist healing movement
which developed as a result is still very active there. This latter
group has been investigated by a team of medical doctors interested
in parapsychology. A similar kind of psychic healing is found in the
Philippines in connection with a union of spiritualist churches there.

Of course mediumship is as old as religious records. The oldest
known writing, *The Gilgamesh Epic* (in cuneiform on clay tablets), tells
of calling up the spirit of Enkidu from the underworld. Saul in his
troubles sought out the "witch" of Endor. The story of his experience, as recorded in 1 Samuel 28:4-25, is as vivid as any account of a
modern séance. The spirit of the dead Samuel was called up and
predicted Saul's defeat and death. One of the main bulwarks of the
Greek social life and religion was the Delphic oracle in which the
priestess or "pythoness" spoke from a mediumistic trance in ambiguous words which others had to interpret. For nearly a thousand

years this was a focal point of Greek piety. Delphi in ruins is still one of the most moving places that I have ever visited. Shamans from time immemorial in all parts of the world have told of going into the world of the dead.

Christianity in Western Europe in the past three centuries offers one of the few examples in religious history of a major religion which became rational and moralistic so that the aspect of revelation was lost. Chinese religion came close to the same thing, but in China where the movement toward rationalism was even greater, that kind of religion co-existed with the popular shamanistic kind. Thus it was in Western Europe and America that churches grew up devoted primarily to getting in touch with the dead, with healing practices a later outgrowth. When organized religion pushes this kind of experience aside, sooner or later it emerges on its own, with or without the blessing of a higher authority.

In the late 1880's, because of the influence of spiritualism, a group of serious scientists in Britain and some leaders in other fields became convinced that psychic phenomena pointed to an existence beyond this life. In order to investigate these experiences they organized the Society for Psychical Research, and a few years later an American counterpart was formed. It was largely through the efforts of these men and women that the genuine data of parapsychology began to emerge. They were deeply interested in survival after death and questioned whether Darwin had found the whole truth.

The societies in both England and the United States undertook a careful investigation of mediums. Some of the remarkable mediums of the time, like Geraldine Cummins and Gladys Leonard in England and Lenore Piper in the United States, were studied intensively. In the meantime the reality of telepathy (the capacity of mind to communicate with mind without using ordinary sense channels) was established, and later that of psychokinesis (the capacity of mind to have an effect on physical objects without the use of any ordinary or known energy). It was realized that, by using telepathy unconsciously, perfectly honest mediums might be reading sitters' minds in séances; or by using psychokinesis without realizing it, unconsciously they might produce the physical effect of an appearance without being in contact with the deceased person. Still, people as cautious as William James became convinced that these individuals were in communication with some reality other than living human beings.

The communications received through mediums were studied

for examples of information that could not have been known to living people. Several apparent examples of such communication were discovered. In addition the communications received by various mediums were checked against each other to see if someone from "the other side" might be communicating with individuals in various parts of the world who were not in touch with each other. Often the messages received by one individual made no sense. But through cross-correspondences, when put together with other communications supposedly received from the same deceased person, they made sense and were characteristic of that person.[6] Some very careful and critical minds have come to the conclusion, on the basis of such evidence, that there is some kind of communication from beyond. Sometimes the evidence reveals something truly amazing, like the dream in which Dante's son was told by his dead father where to look for the lost cantos of *The Divine Comedy*. When this subject is dismissed out of hand, it is usually because the skeptic knows nothing of the material that can come to the best mediums.

The healings done by spiritualists in Brazil and the Philippines are interesting in a similar way. The story of one of the most famous and most investigated of them is told by John G. Fuller in *Arigó: Surgeon of the Rusty Knife*. Arigó professed to be possessed by the spirit of a dead German physician. In ordinary life he was an ignorant peasant, and yet when he went into a trance ready to heal, he seemed well versed in medical terminology and procedure. Both Lyall Watson in *The Romeo Error* and Stanley Krippner in *Song of the Siren* describe their investigations of the Philippine healers. Since teams of doctors and other specialists did their best to uncover fraud, these spiritualist healings seem to present us with something unexplainable, some core of genuine and mysterious experience.

The same thing is true of Edgar Cayce. Perhaps one thing that makes his story appear so incredible is the fact that it happened right here where medical science was developing faster than ever before in history. Cayce was an uneducated man who found that, in a state of trance, he seemed to make contact with the "being" or "person" of sick people and know what was wrong with them, even at a great distance. He would state the trouble in correct medical terms and then prescribe a remedy, sometimes a very unusual one. Healings resulted in a surprisingly high percentage of these cases. Cayce was active in the 1930's and 1940's in the most rationalistic period of American church history.

What he accomplished made a profound impression on many

people who came to know him. For over thirty years stenographic records were kept of his trance experiences. These records have been printed and are available for study at the Association for Research and Enlightenment in Virginia Beach, Virginia. I know several of the leaders of this group quite well and can vouch for their sincerity and openness. Because they stress the reality of the spiritual world and our contact with it in the here and now, many people hungry for spiritual reality have been drawn to Edgar Cayce's ideas. There are now nearly 1,300 organized groups all over the world.

Many genuine experiences of something beyond this present life undoubtedly occur among mediums, but this in itself presents a problem. Most professional mediums have to admit that their powers are not always the same. There is no way that they can exert conscious control over their receptivity or what comes through to them. Unfortunately at times of low ebb there is a temptation to use fraud and most mediums give in to it, at least on occasion. Allen Spraggett, who did the actual writing of M. Lamar Keene's book, *The Psychic Mafia*, has remarked that all mediums lie some of the time and some mediums lie all of the time. This book tells the story of Keene who confessed to his own share in the fraud rampant in spiritualist circles.

There are few things more repugnant than this kind of fraud which preys on bereaved individuals at their weakest moments. If one takes the trouble to visit séances and see the dependence of sorrowing people on the experiences provided by mediums, it is easy to understand the power that a medium can have over someone disturbed by this kind of loss and seeking reason to go on. By the fraudulent act of consciously filling in the gaps in their performance, the medium usually keeps the person more firmly tied to the deceased and less able to turn toward life and go on. Keene concludes his story of the same kind of problems with these words spoken to Spraggett:

I believe that the individual can have his or her own private psychic experience. . . . But when it comes to paying a medium to do it for you—beware! Communication with the dead is something I would urge you to avoid—I mean even the idea of it, the possibility of it. At least through a professional medium. Trying to communicate with the dead has been the downfall of many individuals, as my story amply and tragically reveals.[7]

In my opinion this is good and wise advice. Experiences of those who have died may come spontaneously, as the accounts in the last chapter have shown. But when people go out of their way to make the contact, they are usually indulging ego or power motives and as a result the whole experience turns sour.

On the other hand, people do not go to mediums without some reason. The one thing I have found that drives them to this route is the need to find on-going meaning in life. When our churches fail to put any emphasis on belief in life beyond the grave, they create a situation in which mediums and spiritualism can flourish. Clergy who do not teach and preach about life after death create a vacuum. Individuals who have had post-death encounters spontaneously, as well as those who might seek such an experience, are cut off from the guidance and wisdom which Christian clergy could offer them. People simply do not say much about these experiences around the Church because they find so little acceptance of what they describe.

The clergy are in a different situation, to say the least. They need the critical understanding which is definitely provided by seminary training and theology today. But this understanding is of little help to ordinary people unless it is used along with openness to the experiences that people describe. The clergy need to have a view of the universe which opens up the reality of another world. Only then can they accept all levels of people's experience and help them relate to whatever they encounter, both in this life and in the world beyond.

The first need is for clergy who listen with understanding to mystical experiences. There is then a real possibility that people who have had experiences of the dead will also come for help and guidance. As Kalish and Reynolds point out, in their Los Angeles survey nearly forty-four percent of the people they questioned reported such experiences and only a small percent had them through séances. If there is any place where séances would be available, it is in Los Angeles, California. Apparently the number of people who need acceptance and real understanding of these spontaneous encounters is far greater than most of us have imagined.

Once religious professionals realize how much need there is to listen openly to these experiences, the individuals who have them can then be helped to find the creative understanding that Jesus offered of the world beyond and how it affects our lives right now. We can learn a great deal from the experiences of another dimension of reality which unquestionably come to many mediums. But this should be investigated by competent scientists and not by average individuals, particularly in times of sorrow and bereavement when they need the best help that Christian clergy can give.

Parapsychology and Life after Death

In the introduction to his survey of parapsychology, *Supersenses*, Charles Panati suggests that the 1950's can be called the beginning of the computer age, and the 1960's the beginning of the space age, while the 1970's will be known as the beginning of the psychic age. There is growing dissatisfaction with the dogmatism of psychologists like B. F. Skinner who has stated that mind is a term "invented for the sole purpose of providing spurious explanations." Young people in particular have realized how wrong these psychologists are in denying the reality of people's inner psychic experiences.

In my book *The Christian and the Supernatural* I have described five different kinds of these extrasensory or parapsychological experiences. This book began to take shape a long time ago when I discovered how many evidences of parapsychological events are found in both the Old and New Testaments. I kept running across such experiences which almost always seemed to happen to people who were sincerely practicing their religion and seeking deeper encounters with the divine spirit. But a fuller appreciation of these facts had to wait for scientific research to show that something other than purely physical causes is apparently at work in these five experiences. All of them are found in both parts of the Bible, and they have been tested by careful scientific methods. They are:

Telepathy—mind to mind communication without any known means of contact.
Clairvoyance—seeing objects or events at a distance or otherwise completely hidden from sight in the ordinary sense.
Precognition—seeing into the future, seeing something which has not yet happened.
Psychokinesis—moving, bending, or in some way altering an object without using any known physical force.
Psychic or religious healing—healing by non-physical means.

Scientists have now shown under careful laboratory controls that humans can sometimes act in every one of these ways. In one experiment after another, people have "seen" and described things which they could not see physically. Physical changes have been brought about in both objects and living things simply by someone's concentration, sometimes along with the touch of their hands. Apparently there is some force or power within human beings which is effective in the space-time world and yet cannot be perceived or measured physically.

Once we realize that there is something *not physical* within us which can interact with physical matter, then the hypothesis that we are in communication with another realm of existence seems quite reasonable. There may well be a realm of existence from which other similar realities, including the souls or personalities of those who were once alive, can reach out and communicate with us. In fact the recent developments in parapsychology offer evidence to support the hypothesis I have suggested in Chapter 5. These developments provide one of the reasons for believing that humans are in touch with both the physical world and also with some realm of life which is apparently not physical.

Some very significant research has also been done on the human encounter with death which clearly suggests the same kind of contact beyond the physical world that is shown by parapsychological or extrasensory experiences. Using LSD therapy with patients with terminal cancer, Stanislav Grof and Joan Halifax have observed that the patients go through a series of stages in anticipation of death. It is almost as if they experience actual death in the state induced by the LSD. Many of these patients find that death is something that one can pass through and so they lose their fear of dying. This work is reported by Grof and Halifax in their book *The Human Encounter with Death*. In it they support many of the ideas which are proposed in the following chapters.

It is practically impossible, however, to discuss the evidence of parapsychology sensibly and rationally until we try to work out a view of the world which has a place for such facts. When we have no theory of the world to give us a perspective on them, our thinking tends to play tricks. Often we become rigid in our ideas and thus accept or reject facts according to these ideas. Sometimes we don't use our thinking or reasoning at all and accept superstition for fact without any critical judgment. In neither case are we likely to find the truth. When we leave our reason and critical thinking behind in approaching any subject, we give up one of the main tools for learning from our experience. The data of parapsychology, particularly those that appear to come from beyond death, need to be treated with the same careful analysis and reasoning as any other data. But this is possible only as we develop a point of view which helps us accept the experiences as possibilities and thus gives us reason to examine all the facts connected with these experiences carefully and critically.

It is amazing to me how few parapsychologists have critically examined the various implications of their work or the possible ideas underlying it. Instead they often tend to take them for granted. At a recent conference in Montreal on the subject of parapsychology and life after death, I was the only speaker to emphasize the need to recognize our world-view and to see how parapsychological research enlarges it. The understanding of the facts of parapsychology requires a wider view of the total world than we have held, and these facts provide the evidence for such a view. Carl Jung has probably drawn out these implications better than any other modern thinker. Once one takes the facts of parapsychology seriously and sees their implications, it is no longer absurd to believe in other levels of existence besides the physical one. The realization that very likely we do participate in some other level or realm of existence makes life after death something that is possible to consider. This can be understood and accepted by critical and intelligent people. Parapsychology opens a modern door into the possibility of belief in life after death.

Dreams and Death

The dream has been called the natural altered state of consciousness. Those who have studied dreams find that they provide a wisdom and understanding of reality quite different from ordinary waking consciousness. Dreams often give reflections upon how one is living one's life and suggestions about the direction life should be taking for the individual's greatest fulfillment. It is through dreams, many people believe, that they have contact with deceased individuals, or even experiences similar to those described by Dr. Moody and Karlis Osis. Dreams suggest the possibility of the persistence of the human psyche in two other ways. First, our dream life seems to ignore death, and, second, death dreams usually point to or reveal rebirth and renewal.

Toward the end of his life Dr. Jung was interviewed by the British Broadcasting Corporation (BBC) and a film was produced portraying that interview. Dr. Jung was asked if he believed in life after death. He replied quite flatly that he did. He stated that his reason for this belief came from observing the dreams of people who were on the verge of death. Their dreams seemed to take no note of their approaching death. The data was the same whether people knew that they were dying or did not know that they were about to die. Dreams continued to comment on important factors in the life of the person, such as human relationships, failure to face certain aspects of his or her life, doubts and questionings and emotional problems.

Jung went on to say that dreams seemed to ignore death as a relatively unimportant event. There were no indications in the dreams of dying people that an event such as the termination of life was approaching. Their dream life seemed to convey the idea that the quality of life present during physical life would continue after death had cut them off from outer sensory communication with other individuals. Katherine de Jersey, a well-known and responsible astrologist, has told me much the same thing about astrological charts. They seldom predict death, apparently because death does not seem to be an event of great importance. At the deepest level the psyche seems to have little concern about its continuance. It takes continuance of its life almost as a matter of course.

In addition to such data from the depth of the human personality, it is also important to note that dreams of death seldom refer to the actual death of any individual. Many people who start looking at their dreams become apprehensive when they dream of seeing themselves or someone else dying, being killed, or a victim of violence. Dreams of one's own death, however, are usually saying that some aspect or part of oneself has died or perhaps needs to die. When we dream of another person dying, it almost never refers to that person's death. It again refers to an aspect of ourselves which either is dying or ought to die.

In most cases dreams of other people portray the parts of ourselves that those persons represent. Sometimes a dream portraying someone's death could be a warning that we are allowing a valuable part or aspect of ourselves to perish and that we should protect it. What the dream is saying (whether it indicates that one should go through an inner death and let some part of oneself die, or whether one should seek protection from this death) will depend upon the total life situation of the person having the dream. For our purposes it is significant that such dreams almost never indicate physical death. Indeed these dreams seem to treat death as a symbol of rebirth and the transformation.

One of the most impressive discussions of dreams and death was written by the late Franz Riklin with whom I worked when I was at the Jung Institute in Zurich. As far as I know this paper has never been published. It is entitled "Psychotherapy and Death." In it Dr. Riklin described a series of dreams which one of his patients had shortly before she died. He concluded with these words:

In a dream a few days before she died, the patient was told to eat honey and eggs which would be helpful to her. Again Greek mythology teaches us that these were the food of the gods. . . .

And the last dream in her life was that she was sitting beside her bed where her corpse was lying and she no longer sensed any gravitation or pain and was at the same time in her room as well as in a wonderful sphere of beauty overlooking the world. She felt happy and was very angry that she awakened from this dream again. . . .

But what intrigues one the most is the fact that out of all the dream material I have been able to collect, no evidence is given that death from the point of view of the unconscious means the total end, but is shown as a change, a separation from one's body. The psyche points to the realm of the pneumatic man, often shown as being above the world and in itself a world of beauty. This at least could teach us that the ego—the psychic entity—no longer is identical with all that is identified with its worldly life and passes into a situation of totality above the world. . . .

The psyche, containing the ego as nucleus of consciousness, seems not to be touched by death as modern man mostly thinks. We are herein confronted with a mysterium and I can only say that the unrecognizable may be experienced.[8]

Edgar Herzog has written a masterful study of death dreams in his book, *Psyche and Death*. Dr. Herzog is a student of both anthropology and psychology. His book is a careful study of the reactions of human beings to death as they move from a primitive condition to consciousness and culture. He notes several stages in that development. The earliest primitive response to death is one of headlong flight. The dead are left behind and the place of their dying is forever considered unclean or taboo. He sees a second stage in which individuals try to gain control over death by being the killer. At this stage we find ritualization of sacrifice, particularly of human sacrifice. At the next stage death is seen as the devourer, often pictured as an animal, often as a wolf or a dog or some other animal noted for its capacity to rend and tear and devour. At the same time the horse may be seen as an animal which carries the deceased to the other world. In the final developmental stage death takes on a more human form. The god or demon of death is seen not only as a destroyer but also as the one who leads the dying into another realm of existence.

Dr. Herzog then shows that the same symbols which occur in the myths of primitive people also occur in the dreams of modern people. He notes that the failure to face death and its meaning can result in serious neurotic problems. The healthy person, from a psychological point of view, seems to be one who is able to face death with some kind of hope, recognizing that this is not the complete and final end of individual existence. Herzog sees in Christianity one of the final stages of our human relationship to death and to the life beyond. He writes:

> As is well known it is a leading Christian motif that man's responsibility for the life he leads becomes visible in relation to Death and Mortality, but this idea only appears late in the mythological formulations of the experience of death, and even then is only seen as a faint intuition—and what is true of myths is true of dreams as well.[9]

Evolution and Death

If the human psyche is envisioned as having the same level of reality as the physical world, the problem of death is lifted to another plane. If human beings are caught between two realms of experience—each at least as real as the other—then the dissolution of the physical body and cessation of physical participation in the space-time world need not imply that the psyche itself ceases to exist. Since one cannot verify the idea of psychic dissolution by any critical or scientific reason, there is no critical, *a priori* reason for denying that the individual might have continued existence. Instead, one is free to take up the evidence for survival with an open mind. One may then consider the rare but significant data concerning life after death which occur from time to time. One may also listen to the intimations of one's own heart, as well as trying to take seriously the nearly universal beliefs on the subject of life after death.

Of course, it is possible that we live in a purely physical universe, although it is becoming increasingly difficult to *believe* that such is the case. If we are just so many physically conditioned responses, then these attitudes about life after death and the very data themselves are the result of self-deception, of the neurosis which we call civilization. But in that case, most of what we call "objective knowledge" today would also have to be re-examined, and much of it would probably have to go by the boards.

If it is true that the human psyche has the ability to transcend and move beyond the strictly space-time world, this would indicate that the psyche is not totally conditioned by physical existence. Most of the religions of humankind throughout the ages have offered such a view of the nature of reality until the rational materialism of the nineteenth century swept it aside in cavalier fashion.

Jung sees the human psyche as a meaningful development from an unconscious matrix toward a growing consciousness. There seems to be an evolutionary process going on within these psyches of ours. The universe appears to be moving toward increasing individuality and consciousness. To see this process terminated at death seems to contradict the very nature of the universe which is revealed in us. The growth and development of our individual psyches in the next life seems to be a continuation of the development we see among growing human beings in this life.

This point of view is very different from that of Freud, with whom Jung was once associated. Freud saw human beings caught in a cold war between meaningless and irrational psychic forces, with the rational ego barely able to keep a tenuous balance between them and survive. For Freud civilization was the product of this neurotic tension and the only compensation humans got for living through this meaninglessness. In the end the best a person can hope for is to face death with fatalistic stoicism, just as Freud did so magnificently himself. He saw no other purpose or meaning, however, for the human psyche; it simply disintegrated with death.

Dr. Jung also saw human beings in a state of tension, but a meaningful tension which can lead to meaningful development beyond the confines of this physical life. The individual must not resist this process of growth and becoming, or one can come to real tragedy. This process usually begins as individuals become more conscious of their own inner being and so begin to face the parts of themselves that they have chosen to ignore. Then one usually finds deep within his or her being a latent destructiveness which can be termed the murderer within. Only through a genuine catharsis or emptying of oneself, usually with another person, can one realize the full chaos within. This state of self-knowledge can lead toward a real relationship, in which the courage to bear the darkness and the pain of self-growth is given by relationship with another person who has passed through similar experiences. A stage of self-development follows this, one of self-education. At this point one tries to bring together the fragmented and opposing parts of one's personality. But the person finds that this unifying can seldom be accomplished by one's own effort and determination.

The resolution is usually given as a gift. It comes to the person in conflict much as it came to Job out of a whirlwind. In hundreds of patients Jung observed that this creative transformation came through a transcendent function which suddenly brought the hopelessly fragmented life together. In the coming together of their lives, people's fears and problems were often resolved. The creative center which Jung called *das Selbst* (poorly translated as "the self") he believed to be the same reality of which all the major religions of humankind speak when they refer to deity. He believed it could be experienced and observed by anyone who truly looked for it. The human psyche appears to be a special interest and concern of this reality and so the soul may well share in the ultimate vitality and significance of deity itself. If all this is true, there is no reason to think that the process begun in this life may not continue after this physical life-span is over.

The same growth process is described by most of the religions of the world. While Jung described it in psychological terms, they describe the process in purely religious language. John Sanford shows with startling clarity in his book *The Kingdom Within* how similar the way of individuation and wholeness of Dr. Jung is to the way of life proposed by Jesus in his parables of the kingdom. Both point to an on-going and meaningful life for the psyche in this life and the next. If, however, there turns out to be no life after physical death, then the whole universe appears to be meaningless as well, and our intimations of purpose are only illusion.

When the human psyche is seen as participating in a teleological, purposeful process which is revealed in nature itself, then there is reason to look for its continuance. There would be just cause for surprise if there were an abrupt end of the process. Teilhard de Chardin makes the same point in many of his writings, particularly in *The Phenomenon of Man*. He looks at the process as it occurs outwardly in evolution, while Jung looks at the process from within, observing the developmental process taking place within the individual psyche. They both speak the same message.

In his paper "Stages of Life" in *Modern Man in Search of a Soul*, Jung suggests that old age is a time of withdrawal, reflection and introversion, and thus prepares the individual for the next step forward which could be called the next mutation. The very way in which life moves forward purposefully from stage to stage enables human beings to look ahead to an extension and an expansion of their psychic being after death. This is exactly what most of those who have had near-death experiences claim they have experienced. We shall develop in a later chapter the obvious implication of this idea: the best preparation for this expansion is to live life as deeply, fully and consciously as possible in the here and now.

Reincarnation

There is also some very interesting evidence which leads a number of people to conclude that human personality, rather than disintegrating at death, is reincarnated into some new stage of this present life. The theory of reincarnation is based mainly on the experiences certain people seem to have of a former life. Sometimes they describe having lived as an individual whose life can be checked on, and, in rare instances, intimate details are described which they could scarcely have known in any ordinary way. There have even been cases in which a person exhibited the physical characteristics of the individual who lived at an earlier time.

Those who believe in reincarnation suggest that at death a person enters a non-physical existence but does not stay in that existence long. One soon re-enters the physical world as a different individual. Some people believe that through hypnosis individuals can be taken back through their present lives into the womb, and then back into former existence. Similarly in a trance state Edgar Cayce provided life readings in which he traced the history of individuals back through their previous incarnations.

The most careful study of this subject was made by Dr. Ian Stevenson who is a member of the Department of Neurology and Psychiatry in the Medical School of the University of Virginia. His book *Twenty Cases Suggestive of Reincarnation* was published by the American Society for Psychical Research in 1966. In it he presents data from cases found in Brazil, Ceylon, India, and among the Tlinglit Indians in Alaska. His analysis of the possibility of reincarnation is interesting and is based on careful consideration of the facts.

There is no doubt that such cases demonstrate some kind of continuance of the individual after death. Many people have been attracted to this understanding of the experiences because it gives a way of believing in the persistence of human personality. Whether the facts as a whole, however, support reincarnation as a general theory is another matter. This is a question we shall consider in a later chapter.

Einstein, Modern Physics and Survival after Death

When the facts of the universe itself are looked at through the eyes of the modern physicist, one finds support for the belief in the possibility of life after death which would have seemed unbelievable early in this century. An almost incredible change has taken place in the way it is possible to view this world of ours. Physicists like Einstein, Heisenberg and Planck view the world quite differently from the way it appeared to those brought up in the more commonsense framework provided by Isaac Newton. Present-day physicists often sound more like mystics than hard-headed rational scientists, as Lawrence LeShan shows in *The Medium, the Mystic, and the Physicist*. Some of their statements might well have come straight from classical mysticism.

There is more than one way in which these giants of the scientific world, whether mystical or not, open up the possibility of survival beyond this life. LeShan discusses their approach in an interesting appendix to his book. As far as I have been able to find, this is not only the best but the only discussion of this that has appeared. LeShan points out that Newtonian physics works on a set of assumptions that make it next to impossible to believe that any part of the individual goes on after death.

According to the rules of early classical physics (which are more like refined common sense than the carefully developed thinking of today), something can be said to exist and be real only when three conditions have been met. First of all we must be able to perceive the thing clearly. This means that we must be able to see or taste or touch it, or perhaps smell or hear it, and provide the same experience to other people. Second, if the object is not perceived directly, then we must be able to show that it has had an effect on one of the five senses, and other observers must be able to experience the same effect. Third, we must then be able to account for the various experiences of similar things in a comprehensive theory which describes the reality that has been sensed. In this way, for instance, we can picture the structure of an atom even though we have never seen inside one and probably never will. The problem is that these rules have been applied far beyond their use in answering specific questions about matter.

Classical science *assumes*—as an article of faith—that what cannot be observed or sensed under these conditions simply does not exist. One has no choice but to reject experiences which cannot be repeated. Unique experiences are not subject to the rules of experimentation and so they must be omitted in the final tally of reality. In the classical view reality is made up of things which are simply there and available whenever someone wishes to study them. A "thing" is considered to have no life of its own, no inner force that could cause it to change, to appear or to disappear.

The older science, which was learned so well that it still affects a lot of our thinking, has no place for the experiences we have been considering. Even the clearest and most reliable near-death experience or post-death encounter does not fulfill the requirements laid down for science by Newtonian physics. Within this point of view one cannot learn from experiences that seem to come and go at will and sometimes are observed by only one individual. On the other hand, it is universally observed that dead people decay and sooner or later become only a handful of chemical elements. The conclusion was inevitable "that biological death means annihilation of consciousness and self-awareness of the individual."[10]

Today's physics does not start by *assuming the reality of individual*

things, and then fit them together to learn about the whole. Physicists now start with the whole. They feel that it is impossible to
understand how individual things work until the separate pieces are
seen as parts of the whole, moving and functioning in relation to
other parts. Modern physics has recognized that the whole of anything is more than simply the sum of its separate and individual
parts. Both the whole and the parts that make up the whole must be
understood as on-going events within an entire field of activity.
Once the theory of relativity was stated, scientists began to work
toward a unified field theory. Most scientists now believe that
everything in the universe is interrelated. Time, space, energy and
matter all make up one complete totality. To change or remove any
one part of this whole changes every other part of it.

This point of view can be suggested by the example of a wave
breaking on the shore. The wave is as much a part of the whole
ocean as every other drop of the ceaselessly moving water. When
the wave breaks on the shore, the untrained observer may note that
it ceases to exist at a certain point in time. But this cannot be said for
two reasons. First, the time of an event is always relative to the
observer. The moment of occurrence may be different for each
observer, depending upon one's location and movement, whether or
not one is standing still, or the speed at which one is moving away
from or toward the event. Second, since the wave is a part of the
whole, in a sense it still continues to exist as part of the whole. Its
movement and the event of breaking never stop being part of the
whole system.

LeShan argues that what can be said of the wave is also true of
human consciousness, which behavioral psychologists describe as
nothing more than a wave of physical matter. These behaviorists
insist that consciousness is a by-product of matter (an epiphenome-
non or unplanned outgrowth of matter purely by chance). Within
the total field of reality, however, it is difficult to know what is
essential and what may be a chance by-product. Some of the most
obscure and rare events, such as the disintegration of certain atomic
materials, and certain peculiar properties of light have changed the
entire way that science now views matter.

This view—that our consciousness is merely one unimportant
result of the hit-or-miss operation of the human machine—does not
make much sense in terms of modern physics. In the first place,
those who suggest this view do not give enough consideration to the

importance of the observer in discovering what is going on in any process. Not only the method, but the location and timing and movement of the observer make a real difference in what is seen or learned about anything. If this is true of objects and physical processes, it is far more true of human elements, particularly consciousness. We don't even understand what consciousness is, and yet there is no way to learn about it except to use our consciousness to observe itself and to interact with the same element in other human beings.

As I try to use my consciousness in this way, I again and again realize how differently different human beings must be treated if they are going to reveal the reality that is within them. I discover that there are many semi-conscious creatures like myself who are not entirely predictable (despite the opinions of B. F. Skinner). At the same time I find that it is very hard for us to get over the notion that having a physical body puts human beings in the same category as electrons or masses of rock. People do seem to be different from physical objects, although even electrons and masses of rock can be unpredictable enough.

In addition, the very act of observing a process usually alters it, particularly in sensitive materials. For instance, the use of a light for observation can have an effect on objects or people that are being observed. The same thing seems to be true of the mental activity to which people or objects are exposed during concentrated observation. In repeated experiments it has been shown that conscious concentration can have an effect on physical objects without the intervention of any known physical energy. The fact that the same results have been found by some of the most careful investigators makes it seem very likely that our expectations can influence the object or person we are trying to observe.

Finally the physicist today finds it difficult to determine when something has ceased to exist. As we have seen, the idea that there is a point in time at which a wave disintegrates on the shore and is no longer a part of the whole ocean makes very little sense in modern physics. For essentially the same reason it makes little sense to speak of the extinction of a human consciousness at a certain time and place, and to say with certainty that it no longer exists. One might say that since we human, conscious observers are a part of the whole field, something about our consciousness continues to exist as a part of the total space-time continuum.

This is the kind of existence after death which LeShan suggests, mainly on the basis of theoretical physics. It does sound rather thin and not too satisfying an existence just to be part of the whole. He points out, however, that the mystic often experiences this whole and does not consider it a lesser consciousness, but a higher one. In a certain way the mystical view anticipates the physicist's understanding. LeShan makes a plausible case for such a continued existence as part of the space-time continuum, or the total field. He suggests that perhaps in it we will retain the level of consciousness we have achieved in our life on this earth.

Whatever else his argument does, it opens our eyes to the fact that survival beyond this life has meaning in terms of the interrelatedness of field theory. It also shows that there is no real reason to accept the *dogmatic* denial of life after death which the former classical physics almost necessitated. LeShan's thinking has a great deal to offer anyone who is interested in the implications of Einstein and modern physics for the whole of life. This newer understanding does help by suggesting ways to free us from our set ways and from many prejudices. Whatever else it does, it certainly shows that it is no longer absurd to look into the subject of life after death. It also enables us to listen more openly to the data presented by Moody, Osis and others and to realize the meaning of such data for the whole of existence. Let us look at one more area of experience which can perhaps offer even more understanding of this meaning.

Mysticism, Meditation and Poetry

There is apparently a very interesting relation between mystical experiences and people's attitude toward this world and toward survival after death. For a long time we have been so suspicious of these experiences that we have not really looked at their effect on the lives of the individuals. In the survey by Andrew Greeley, which I have mentioned, there has been some careful study of this subject by a team of competent investigators. Their findings are described in Greeley's book *The Sociology of the Paranormal: A Reconnaissance.* Several things were discovered that are quite contrary to some of our ideas about mysticism.

First of all, far more people reported mystical experiences than even the investigators expected. Very often they described a new sense of life, which was essentially the same as the sense of being twice born described by William James. In the analysis of the data it was found that there is a close correspondence between this new sense of life and belief in survival after death. Emotional balance and well-being were also tested in the survey, and a very high correspondence was found between belief in life after death and emotional well-being. This relation between mystical experience and emotional balance appears to depend upon the belief in survival, and not on a sense of being twice born.

Thus this study, which was carefully based on a random sample of the American population, gives no support at all for the notion that mystics and people who believe in survival after death are psychologically immature or simply softheaded.* As Greeley concludes from the evidence, the sense of having touched a new level of existence in mystical experiences opens people to belief in a life beyond this one and this deepens their sense of psychological well-being. People with this sense of destiny and continued meaning are likely to be a lot less neurotic and much better balanced than others who feel that this is the only chance for achievement they will ever have.

In addition there seems to be some relationship between people's mystical experiences and their consciousness of death. These individuals seem to think and talk about death more than other people, but they seem less afraid of the prospect. In Greeley's words:

> They are more aware of death, but this awareness does not seem to be morbid. As one very active young woman put it, "I am not afraid of death, but it's very much on my mind. Sometimes to think about it makes me relaxed and peaceful."[11]

Some of those who were interviewed reported that they had had a near-death experience, and stated that this was what had triggered the mystical encounter. Thus the near-death experience seems to

---

*Herman Feifel, author of *The Meaning of Death* who is well known for his work in suicide prevention, took part recently in a program on public television on ways of helping the dying and their families deal with the situation as constructively as possible. When Feifel was asked about such experiences as those described by Moody and others, he cut off any discussion immediately, making no effort to conceal his impatience with people who feel a need to believe in life after death. Two other similar television programs appeared about the same time. None of them showed any concern with the question of survival after death. There seems to be a feeling that those who allow this belief to affect them are simply individuals who cannot cope with life as it really is.

generate mysticism, and the mystical experience seems to generate confidence in survival after death. The work of Greeley has been replicated and been verified by a study done in England by Ann Morisy and David Hay working out of Manchester College in Oxford and the School of Education at the University of Nottingham.[12]

While there has been no comparable study of the results of meditation, my own experiences and others that have come to my attention make me quite certain that in many instances the same facts would be found. Meditation is simply a process by which the individual tries to become open to the possibility of mystical experience. It is an attempt to open a way for religious experience, to give the individual a direct relationship with religious realities. Religious belief by itself does not seem to give much in the way of experience, but religious *practice* does.

In my book *The Other Side of Silence*, which is a study of Christian meditation, I have discussed the problem with the word *mysticism*. Basically this is the problem of what one is looking for in religious experience, and thus in the practice of meditation. Mysticism means different things to different people, and the kind of experience one has in the mystical state influences the way one views the world. In addition, the way a person views the world and what one is looking for in meditation can have a real influence on the experience that results. There is one kind of mystical experience which brings the person to an imageless union with the universe which is an experience of merging with the cosmic mind. One sees everything as part of the whole and tries to give up every attachment to become joined with the whole. One's ego and individuality are lost in absorption with all the rest. This view of mysticism is generally characteristic of Hinduism and Buddhism. Many people think that this is the only kind of mystical experience.

There is another kind, however, which seeks to find relationship with the center of all things. Since that center is Love, it requires that there be individuals who can be loved and who retain their egos in order to interact with Love. Except for brief ecstatic moments one cannot merge into that center and fulfill this requirement. Instead, one uses images and pictures to develop interaction and growth in relationship with the Other, the Divine Lover. Images provide a way of stepping into the dimension of reality where the Other can be found. The spiritual world reveals itself in the concrete images of dreams, and one can then work with them in meditation to realize the deepest levels of relationship with the Other.

The general mainstream of Christian devotional life has emphasized the value of the dream, the vision and the concrete image as facilitating one's experience of God. We find this tradition in Origen, Gregory of Nyssa, Chrysostom in the early years of the Church's life, and in later years in Julian of Norwich and Ignatius of Loyola and William Law. This Western mysticism is a development of Plato's idea that one encounters spiritual (ideal) reality rather than being absorbed into it.

There is another tradition in the West which is similar to the mystical views of Buddha. This practice and understanding emphasize imagelessness and merger with the *One*. It springs out of the teaching of Plotinus and Proclus and is found in the Pseudo-Dionysius and in *The Cloud of Unknowing*. It has exerted a powerful effect upon St. John of the Cross and upon many of the popular devotional manuals right up to the present time.

Each of these views expresses a truth about the reality of the universe and God. These views are complementary and not opposed to each other. They speak of a reality too large for our little minds to encompass. It is not really surprising when we realize that scientists cannot even understand what light is. They know from their experiments and from the equations of quantum mechanics that light can ✓ be experienced as either a ray or a particle, and they do not understand how this can be true. In a similar way we find that there are two different experiences of spiritual reality and that they are both true.

When we are caught up by the first view, our individual survival does not seem very meaningful. But when the other view is opened up to us, we understand that there is a real possibility of relationship both with the Divine Lover and also with other persons who have died, and it is easy to see the importance of having our individuality preserved. The experiences of the first kind of meditation reveal the almost overwhelming unity and power of the whole that one will come to know more fully in the next life. The experiences of the second kind give hints that the individual growth and development that we begin in this life will continue in the next. Each experience can open up an aspect of reality to us. T. S. Eliot in his incomparable poem *The Four Quartets* has described this paradoxical nature of the mystical vision.

Those who use the practice of meditation to open themselves to realities beyond the ordinary world of space and time can get a foretaste of life in another dimension. At times the experience may consist of quiet and a sense of being a part of the whole. At other times images from a dream, or those produced directly by the imagination, may reveal another level of experience and even bring one to an encounter with the Divine Lover. *The Spiritual Exercises* of St. Ignatius of Loyola offer one example of the way images may be used in meditation to bring us to this encounter.

The more one deals with the reality found in meditation and religious practice, the more confidence one has that it *is* a reality which is being revealed in these practices. One also becomes less caught by the idea that existence is limited to this ordinary world of asphalt and mud and stone walls and automobiles. In my parish in California I recall visiting one unsophisticated and none too faultless couple during the last illness of first one and then the other of them. They had kept up a steady and daily religious practice, one of the few who did in a parish that sometimes numbered 1,500 members. I was amazed to see the ease with which they both accepted their own death, and the confidence the husband showed as he faced the loss of his wife after sixty years of marriage. These two seemed to know another world, and they did not fear leaving this one or letting death separate them for a while.

My own religious practice, at its best and deepest moments, has led me to an experience similar to that described in Moody's book as a being of light, a loving and non-judgmental being of light. While these experiences have kept my life running through many difficult times and inner battles, still it strengthened my confidence in them to know that others had described experiences of this kind in such similar terms. One does not have to die to meet the being of light. When we actually encounter this reality in prayer and meditation, our fear of losing hold of life has much less power. In one sense meditation is a process in which one takes the time to die to this world and taste another, and so final death is not so awesome.

The same understanding of God and his universe is revealed in the greatest poetry. Dante's unequaled vision of the next world poured out in poetry from the imaginative depth from which all true inspiration springs. The greatest poetic and literary work in the German language, Goethe's *Faust*, ends with the vision describing the Virgin Mary and her angels carrying Faust off to heaven. Some of Shakespeare's plays reveal the same kind of understanding, as

James Kirsch has shown in *Shakespeare's Royal Self* and also Martin Lings in *Shakespeare in the Light of Sacred Art*. But even these works do not surpass William Blake in revealing this other dimension through his incomparable art and poetry.

William Blake realized exactly what Newtonian physics would do to the minds of men and women. He knew better than Newton who still saw himself as a real believer. Blake vigorously opposed the rationalism and materialism of Newton and the Enlightenment which he saw imprisoning humans in a world which these ideas had created, at the same time limiting infinite reality by man-made laws. He realized that imagination is the faculty which can open up this infinite reality to individuals. In his own words, which are better than mine:

> Vision or Imagination is the Representation of what Eternally Exists, Really and Unchangeably.... The Nature of Visionary Fancy or Imagination is very little known and the Eternal Nature and permanence of its ever-Existent Images is wrongly considered as less permanent than the things of Vegetative and Generative Nature.... The Imaginative Image returns by . . . Contemplative thought; the writings of the Prophets illustrate these conceptions of the Visionary Fancy by their various sublime and Divine Images as seen in the Worlds of Vision.[13]

Carl Jung came to much the same conclusion as he tried to heal sick and confused people by helping them deal both with human relationships and with the world of inner vision. Like Blake, Jung believed that as men and women enter this inner world they are able to change themselves and the world at the same time. Blake said the same thing in these words:

> If the spectator could enter into these images in his imagination . . . if he could enter into Noah's rainbow or into his bosom, or could make a friend and companion of one of these Images of wonder . . . then would he arise from his grave, then would he meet the Lord in the air and then he would be happy.[14]

Jung's active imagination, the imaginative meditation of Christianity, and the poetic fancy of William Blake all point in the same direction. All three are aimed at revealing the same reality, the reality we will come to know more fully when we die.

The Consensus of Humankind

Jung once wrote that, except for those groups whose tradition originated on that little peninsula of Asia known as Europe, all people everywhere believe in another dimension of reality. Could it be that we peoples of European heritage are wrong? Is it just possible that we do not perceive all there is to know about reality, and that for this reason we are suffering from a strange malady in both head and heart? The madman is sick because he fails to perceive ordinary reality. If the spiritual is just as real, and has just as much effect on us as any other reality, could it be that our neglect of this reality is causing some of our many physical and social problems today?

In 1900 it may have been possible to believe that we in the Western European tradition had finally arrived at the truth and could look down on the rest of the world, with its funny beliefs in spirits and flying off into a reality beyond the horizon and coming back from the dead, as childish. In these later years of our century it is harder to be sure that we are the only ones who are fully conscious, fully mature. Other peoples have believed for a long time that there is another reality besides the tangible, objective one that we have tried to deal with without letting anything else interfere. The belief of the rest of the world suggests that we are trying to do the impossible. This other reality, it is believed, is not only the "place" or kind of existence one steps into at death, but is also an ever-present influence on our lives and actions. It can help and fulfill us or disrupt and destroy our lives. This was also the conclusion reached by Carl Jung on the basis of his extensive experience with human beings.

The events of our own time make it difficult to believe that our position is so superior that we can keep on ignoring this understanding. Western peoples have fought two of the most savage and uncivilized wars the world has ever known. They are plagued by senseless and primitive violence in one place after another, and by the wear and tear which Western culture inflicts on both the psychic and the physical environment. In addition, the developments of modern science have knocked away the underpinnings of our certainty about the physical world. What appeared to be final truth in the 1890's is impossible to maintain in the 1970's.

When one truth crumbles, other related truths are likely to

crumble with it. The certainty of science about the nature of space and time has crumbled, and with it we have lost the dogmatic certainty that there is no possibility of survival after death. We are left in the position of Heisenberg who felt that science has become so skeptical that it is skeptical of its own skepticism. He went on to write that the natural words like "soul" and "spirit" probably tell more about reality than the exact words of physics which have been defined to the point of rigidity.

If even our own science urges us to be open to the possibility that reality is not limited to just what we can see and touch, then we can begin to look again at the consensus of human belief with a new confidence. This is particularly true since the research in parapsychology has begun to provide evidence which seems to support many of the ideas about life after death which have come from the experience and the thinking of believers around the world. Humankind may not have been practicing self-deception after all in believing in another life. There are as many good reasons for believing this as for doubting it. No, there are better reasons for believing in survival after death than for doubting it, if one takes all the data into consideration. With the possibility of openness about the question of survival, and even of confidence, let us go on now to consider what our existence after death might be like.

VIII. Survival: Persistence and Transformation

For a long time I have struggled with the need to develop some picture or view of the kind of life that we may find on the other side of death. Most of us, I find, share a common need to see meaning in our lives that continues on beyond our present existence. The studies that are now being made of people's experiences at the time of death make me even more convinced of our need for an understanding of the nature of the afterlife. Even so, it seems presumptuous for an ordinary human being to attempt such an overwhelming task. How can any of us hope to picture or understand what lies beyond the limits of this world and this life?

Through the ages, however, there have been many, varied ideas about human beings and the future they would find in the life to come. When we compare this thinking with the meager fare that is offered by so many churches today, it appears that there is need to go back into our Christian tradition and sort out the views and ideas that once flowed so freely. At the outset we need to remind ourselves that ideas like these are not created in a vacuum. They originate from some kind of human experience. But since we cannot be sure about the experiences behind these ideas, what sort of picture or understanding can we expect to gain from considering them? Some of the things that scientists have learned in this century suggest quite clearly the possibility of an answer.

For one thing, science has learned that we can go only so far in understanding the nature of light. After all the experiments and all the painstaking calculations, there is a point at which one is caught in insoluble problems. Light can act both as a wave and as a particle, and it defies every attempt to explain how it can be both things at the same time. Although both things can be dealt with in a complex algebraic equation, our minds cannot comprehend what the equation expresses. All we can do is report what it says in terms that seem contradictory to the human mind. Physicists tell us, however, that the two descriptions are not actually contradictory, but complementary. Both descriptions are needed; by complementing each other they reveal what is really true about light. If we insist that light must conform to our limited human perception and imagination, we learn only part of the story. Because we do not understand the nature of light, we do not suggest that it does not exist.

What is true of light, which is one of the simpler and more basic elements of the universe, is also true of a clod of dirt. Locked in that apparently simple bit of matter from the garden is such complexity and mystery as to stretch our imagination to the breaking point. Inside the tiniest fragment of it we now know that there is a whirling universe of countless particles in continuous motion. We have begun to realize how little we do know for sure, and how much room there is for wonder at the mystery of all things, as we have come to understand what is going on inside such seemingly solid lumps of matter.

When it comes to human beings, their basic nature and what may lie beyond the grave for them, we can be sure of one thing. We will find that the complexities, the wonder, the apparent contradictions are infinitely greater. Human life is the most complex and highly developed aspect of the physical world. Our brains are instruments of unbelievable refinement, far more complicated than the most highly developed computers. In every way we humans are harder to understand than light or energy or matter. In approaching questions about the nature of human life and its persistence after death, we can be quite certain that *any simple, clear, and precise description of the nature of life after death will be only partial, and therefore false.* Even if God in his infinite wisdom were to reveal the full and ultimate nature of reality and of himself, we would certainly not understand that revelation completely or be able to convey it with total clarity.

The best we can hope for is to discover some indications, some images and hints of what life and existence can be beyond the grave. We can clear away some of the many absurd beliefs that surround this subject. We can learn what happens when men and women believe that they can understand everything about either God or their own ultimate destiny. In the end, I believe, we will be able to reach some very probable conclusions about the quality and characteristics of the life that may be found after death.

We shall not be looking for final, unchangeable answers, however. People who want absolute certainty, even about things in this present life, usually seem to be hiding from their own insecurities. They are afraid, and so they demand of God the certainty he cannot give to our limited human minds and spirits. Only God has that kind of knowledge about the universe he has made. When individuals assume that sort of complete or logical certainty and make dogmatic statements about religious matters, they are generally hiding their doubts. Sometimes they are making an effort to control the minds of unsuspecting people who are easily led. Whenever these dogmatic people suggest that the listener should be guilty for doubting their declarations, we are dealing with brainwashing.

There are obviously good reasons for inquiring about the methods that people use to decide what may or may not be true in this world, and also beyond it. Let us ask, then, how we shall go about considering the ideas about life after death which are found in Christianity and in nearly every other religion the world over.

A Theological Approach

It may seem foolish to try to define a theological method in a few paragraphs, but it is even more foolish not to make the effort. Religious investigation requires ground rules just as much as scientific research. If I do not state them and share my method of thinking, I risk letting facts be replaced by presuppositions of which I am not even aware. Working with ideas without asking where they come from and why they seem to have meaning can lead us into blind alleys and to all sorts of nonsense.

There are four basic avenues to approach religious understanding which I propose to use. Three of them were suggested by Baron Friedrich von Hügel, and I have added a fourth element or way of approach which was not available when he was writing. Von Hügel suggested that first of all we need to know our own religious traditions deeply and well. No individual or single group gains enough experience to plumb the depth of the spiritual aspect of reality alone or independently. New research in physics or chemistry can begin only on the basis of earlier discoveries. In a similar way religious understanding has to be built on the accumulated wisdom and understanding of the great religions of humankind.

My own thinking is based on an understanding that the New Testament and Jesus of Nazareth give us the most complete and adequate picture of spiritual reality available to us. My considered opinion after examining the great religions of humankind is that in Christianity we have the best picture of God, of the spiritual nature of human beings and the spiritual world that surrounds them, that has yet been given. I hold this belief in spite of the distortions of which the Christian Church has sometimes been guilty, even in our own time. One needs, however, to know other religious traditions in order to appreciate one's own.

In addition to knowing our tradition, its sources and its history, one needs to develop a capacity for critical thinking. As von Hügel showed, there is tremendous value for religious understanding in the scientific method, in its way of looking critically at all the facts and remaining open to new data. If God really did make this world of ours, then the deeper I probe in an effort to understand various aspects of this universe, the more likely I will be to find the awesome mystery, the very finger of God. Scientists have the same human need for certainty as the rest of us, and unfortunately, as I have noted, they sometimes give in and find ways to avoid facts which do not fit their theories. If we can keep from making this mistake, we will find that open seeking will ultimately lead to God, if such a reality exists at all. There is no need for the genuinely religious person to fear either facts or theories. God gave us inquiring and questioning hearts and minds to be used, and our science and scientific methods are a way of learning about God and his universe. They are also one of the best ways we have to avoid illusions and absurd ideas and to keep from becoming prejudiced and one-sided.

The third element that is important in religious and theological investigation is one's own experience. So long as people accepted authority and reason as the only real basis for religious understanding, experience seemed to have little place in religious thinking. The modern world, on the other hand, finds it very difficult to believe anything which cannot be tested in someone's experience. Our experiences of the spiritual world, in fact, give us one real way to make contact with our religious tradition and realize our belief in it. Both unexpected mystical experiences and those found through ritual and dream and meditation can lift us out of our ordinary perception of reality into another dimension of experience.

Without meditation and the things that happen to me through this process, I would have very little to say about the nature of life after death. As I enter into the deepest experiences of meditation, I find direct contact with an Other who reaches out to me and lets me know the reality of this other dimension of experience in various ways. I also see how similar my own experiences are to those of people on the verge of death and those described by people who return from a close encounter with death. In this way I begin to get a vision of what life after death may be like. The experiences described in the New Testament and throughout the history of the Church begin to sound like actual happenings. My own experience of something quite beyond this present existence, something from a Divine Source, adds credence to our entire tradition. Theologians and religious philosophers who do not have their own personal encounters with the Other have little occasion to voice negative opinions about life after death or any of the other experiences described in that tradition.*

The fourth element which I find necessary in order to approach religious matters with any degree of wisdom is a knowledge of the depth and complexity of human beings. One must know as much as possible about the range of human experience, the extent of people's agony and their aspirations, their dreams and religious experiences, and have some feel for the hidden and mysterious aspects of human personality. We humans are far more than our conscious minds. We are more than our clarity and logical understanding. There is substantiality to the psyche. Within each of us there is a soul with fears and doubts and hidden motivations, with capacities for revelation and communion with a dimension of reality other than the ordinary physical one. Wise spiritual directors of all times and places and religions have known and understood these depths, and have minis-

---

*It is interesting that the new data about the possibility of on-going life beyond the grave does not come in most instances from theologians, but from medical doctors, experts in sociology, psychology and parapsychology. Andrew Greeley is one exception, and he is a sociologist as well as a priest. All of these people are using the scientific method of free inquiry as best they can in order to learn more about the nature of human beings and their destiny.

tered to them.[1] Almost instinctively they have understood the depth of human beings and known how to approach the needs that arise from within us.

In this century the depth of the human soul has been studied as never before. No one has done more to contribute to this study or written about it more widely than C. G. Jung. The twenty volumes of his collected works give an understanding of human personality, of our souls, in a way that has never been available before. In addition his autobiography reveals his own experiences and his struggle in such personal depth that he felt it should not be included with the studies of a more scientific nature.

Jung seldom ever intended what he wrote to be taken as final truth. It was to be tested according to the canons of religious tradition, critical thinking, and human experience. Jung offers data and hypothesis, and this understanding provides a starting point, an essential basis for theological inquiry. One who is trying to learn about hidden realities such as God or an existence beyond this world must start with an understanding about the hidden depths of human beings. Anything we learn has to come from human beings themselves, and this knowledge which has been unearthed by scientific methods gives us the only basis available at present for sorting out fact and reality from illusion and self-deception.

In addition there is not much point in getting religious knowledge unless it can be communicated to others, and this requires an intimate knowledge of oneself and other human beings. We are more than our logical minds. The same understanding is generally essential if one is trying to lead others upon the religious way. And finally in approaching our questions about life after death, the more we know about the inner depth of human beings as they live and interact in this world, the more we may be able to understand about their continued existence.

These four elements of religious understanding are almost constantly in conflict and friction. Only at rare moments are they all in harmony. The very tension between them keeps us alive and open to the rich abundance of God's world, both physical and spiritual. The friction keeps us humble and growing in our knowledge of both realities and of God.

If we use only one of these ways of learning about the reality around us, we are very likely to come up with narrow, one-sided ideas that do not make much sense. This is particularly true in religious matters. If one is guided only by tradition, there is a tendency to become rigid and dogmatic in one way or another. One may also be caught by superstitious or inhuman ideas. The person who depends only on logical, critical methods runs the risk of becoming caught in either agnosticism or a cold and bloodless deism. On the other hand, the idea that experience provides the *only* test can lead to rejecting any kind of structure and thus to superstition and all sorts of enthusiastic excesses. Reliance solely upon knowledge of human beings and their inner, psychic structure can create so much interest in one's own depth that the outer world is neglected and the person develops gnostic and self-centered ideas that are unhealthy.

In going over the recent discussions of life after death by both Catholic and Protestant writers, I find that they are mainly based on only one or two of these ways of approaching religious realities. Therefore they are one-sided and inadequate, even inhuman. An excellent survey of these ideas is provided by E. J. Fortman, S.J. in his book *Everlasting Life after Death*. The range of opinions he presents is dismaying. In one case he calls attention to four Protestant theologians who base their ideas on the same passage in Paul's letter and come up with four different opinions about the afterlife. Fortman observes:

> If their basic principle of *"sola Scriptura"* leads to such divergent interpretations, perhaps they should think of supplementing it by recourse also to the interpretations of the Fathers and of the Church's Creeds.[2]

These four—Oscar Cullmann, Helmut Thielicke, J. M. Shaw, and Russell Aldwinckle—are all quite conservative. There are also the various liberal theologians who feel that there isn't enough material to write much on the subject of life after death.

Fortman's suggestion, of course, is a good one, but to my way of thinking he doesn't go quite far enough. This tradition itself needs to be explored by the best of human critical thinking, in the light of the deepest human experience of God and the divine, and related to the best knowledge we have of human personality. At the outset we need to realize that these four aspects can be related without diminishing the value of biblical revelation or the tradition of the Church. On the contrary these are simply four ways that are available to us for learning about most of the things our tradition describes. The possibility of integrating these four aspects gives us a real chance of finding a total picture of the reality of the spiritual world and the One who can be found there as its source and center.

This is God's world. It is both physical and spiritual. We human beings share in both, and if we are to show sensitive and alert individuals a way to the source of their lives in spiritual reality, we need to present as total a picture as possible. We live in the midst of a rich, complex, and incredibly mysterious universe. To understand it and share that knowledge we need to use all of our capacities and all the ways available to us for coming to that knowledge.

Jesus of Nazareth told the story of the Father's love for the prodigal son to give us an inkling of what we might find in this universe. But the story that he lived out for us in his death and resurrection was far better. In Jesus God reached out to share his love in a personal way with lost human beings, broken by life and dissatisfied. He offered his love in order to rescue them from their lostness. So great was that love that Jesus—whose nature the Church believes is the same as that of God himself—died and rose again to rescue human beings from the control that death and evil had over them. This is the central revelation of Christianity, the revelation which is expressed in essence in the dogmas of the incarnation and the atonement. The entire Bible needs to be looked at in the light of this central revelation. The Bible needs to be understood as an introduction to the loving nature of God, as one of the main ways of learning about the quality which Dante described so well in the final lines of *The Divine Comedy*. Dante's vision came as he was brought to the very center of paradise to behold the triune God. What he experienced was inexpressible. All he could say of it was put in these words:

High phantasy lost power and here broke off;
   Yet, as a wheel moves smoothly, free from jars,
   My will and my desire were turned by love,
The love that moves the sun and the other stars.[3]

As we try to understand the nature of life after death, we need to keep this central revelation in mind. We need to use our heads and ask how this revelation in Christ fits our own experience and our knowledge of human beings. How does our knowledge in these areas add to what this revelation tells us about God, about the physical and spiritual universes in which he reigns, and how we are to share them with him in life after death?

Nothing I have worked on previously has been as difficult as the effort to put together these ideas and pictures of what we may find in eternal life. My own thinking often fails me. And at those times (I say this in spite of my reluctance to sound unduly religious or even pious), I go on only because of the encouragement I find in my contact with the Other, the risen Christ. In times of quiet and interaction, often in the middle of the night, I experience something of the reality that is waiting, desiring to be experienced. Particularly in the pages that follow I have not only tried to use my intellect and my knowledge of our Christian tradition and of human beings and our souls, but I have had to let my experiences of the risen One throw light upon these efforts. The process that has gone on makes me wonder if theology may not be a futile intellectual game unless it involves the whole person and so becomes a confession of faith. If the theological writer is not emotionally involved with God, can he really know that of which he speaks? Or is he like a blind art critic who must rely entirely on the opinions of others in order to say something about works of art?

Let us turn now to see if the use of these four approaches can open up a view of the reality that lies ón the other side of death.

Immortality

Originally I intended to call this chapter "Immortality and Resurrection of the Dead." However, as I considered the current theology more fully, I realized that both of these words are so loaded with emotion and prejudice that their meaning has become almost too confused to shed light on the subject. Still, these are the words commonly used to represent two opposite approaches to the nature of life after death. It is my basic contention that the ideas of *immortality* and *resurrection* are not contradictory, but rather complementary in the same way that modern physics uses two opposite descriptions to represent the nature of light completely. Let us look at what each of these words actually represents about the nature of the life beyond.

Among nearly all primitive peoples, both ancient and modern, there is a belief that a substantial part of each person continues on after the death of the physical body.[4] These peoples almost invariably see things from within a world-view which does not distinguish clearly between the physical and the non-physical (spiritual or psychoid*) realms of reality. They are quite aware, however, that something significant happens to the soul at death. Most primitive peoples see life after death as less satisfactory than their physical existence in the here and now. This is one reason for the elaborate precautions they take in burying the dead. They want to be sure that the souls of the departed do not return to bother those who are still living. The primitive view of the afterlife is often very similar to the Hades of the Greeks or the Sheol of the Hebrews. Such a shadowy existence is gray and dull. People are only half alive. As the early Hebrews stressed, in the unsatisfying life of Sheol one could not even praise God.

Among ancient peoples two pictures emerged to convey another level of experience and understanding about the state of the deceased. The Hebrew and Semitic peoples came to the idea of the resurrection of the dead in which the just were raised to a new life, either in a new and transfigured earth or in another realm of being. A different idea, the idea of the immortality of the soul, developed among the people of northern Asia. They came to believe that one's soul could continue to grow in the next life as well as in this one, and that the individual could come to a full and rich immortal life.[5]

Resurrection stresses the value of transformation given in the next life, a transformation which is not earned but is a gift simply given through the grace of God. Immortality, on the other hand, points to the substantiality of the soul and the importance of its persistence and its potential for growth. It stresses the importance of our working at our own growth both in this world and in the next.

Eliade has shown that there is a widespread group of practices which he calls shamanism. The basic idea of shamanism is that humans are caught between two worlds, a physical one and a spiritual one. The shaman is the one who has journeyed into the spiritual world and met there the forces of evil, has been dismembered and resurrected, and then has been enabled to return to be a guide for others in their dealings with this spiritual world. The shaman also helps people in sickness, which is usually viewed as

---

*"Psychoid" refers to a realm of being which is not physical. This realm contains realities which are psyche-like and non-physical. They exist in a realm similar to the physical one which we are aware of in our everyday sensory life but different from it. I have described this at some length in *Encounter with God* and *The Other Side of Silence*.

caused from the spiritual side. He or she (for shamans can be of
either sex) is also the guide to help people through the perilous
journey at death and lead them to paradise. The practices of
shamanism give the germ of what was later developed into the full-
blown idea of immortality. In both the mystery religions and in
Orphism there were the beginnings of this belief in the persistence
of the soul. In these religions the attainment of immortal life de-
pended more on initiation and following the practices of the cult
than on moral development.

The philosophical idea of immortality was given its classical
statement by Plato in the *Phaedo*, his description of the last days of
Socrates. Plato, in fact, could even be called the philosopher of the
shamanistic world-view. He saw human beings participating in two
worlds. There is no doubt that in much of his writing Plato considered the physical world the inferior one. He held that matter is
chaotic and that this keeps the perfect spiritual forms or *ideas* from
being fully expressed. Thus he tended to devalue the human body
and its physical existence. Because of his influence many people
came to see the body as the prison house of the soul.

Yet at the same time Plato was convinced that human love is
one way of encountering the divine which can lead people to God.
This understanding is developed in his fascinating dialogue *The
Symposium*. The process starts when a person falls in love with the
beautiful body of another individual, and then comes to appreciate
the soul which is the source of that body's beauty. Then the lover
who continues to love is led on to love the God who has made that
beautiful soul. Plato also felt that one's soul had existed before and
that it lived first in one human body and then in another. This idea
of the transmigration of souls, or reincarnation, led him to believe
that many of people's capacities came from a previous life. They
were reawakened in an individual as one recollected what had been
known in a previous life but had been forgotten upon re-entering
the world.

Plato, magnificent man and great thinker that he was, could
hold all these various ideas together in tension without becoming
absurd or foolish. Many of those who followed his thinking, however, did not have his breadth of wisdom or his sanity. They ignored
his view of love as an avenue to God, with the body mediating the
divine. They began to see the body only as the prison house of the
soul and to consider physical matter the actual source of corruption

and evil. A group of religious sects developed to teach men and women how to free their souls from entanglement in this material world. By following ascetic practices the soul could be separated from the physical body and prepared to go on into the next life. Sexuality and conceiving new physical life became supreme evils because they brought new souls into contact with evil and corrupt matter.

These sects believed that people's souls belonged in a purely spiritual realm which was entirely separate from the physical world and had no relation to it. They taught that human beings had become caught in physical existence accidentally. A cosmic catastrophe, an explosion in the realm of spirit, had somehow occurred. Bits and pieces of soul-matter had been thrown out into space. As they came into contact with matter, human bodies were formed. Only these bits of soul-matter were considered valuable. The main purpose of human beings was to release them from involvement in physical bodies and the physical world and start them back toward the spiritual realm where they belonged.

The way to find salvation was to free oneself from all interest in the physical world and all emotional involvement in it. Obviously all sexuality had to be eliminated since through conception it only resulted in attaching more soul to matter. The first task of the individual was to understand the evil nature of the world, and then the various levels of spiritual reality through which one had to ascend to get back to the realm at the center of that reality. By knowledge and by learning to live by strict practices, the soul was prepared to make its way to a life of pure spirit. Since this was basically a way of self-help based upon knowledge, the general point of view was known as Gnosticism, a form of *gnosis*, the Greek word for knowledge.

In the early days of Christianity gnostic religion began to attract more and more people in the Roman Empire. Before long it became one of the chief competitors the Church had to face. Gnosticism even tried to take over the Church itself. The early Church Fathers, Irenaeus, Tertullian and others, fought tooth and nail to keep the Church from being taken over by a gnostic point of view. In the Apostles' Creed Christian leaders took a firm stand against Gnosticism. They started by stating their belief that God had created both heaven and earth, showing that the physical world must be essentially good. The final words express their belief in "the resurrection of the body and life everlasting." In these words the Church denied the kind of belief in immortality that was taught by Gnosticism, but *not the idea of immortality itself*.

The early Church shared the world-view of that time, with its belief in a spiritual world as well as a physical one. In this understanding they had no quarrel with the gnostics. However, the Christian belief was fundamentally opposed to the Gnostic idea that there was no communication between these two modes of existence, and that only the spiritual one was good.* The Christian belief held that the two interpenetrated and intermingled. The human soul shared both of these worlds, and God spoke to men and women in dreams and visions and touched their bodies and souls to heal them. The early Christians also saw the physical world and the human body, sexuality and emotions as good creations of God. They saw the body as a concrete expression of the soul in actual human beings and felt that it had enough eternal value to be resurrected and go on into the next life. Certainly it should not be cast away and lost. Unfortunately the Church sometimes valued the body more in theory than in practice, as Augustine showed in his diatribe against sexuality.

*Much the same point of view which Gnosticism expressed about the evil nature of the physical world is also found in Hinduism and Buddhism. In the popular versions of these religions the physical world is generally seen as illusion. Only the spiritual realm is considered real. One's task is to separate the soul out from illusion in order to help it find salvation. Since the real purpose of developing an ego, according to this view, is only to deal with the physical world, the ego must do its work and then fade out of the picture if one is to come to enlightenment and be delivered from illusion.

The world is a vale of pain and sorrow, of agony and self-destructive passion. There is no choice but to get off the world. This is the goal of life, to separate from the sorry illusions of the physical world. It is accomplished by eliminating all emotion and even losing one's ego consciousness. Bliss in Buddhism comes with losing all ties to the world, even consciousness, and merging with the imageless, cosmic mind in *Nirvana*.

The idea of resurrecting this human body as a valuable addition to eternal life at any stage is simply unthinkable in these traditions. The whole physical world is essentially a prison to which one returns again and again to work out one's *karma* in the hope of finally being released from any body and from this earth. The great religious leaders like Buddha did not carry this idea to the inhuman extremes which are possible. Buddha spoke of the compassion which brings the *bodhisattva* back into the world to help others toward enlightenment. The *bodhisattva* is one who can enter into the bliss of *Nirvana*, but chooses to return because of his compassion for other people. It must also be realized that there are as many varieties of Eastern thought and religion as there are of Western. While this is the general framework in which Eastern religions have developed, what I have said may apply to the majority of groups and not to all.

The physical world itself was considered valuable and worth saving. At the right time God was going to redeem and transform it. In fact this world was good enough for the reality of God to become incarnate in it. Thus in its very essence Christianity denied the idea that physical matter is evil by nature. Rather, it saw evil in any action or process that turned human beings away from relationship with God. At the same time the early Christians continued to maintain the value of the spiritual world. They saw in it not only angels and seraphim, departed human beings and principalities and powers, but, most important, this was where the triune God was found. Through contact with the world of spirit human beings could have fellowship with God, the supreme good, in this present world, and they could expect more complete fellowship with this reality in the life after death.

The Church Fathers did not believe that people earned such a place in the life to come by their own power and knowledge, but by keeping themselves open to the transforming power of God. As Robert Wilken has shown in his excellent article, "The Immortality of the Soul and Christian Hope,"[6] all of the early Church Fathers believed and taught both the immortality of the soul and the resurrection of the dead, and they did not see these ideas as inconsistent or contradictory. These early Christians were real human beings struggling with their own and other people's fear of death. They found that in order to deal with the fear of death, they needed to use both arguments, to show both the soul's immortality and its capacity for resurrection.

One of the most profound statements of this attitude is found in Gregory of Nyssa's book, *On the Soul and Resurrection*. Gregory was not writing theology as an intellectual pursuit in this work. He had lost both his brother, Basil the Great, and his sister Macrina, and he was writing to sustain his own hope as well as to share with others the hope that he found. Like most of the early Christians, he saw immortality not as "a philosophical idea but an article of faith. Indeed it was self-evident to the Fathers that the immortality of the soul was a doctrine derived from the Bible."[7]

Three passages were most often referred to by the Fathers to support the doctrine of immortality. In Philippians 1:21-24 Paul was wondering whether it would be better to stay alive or to die and be with Christ. In 2 Corinthians 5:1 Paul spoke of a house not made by human hands, an eternal house in heaven. And in Matthew 10:28 Jesus told the disciples not to fear those who can kill the body but cannot kill the soul. In addition there are several passages in the Bible which refer to resurrection of the dead. What has this idea meant to Christians in various times and places?

The Resurrection of the Dead

If it is difficult for sophisticated modern men and women to have a place in their thinking for immortality, most of them have even more trouble accepting the idea of resurrection of the dead, particularly resurrection of the body. For a long time the Church avoided dealing with the discussion of resurrection in the New Testament, but modern scholarship has shown that we cannot eliminate this idea from the New Testament without doing violence to its whole message. Oscar Cullmann in particular has emphasized the need for Christians to take resurrection into account, and he has had great influence. Unfortunately most of the writers who point to the importance of resurrection for Christian thinking are trying to deny the importance of the idea of immortality in the Bible. Besides this, the tradition of literalism in Christianity has created problems for many people by stressing the last days, the second coming of Christ, and the end of the world as necessary conditions for resurrection to take place.

The most important support for some idea of resurrection is, of course, the resurrection of Jesus. He did not return to his disciples as a ball of fire or an inner voice, but as a resurrected body which could be handled and touched and which consumed fish. And yet this body had strange qualities about it. It could pass through solid doors and appear and disappear in an extraordinary way. Finally it was seen for the last time as it ascended into heaven.

There is little doubt that these appearances of Jesus were the cornerstone of the faith of early Christianity. They convinced the disciples that Jesus had conquered death, and with this conviction they were able to go forth and outlive, outthink, and outdie the ancient world. Something remarkable happened in these resurrection appearances, although it is difficult to describe exactly what it was. The apostles wrote of their conviction that Christ has conquered death and evil not only in their lives but also in both the outer world and the spiritual world. They were able to see the concrete reality and power of God's conquering spirit manifested directly in the physical world. Their writings express the basic idea that at death all Christians will be given a resurrected body and a life similar to what they had seen after the death of Jesus. This is quite a different idea from that of merging into the nothingness of a blissful *Nirvana*.

Jesus also spoke of the resurrection. This idea was quite common among the Semitic people of the time. It was one solution for the unsatisfactory prospect of Sheol. In fact, one of the basic differences between the Pharisees and Sadducees was that the Sadducees, who based their beliefs on the first five books of the Bible, maintained that there was no resurrection. Paul took advantage of this disagreement when he was in prison in Caesarea and divided his opponents over this issue. The Book of Enoch, written in the century just before Jesus' ministry, gave an elaborate account of how resurrection took place and the nature of life after death. It described heaven above the earth and Gehenna, a place of fire and torment below. Some people understood that resurrection would occur for everyone at the same time on the day of the Lord when God's kingdom became a reality, while others felt that each person would be resurrected individually at death. Both ideas seem to be found in Jesus' statements.

The party of Herod, the Sadducees, tried to trip Jesus up by asking him what would happen at death to a woman who had been married successively to seven brothers. They wanted him to tell them which of them she would be married to after resurrection. He told them that there was no giving and taking in marriage in the resurrected state. God, he said, is the God of the living and not of the dead, and he let them know that it is a real mistake not to realize that there is life with God after death (Matthew 22:23-33; Mark 12:18-27; Luke 20:27-40). In the story of Lazarus and the rich man Jesus suggested that both men went to some kind of resurrected life immediately, one to joy in Abraham's bosom and the rich man to fiery torment. When the rich man pleaded that someone be sent to warn his brothers, Abraham looked at him from afar and said, "If they will not listen either to Moses or to the prophets, they will not be convinced even if someone should rise from the dead" (Luke 16:19-31, JB).

Jesus told a group of Pharisees that good people would be recompensed when they rose from the dead (Luke 14:14). In the account of the raising of Lazarus he told Martha that her brother would rise again, and Martha said to him, "I know he will rise again

at the resurrection on the last day" (John 11:21-25, JB). For people
living in Palestine in the first century this way of speaking about
resurrection was probably the idiom used to speak of life after
death. The way this idea was expressed had important implications
which we shall look at later.

The early Christians believed that the kingdom of God or the
kingdom of heaven was about to come. Whatever Jesus had meant
by saying that the kingdom of God was at hand, after his death the
disciples concluded that the end of the world was about to occur.
They believed that Jesus would then return in clouds of glory just as
the two angels had told the group immediately after his ascension
(Acts 1:9-11). Jesus did discuss what was going to happen in the
apocalyptic sections in each of the Synoptic Gospels (Matthew 24;
Mark 13; Luke 21). In these talks with the disciples he spoke of
something coming to an end, saying that there would be a time of
great tribulation and that the Son of Man would then come in glory.
But he insisted that no one could know the day or hour when these
things would happen, and that not even the angels or the Son had
that knowledge, but only the Father. In 1 Corinthians 15 and 1
Thessalonians 4 Paul went on with what Jesus is reported to have
said in these passages and discussed how the dead would be raised
to new life. He believed that this would happen when Jesus returned to this earth and had power over it.

The final and most complete statement in the New Testament
about the second coming and resurrection is found in Revelation 19
and 20. John's final vision showed how Jesus would return after the
world had suffered great troubles and distress. Satan would then be
chained and sealed into the abyss, and all the righteous and the
martyrs would rise from their graves to reign with Christ for a
thousand years. At the end of the millennium Satan would be
released, but when Satan gathered his forces for one final attack, he
would be defeated and thrown into the fiery pit. All of the dead
would then be raised. The wicked would be judged and, along with
Death and Hades, cast into a lake of fire. In John's vision a new
heaven then appeared, and a new earth, the new Jerusalem adorned
like a bride, came down from God, making a place where God
would live forever with his people.

There have been groups of Christians from the very beginning
of the Church who maintained that the Book of Revelation spoke of
literal truth. They have looked, and many people still look, for the

signs of this final conflict. I once attended a lecture at a Bible college and heard the speaker cite various sources to pinpoint just when this time would come. People who hold this view are known as millenarians or chiliasts, from the Latin and the Greek words for a thousand. This was once the view of many Christians, but after Augustine had identified the Church with the kingdom of God, present here and now in *this* world, the idea that God's kingdom would come only after Satan and all the wicked people had been disposed of was no longer considered orthodox.

Today many enthusiastic Christians and most of those who interpret the Bible literally have seized upon this aspect of the New Testament and made it central to their understanding of Christianity. There are people in almost every denomination who find confident hope of a future life in this belief. And, of course, if there is a chance that the world is about to come to an end as the Jehovah's Witnesses maintain, then it is a good idea to know all that one can about the life to come.

Therefore, for many people the idea of resurrection and belief in a future life depend upon certainty about this understanding of the second coming of Christ and the judgment that will occur at that time. In the case of immortality one does not have to accept the entire gnostic view in order to see the validity and the value of the understanding that is given by the idea of immortality. The same thing is true about resurrection. One does not have to take the whole millenarian idea or schema bag and baggage in order to see that there is real value expressed in the image of resurrection.

In essence the idea of resurrection speaks to three very important Christian truths which are not emphasized in the idea of immortality. It speaks first of all of the value of the body and our emotional life, its images and passions, which are intimately related to our physical bodies. These elements of our being are anything but insignificant; they have eternal consequences. We do not divest ourselves of what we have been when we die. In one sense the image of resurrection provides some of the same meaning for the Jew and Christian that the concept of *karma* offers to the Hindu and Buddhist. The human body and its emotions have eternal value. They continue with us. We do not slip out of them as a butterfly does out of its cocoon.

Resurrection also speaks of transformation. Unless there is a possibility of change, renewal and transformation, people will find

themselves after death in a boring, Sheol-like existence. And transformation cannot occur unless our individual structure is resurrected
to be worked on once more. The life that has gone before is never
quite good enough. Human life, if it is to continue and be worthwhile, demands resurrection to a new level—transformation.

Finally, resurrection speaks about the action of God. Human
beings do not achieve resurrection by their own efforts. It is given.
Jung has pointed out that seldom, if ever, do human beings come to
wholeness and renewal unless it is given from a source beyond
themselves. Really satisfactory life is not inherent in our human
condition. It is a gift of grace from beyond the human being. Simply
the fact that we do find this grace, even now and then, in our
present, earth-bound lives is one reason for believing in a God who
wants us to go on to a new level of life in this universe of his.

The Human Condition

Most people find that life is very difficult. For twenty years I
was rector of quite a large parish, and I have lectured all over this
country and in several others. Wherever I go I find human beings
and their problems very much the same. When I listen in depth to
individuals, I find very few men or women who find life really
satisfying. Like the great British philosopher John Stuart Mill, they
cannot even imagine a life which would satisfy them. Most men and
women, in fact, are trying to hide from the conflict and pain that
looms up and overshadows them if they have to be alone and quiet.

We are all aware of the obvious escape routes that many people
take to avoid facing themselves in solitary silence. We pay attention
to the statistics about alcoholism and drug addiction. But we tend to
forget that our busy-ness, including television addiction, also represents a serious spiritual problem. Most of us would be terrified out
of our wits to face solitary confinement. But people who never take
time alone to face what lies within cannot know their own need, nor
do they turn to find the reality that could help them prepare for
continued life and growth.

For twenty-five years I have been listening to the loneliness
and agony of human beings. One reason many people are willing to
talk to me is because I have had to deal with my own inner darkness
and conflict, and so I know that I am in no position to judge any
individual. In a recent book, *Discernment: A Study in Ecstasy and Evil*, I

presented a picture of my own soul as I have come to know it through years of listening to my dreams and becoming open to new depths through meditation and prayer. I find that most people are much like me. In the often hidden depths of themselves they are as complex as I am. They have many powers and forces fighting for control of their lives. There is also a principle of separation and destructiveness which tries to seize these inner powers and use them to destroy rather than for creativity and love. This is what Elisabeth Kübler-Ross has called the Hitler within.

When we are honest and look at the totality of our inner life we find anything but sweetness and light. After many years of struggle I have found only one reality and power which can bring the parts of me into harmony and keep me from being taken over by the powers of dark destructiveness. This is the power of Love as I find this reality incarnated in Jesus of Nazareth. I find that, because he was victorious over evil and death, he can help me bring my fragmented soul together and rescue me from being separated and dragged down in one way or another by evil.

For myself I can think of nothing worse than having to face an immortal life in which I had to fend for myself, in which I had to struggle alone against the powers of evil within and outside of me. This would indeed be hell. The powers which I encounter within are more powerful than I am. As Paul wrote in Ephesians 6:12, we struggle against "the spiritual army of evil in the heavens"(JB). If I cannot find the fellowship of One who has conquered this darkness, then immortality would be a horror worse than anything else I can imagine. In that case, it would be anything but a blessing. I need transformation and renewal, protection, new life, resurrection. I need it in this life and I will need it even more in the immortal life to come.

In an article in *The Christian Century* Robert Herhold wrote that the ideas of Elisabeth Kübler-Ross about immortality have robbed Easter of its meaning. He said that there would be no need for Easter if human beings were immortal. Nothing could be farther from the truth. Mr. Herhold does not seem to know the reality of the spiritual world whose forces well up within us. The possibility that we may well be faced by immortality whether we can stomach it or not, makes the resurrection of Jesus a vital necessity.

I can begin to know that the power of Easter is available to me in this life. Christ who has conquered the Evil One and Death (in the sense that the early Church spoke of Death as almost a person) can rescue me from the forces which would drag me down to eternal agony. When I know this almost daily resurrection, then I can realize that the power of Easter is also available to me in a life of immortality. I bring all of me into immortality, and so I need to be resurrected over and over again. Even after death I can continue to be recreated and keep on approaching the full reality of becoming one of the sons of God.

Death strips me of my defenses and I must face myself, total and naked. Then there is no way to hide from the dark depths of myself. If one honestly faces the likelihood of being immortal, it is a frightening, almost intolerable prospect if we find no possibility of transformation and resurrection. *The Tibetan Book of the Dead* suggests that other cultures may have realized much the same thing. This book offers instructions to guide the dying person into the intermediate state of *bardo* before that soul turns to take up its dwelling in another life. It sees a path through great dangers, even horrors. Perhaps the thought of annihilation seems preferable to facing either the prospect of such dangers or the idea of an eternity of boredom and stagnation. Sometimes I wonder if our present secular and materialistic denial of life after death is not in part a way of avoiding the necessity for transformation with which immortality confronts us. If immortality is what lies ahead, then I must have transformation and resurrection—or annihilation would be better.

Making the Connection

Immortality and resurrection give different glimpses of the life beyond death. Immortality speaks of the persistence of human beings and human personality. All of the evidence seems to support some kind of survival and persistence after death as natural to human beings. The same evidence comes both from modern research and from nearly every major religion of this world. It is difficult to deny once one is freed from our narrow materialistic world-view. But immortality is not enough. It is apparently essential and natural, but not enough.

Immortality requires a place, a realm, or a world in which it can happen. There is a spiritual realm or world into which we step when we die. We get a taste of that realm or world in our dreams and we have contacts with it in our deepest religious and mystical experiences. What happens in that world of spirit has been suggested by von Hügel in his superb discussion of eternal life. Leonard Biallas has summarized von Hügel's conclusions in these words:

> Neither an eternal life that is already fully achieved here below nor an eternal life to be begun and known solely in the beyond satisfies man's mystical longing. Only an eternal life already begun and truly known in part here, though to be fully achieved and completely understood hereafter, corresponds to the deepest longings of man's spirit as touched by God.

> Then the resurrection becomes a present reality, bringing fullness to each moment. It is the climax of a process of healing, the end of the journey toward wholeness, anticipated often during one's lifetime, in which a person is once and for all united with the one he loves and for whom he longs. Resurrection is the only thing that can ultimately satisfy a person's longing for the Absolute and heal his anguish of separation and isolation from this Absolute.[8]

It is difficult to believe in growth and transformation without some kind of belief in the persistence of the soul. As I have suggested, these gifts come from a source that shows a desire to relate to human beings both now and hereafter. It is even more difficult to endure the idea of persistence without some kind of belief in transformation. When one sees eternal life as a combination of persistence and transformation, then one does away with most of the absurdities which are found in the literal acceptance of only one aspect of this bipolar reality.

It is then necessary to realize our need to work as best we can to prepare for the life to come, and to see that we will have to continue to work at growth in that future life. At the same time one will understand that the real consummation of life is given by the merciful action and grace of God alone. Then one does not see growth as opposed to static perfection. Both are aspects of eternal life.

There is need to reach out in mystical practice to touch the spiritual world, and yet one is never closer to it than when one loves the unhappy and incomplete humans on this earth and tries to meet their needs. Christian mysticism is the other side of the coin of the Christian ethic of love. The kingdom of God realized here and now in trying to perfect human society is not opposed to entering or approaching that kingdom in life after death. Social action is not contrary to mystical vision. Both are parts of the greater whole.

It is so difficult for human beings to allow the complexities of life to stand just as they are. We try to reduce matter to simple units, and we try to do the same thing to life. But neither one can be reduced to neat and simple categories. Eternal life, in particular, is paradoxical. It involves both immortality and resurrection. Eternal life is both simultaneous and successive. It must be worked for and it is a free gift. It is both present in this world and found beyond this world. There is both a real and good physical world, and a real and good spiritual one, and the two interpenetrate, sustain and enrich each other. One prepares for eternal life not only by turning inward in mystical and inner devotion, but also by the ethics of love, moral integrity and social action. There is a kingdom of heaven possible on this earth and also beyond. Eternal life is static in its perfection and it also demands growth if we are to participate in it.

If we pick at these complementary aspects of eternal life and try to make them fit into our logical, either/or categories, we fail to understand the rich abundance and mystery of reality. We are then likely to fall into absurdity. Modern physics and mathematics have taught us an important lesson by showing us that both physical and mathematical reality are more subtle and mysterious than our crude methods of understanding can comprehend. We can no longer honestly say that we can understand either matter or mathematics completely, exhaustively. We cannot define reality. We have no final knowledge; we can only describe with wonder the reality that is presented to us. We can approach eternal life, life after death, in the same way. We come to the same kind of solid but incomplete knowledge. There will always be mystery and new levels of knowledge and experience as we learn about this world and the life beyond death.

Our personalities do survive and persist after death. There is a real spiritual world into which we step at death, and in that new existence there are possibilities of transformation beyond our wildest imagination. There is a guide there to lead us on toward that complete and total fruition of life without bounds, the risen and resurrected One himself. What then is the nature of that kingdom to which he leads us both now and hereafter?

IX. What Is Heaven Like?

The central message of Jesus of Narareth is about heaven. To the people who heard him it was an amazing message. It was different in two ways from anything they had heard before. They knew about hoping for heaven in the future and trying their best to earn it and avoid punishment. But Jesus spoke about finding heaven within and around and among us, as well as in a future that is hidden from us. Heaven, he said, is at hand. He also showed, in words and actions that could be understood, that heaven is the kingdom of a loving, caring God. Jesus used every avenue available that would open human understanding to know the reality of the loving Father and to realize that God cares and seeks us more than we seek him. He is always present with us. Prayer just helps us to be aware of him.

Günther Bornkamm, in his profound book *Jesus of Nazareth*, brings out clearly the uniqueness of these two elements of Jesus' message and shows how essential they are to his entire purpose and ministry. In the New Testament the nearness of the kingdom of heaven is emphasized from the very beginning of his ministry. In the words of Mark:

After John had been arrested, Jesus came into Galilee proclaiming the Gospel of God: "The time has come; the kingdom of God is upon you; repent, and believe the Gospel" (Mark 1:14-15).

Or as Matthew wrote, "From that day Jesus began to proclaim the message: 'Repent; for the kingdom of heaven is upon you.' " Heaven, Jesus taught, can be shared in the here and now. It is both the immediate goal toward which we work in this life, and also the gift we hope to be given in the end.

His understanding of the nature of God was also unique. Bornkamm writes:

> [This is] shown in the expression by which Jesus chooses to address God in prayer, an expression which would have appeared to any Jew too unceremonious and lacking in respect. Abba—Father, this is the word Jesus uses (Mk. xiv.36), and which the Hellenistic Church has taken over in its original Aramaic form from the oldest records about Jesus (Rom. viii.15; Gal. iv.6). It is the child's familiar address to his father here on earth, completely uncommon in religious language.[1]

The word *abba* is used like "daddy" or "papa" in English. It expresses the way a small child would turn to a loving father who can be completely trusted. The way Jesus spoke this word in the garden of Gethsemane reinforces all that he taught and expressed in other ways about the loving nature of God. This simple word *abba* speaks volumes about the closeness of God and his kingdom, and how we can turn to him with confidence and trust. He makes the kingdom of heaven available to us now so that we can find the One who would share his life with us and bring us to fulfillment in that kingdom.

Wherever the idea started that Jesus was simply a social reformer interested only in this-worldly ethics, it was not based on knowledge of what the New Testament actually discusses. A glance at the references listed in a concordance for "heaven," "kingdom" and related words leaves no question about Jesus' message. It had to do with heaven, as well as with life on earth. As I shall show, Jesus was speaking about a heaven which is both now and hereafter, both immanent and transcendent. But first of all let us look at the sheer mass of evidence, the number of times in the New Testament that Jesus and the early Church writers refer to heaven and the life of that realm.

More than five different words or phrases are used in Greek to speak of this spiritual reality. Sometimes it is simply called heaven or the kingdom of heaven, or sometimes the words for resurrection and rising from the dead are used. Eternal or everlasting life and the kingdom of God are also used to suggest the nature of the divine spiritual reality. In some cases a writer adopts a characteristic phrase which becomes almost a trademark. The kingdom of heaven is the expression found most often in Matthew, while John's favorite phrase was eternal life. The following tabulation shows how often these expressions were used in the Gospels and how often they occur in the other New Testament writings.

The Puzzle of the Kingdom of Heaven

Modern biblical studies have opened up a great deal of important evidence which can help us to understand what Jesus meant by the kingdom of heaven or the kingdom of God. A number of years ago when I became interested in finding more insight into these teachings, my good friend and colleague John Sanford was already pursuing the same interest and we discussed many ideas about it. His studies of the results of biblical criticism had shown him the confusion which exists among modern students of the Bible because of their studies. He had come to the conclusion that these scholars cannot comprehend what Jesus meant by the kingdom of heaven because they have lost touch with the world-view of Jesus and the first century. They cannot see that he was speaking about another dimension of reality, a spiritual and non-physical reality which penetrates and interacts with this world of physical things.

Many of these thinkers seem to agree with Rudolf Bultmann that ideas such as the kingdom of heaven are myths which must be discarded. Bultmann of course is right when he states in *Kerygma and Myth* that we must understand Jesus as speaking to the people and the ideas of that time. But he is wrong in thinking that modern men and women are in such a totally different frame of reference that they cannot be open to the world-view of Jesus and his time. As I have already suggested, many thinkers in other fields have been forced to accept some idea of spiritual reality in order to deal with themselves and their world. This fact is shown more fully in my book *Myth, History and Faith*.

Mr. Sanford's studies reinforced his interest in the ethical and psychological aspects of Jesus' teachings about the kingdom of heaven. In 1970 his excellent book on this subject, *The Kingdom Within*, was published. In the original draft he included a chapter providing somewhat technical evidence from modern biblical studies to support his approach to an understanding of the kingdom. His publishers, however, wished to keep the book popular and cut out

References to Eternal Life, Resurrection, and the Kingdom of God or of Heaven in the New Testament

	Gospels	Other New Testament Writings	Total
Eternal or everlasting life——*zōè aiōnios* *	25	18	43
Life (in the sense of eternal, everlasting, or heavenly)——*zōé*	20	30	50
To live (in the sense of being resurrected, finding eternal life) ——*záō*	9	9	18
To give life (in the sense of resurrection or eternal life)——*zopóieō*	1	5	6
Resurrection——*anástasis*	14	26	40
To rise or be raised from the dead ——*anístemi ek nekrōn* **	23	12	35
——*egeírō ek nekrōn* **	32	42	74
To bring back from the dead ——*anágō ek nekrōn*	-	2	2
The kingdom of God——*basileía toû theoû*	60	24	84
The kingdom of heaven——*basileír tōn ouranōn*	32	-	32
The kingdom (eternal or of heaven or God)——*basileír*	15	5	20
Heaven or heavenly (in the sense of God's kingdom)——*ouranós*	97	135	232
Immortality——*athanasía* ***	-	2	2
	328	310	638

*There are also five references in the Gospels and fifteen in the other writings to eternal habitation or house, eternal glory, salvation, inheritance, punishment, judgment, fire, destruction, etc.

**In a few instances the words "from the dead" are omitted, but are clearly implied.

***Paul also speaks of immortality as "incorruptibility" *(aphtharsía)* in six places in his letters, but these references also contain certain of the other words listed above and are included under those headings.

this chapter. Mr. Sanford has given me permission to use this material, which has never been published before, as an appendix to help the reader appreciate the reality of the kingdom of God, or of heaven. While the purpose of Mr. Sanford's study was different from our inquiry into the objective reality of the kingdom beyond this world, the evidence he presents helps us to see the kingdom as both a future spiritual reality and a present one. He has summarized his findings in these words:

The kingdom of God is a non-physical reality, a personal state of being, an archetypal spiritual realm. When the kingdom emerges into a man's life it brings with it wholeness and creativity. The kingdom, as the spiritual rock on which a man's personality is based, is transcendental because it is of divine, not human origin. God created our lives, not we ourselves. It is transpersonal because this inner reality of the kingdom is not "my" kingdom, but "the" kingdom. The individual who belongs to the kingdom does not follow his own plan of life, but must fashion his life according to the larger reality within himself.

The kingdom is a psychological reality in that it is personally experienced by each individual. It is a mystical reality in that only an *experience* with the kingdom can reveal what it is, and no words, including these, can do more than vaguely adumbrate the kingdom to those who have not been initiated into it. The kingdom is an objective reality because it is not subjectively created by man's experience or wishes, any more than a man who has seen the Himalayas for the first time can say that he has created them. The kingdom is an inner reality in that a man perceives it not out in space and time through the media of the senses of the body, but in the inner dimension of life, via the illumination of his soul.

At the same time the kingdom of God has a great social significance. The one who experiences the kingdom is called upon to translate his relationship with God into social concerns, and to seek to make the outer order and fabric of men's lives conform to the inner archetypal order of the kingdom within. The kingdom thus has a universal significance and is the impelling force calling upon men to establish a social order grounded upon God's will. But it can only be realized socially through individuals, and cannot be established through collective media. The one who enters into the kingdom enters into a personal, individual relationship to God, his neighbors, and himself. He becomes an *individual* man, that is, an undivided person, whose outer personality and inner self are in harmony, and who is distinct as a person from the collective psychology around him.

All of this describes the kingdom as a present spiritual reality, but the kingdom as a spiritual reality also has an eschatological character. It is a present state insofar as it is a reality which already exists within men, and in which those men can participate who are conscious enough and have formed their lives according to its pattern. But the kingdom in another sense is still to come in the future for it cannot be said to be completely established until all men belong to it. Therefore the kingdom is eschatological in nature insofar as it embodies God's plan for man, a plan not yet completed and so still to come.

We are trying to understand the nature of the kingdom of heaven as best we can. What can one say about this state of being, the existence to which we believe we can look forward in the life to come? As we try to discover what can be said about this last state, we must keep in mind the fact that Jesus taught us to pray that God's will may be done and his kingdom may come and be accomplished on earth as it is in heaven. We cannot realize this kingdom on earth unless we have as clear a vision as possible of what the kingdom of heaven is like. Our social action depends upon our vision of heaven.

Making Contact with the Kingdom

The most obvious and striking feature of Jesus' view of life after death and the final state of our existence is that it is a *kingdom*. It is therefore social in nature. Jesus did not talk about some mystical flight of the alone to the alone. Although, as we shall see, finding the kingdom may involve such experiences, Jesus saw our final state as essentially a fellowship. He stressed our social nature, the fact that we cannot be fully human unless we have each other. In the Lord's Prayer Jesus used the word *our* over and over. He told us to pray to *our* Father, to ask for *our* daily bread, and to be forgiven *our* sins. It is *we* who are to forgive those who sin against *us*, who ask that *we* may not be led into temptation, and that *we* may be delivered from evil. Human beings need each other as well as God if they are to be completely human and come to their full potential as sons and daughters of God.

The early Church used the image of the holy city, the new Jerusalem, to express the same idea about the kingdom of heaven.

Heaven requires love for other human beings like myself as well as for God. As difficult as it sometimes is for me, with my introverted nature, to realize this, it requires sharing both ways. Our love for other humans is what opens us to deeper, more genuine love for God. And as my love for God grows and deepens, I become more and more able to love all the shapes and sizes, kinds and colors and types of human beings who will one day share with me in the city of God. As C. S. Lewis stresses in his imaginative trip to heaven in *The Great Divorce*, heaven is a reality to which we must adapt and adjust, and one adjustment we must all make is to grow in the relationships of that society.

Love, of course, is the first essential quality of God and his kingdom. Only as we grow in love do we find the doors of the kingdom opening to us. And in order to love we need one another. Heaven, it appears, is the place where we develop and grow in relationship with other human beings who have stepped beyond death, interacting with each other, with the spiritual entities of heaven known as angels, and with the triune God.

The second basic thing about heaven is its spiritual quality. It is a non-physical or psychoid reality which is different from the world of matter. We Westerners have trouble imagining a truly spiritual world, one that is as real or more real than the physical world that can be seen and touched. John Macquarrie, professor of divinity at Oxford, is typical of religious thinkers who are still caught in the materialistic framework of yesterday's science. In the November 1977 issue of *The Expository Times* Dr. Macquarrie tries to answer his critics who feel that he eliminates any basis for life after death from his view of Christianity. His answer is very thin, and he frankly admits that he can't imagine any kind of existence other than physical. His philosophical existentialism blinds him to any possibility of life without a physical dimension.

There is a good deal we can learn about the reality of the spiritual world from Eastern religions. For centuries Eastern peoples have been portraying what they find in the spiritual realm in elaborate mythologies and rituals, and they have developed techniques for working with one's soul to a fine point. Of course the Eastern point of view, particularly its neglect of the reality and importance of the physical world, presents real dangers. But one does not have to take the whole package in order to learn things of value about the reality of the spiritual world. Without some grasp of the reality of that world, it is very difficult for intelligent people to see how there can be any kind of real life once one's physical body is dead and gone. Life itself then begins to lose its meaning.

I worked for a good many years with some of the individuals who had been closest to Jung before I finally grasped Jung's basic idea that there is a real dimension of experience which is *not* physical. The realization finally dawned on me that I had been participating in this other, complex aspect of reality as I listened to my dreams and religious experiences and shared in ritual. I also participated in this other aspect as I allowed my imagination free rein and allowed myself to love all manner of other human beings. I could then see that children are often close to this realm, as close as lovers are to each other. Watching my own children began to bring this realm very close to me.

As I woke up to the fact that these are exactly the experiences religious people have been describing almost from the word go, I started to study what they have said, and at least certain people still say today. In ecstasy and trance, I found, people can be open to this kind of experience. The use of an oracle can sometimes give hints of it. As we have seen, it comes uninvited to many of the individuals who have near-death and spontaneous religious experiences. But Christian meditation is the religious practice designed to open one to this dimension of reality. As I step through the silence in meditation into a realm of dream-like images (like the images of a strikingly clear dream), I find that negative experiences can sometimes come to me into this other realm more quickly and dramatically than any other. In psychosis and neurosis, in fact, there are sometimes overwhelming experiences of the destructive side of this realm that leave no doubt about its reality. However, this is not a very pleasant way to reach this realm. I do not recommend it.

In addition, there are some very questionable and dangerous ways of getting in touch with this dimension of reality. Many religious groups have used drugs to open people to such an altered state of consciousness, and this has become a common method of young people all over the world hoping to escape from the confines of physical reality. Hypnosis also has been used to induce these experiences. Mediums, as I have already shown, may often be in touch with this other dimension. These practices can lead individuals into dangerous or meaningless places, and it is questionable whether they can lead to any creative growth. They do give evidence, however, that we are in touch with another dimension of reality.

In all of these ways one finds that there is a spiritual realm which is as complex and varied, as interesting and mysterious, as substantial and unyielding and often as uncaring and dangerous, as the physical realm we now experience. It is this realm that we may touch from within ourselves. John Sanford calls it the kingdom within. It can be tasted now. We can get some understanding of its nature in the here and now as we move toward the consummation of life.

Luke reported that when Jesus was asked when this reality of the kingdom would come, he replied:

"You cannot tell by observation. . . . There will be no saying, 'Look, here it is!' or 'There it is!'; for in fact the kingdom of God is within [or among] you"* (Luke 17:20-21).

Whichever he meant, *within* or *among*, Jesus clearly suggested that the kingdom of God is available now, as well as in eternity. In his discussion in the appendix, Mr. Sanford has carefully analyzed this phrase, showing that the kingdom of God can best be understood as a spiritual dimension, and that there is no good reason why this understanding must be discarded. Every one of the early Church Fathers interpreted this passage in Luke as "within you," now and forever. This is one more piece of evidence supporting the idea that the kingdom can be found inwardly, through the human soul. It suggests that people learn something about God's eternal kingdom through their own souls, their own inner experience.

The Nature of the Kingdom

There is a delightful old French story about Acousin and Nicolette who were very much in love. When the hero was chided by a priest about his affection for Nicolette and told that he might go to hell unless he took care, Acousin replied, "Oh! I don't want to go to heaven and be stuck with the old men and beggars and cripples, the pious old maids. Let me go to hell where I'll find knights and warriors and people who are bold and adventurous. I

---

*I have given preference to the first alternative translation provided by *The New English Bible*. Other versions from the King James translation to the latest edition of the New International version give out-and-out preference to the idea that the kingdom of God is found *within* us, as did essentially all of the early Fathers of the Church.

want to go to the place where the ladies are beautiful and gay, and where I won't be bored!" Caught up as we are by worldly values and worldly things, most of us share some of the same feelings. We even wonder what is the point of heaven if it is going to be like an old folks' home, with nothing to do and no place to go.

I have to admit first to myself that these are not very mature feelings. But there is another reason why most of us have them. We have not listened to the picture which Jesus gave us of God's kingdom. He spoke about that kingdom so many times that one gets lost among all the images the New Testament includes. We need an over-all view to realize that the ideas fit together into a whole picture. Both Matthew and Luke included such a statement. It is found in the beatitudes in Matthew 5:3-12 and Luke 6:20-26. For our purposes the longer and more developed version in Matthew offers a sort of blueprint or working plan which shows us how the whole structure goes together. Whether this passage is directly from the mouth of Jesus or a summary by those who knew him well makes little difference. Either way, it summarizes Jesus' teachings about the kingdom, about the qualities that make for blessedness or true happiness, and the results that can be expected. The blessed or fortunate are those who have touched ultimate meaning. They have opened themselves to the final and permanent reality found in the kingdom.

This passage is so important that I quote it in full from *The New English Bible*:

How blest are those who know their need of God;
    the kingdom of Heaven is theirs.
How blest are the sorrowful;
    they shall find consolation.
How blest are those of a gentle spirit;
    they shall have the earth for their possession.
How blest are those who hunger and thirst to see right prevail;
    they shall be satisfied.
How blest are those who show mercy;
    mercy shall be shown to them.
How blest are those whose hearts are pure;
    they shall see God.
How blest are the peacemakers;
    God shall call them his sons.

How blest are those who have suffered persecution for the cause of
   right;
   the kingdom of Heaven is theirs.

You will notice that result or reward is the same in the first statement and the last one: the kingdom of Heaven is theirs. These two
identical promises enclose the other six like parentheses. It seems
reasonable to suggest that the six intervening statements are descriptions of God's kingdom, the kingdom of heaven. In this passage, as I see it, Jesus is telling us what heaven is like. He is describing the kingdom of the Father—the kingdom of *abba*. This is the
nature of the heaven that the loving, caring, father-mother God has
provided for us, asking only that we accept and seek it. We can taste
it a bit now and fully after death.

Certainly the results that Jesus suggested don't happen very often on earth. Those who mourn and are sorrowful are not too often
comforted and consoled in this life; mostly they go right on finding
life a painful struggle. The gentle in spirit, those who have been
called the meek or the poor in spirit, do not noticeably inherit the
earth in most places in this world. The merciful often lose their
shirts and come out on the short end of business deals. In view of
the world hunger problem, it is not too evident that the hungry and
thirsty are filled physically. And those who hunger for spiritual satisfaction, like Martin Luther King, often end up with a bullet in the
head, or beaten in some more degrading way. Jesus was quite naive
if he believed that these first four rewards were to be earthly ones,
so naive that we should be wary of taking him seriously. The last
two promises, however, do not really make sense except in the context of life after death. It would certainly be wonderful to see God
and be called a son or daughter in this world, but fulfilling this
promise makes sense only in the kingdom.

In fact, the whole set of beatitudes makes real sense only if
Jesus was describing the nature of heaven. He did this by describing
the actual qualities of life which lead to heaven. Then he described
the results which are found among those people who are able to live
in contact with God or the source of ultimate meaning. This present
life has to be lived here and now on this planet. Not even these direct contacts that God does give us now and then can make it possible to live out these qualities of life as are given to us in the

beatitudes and achieve the results which are mentioned there. In all that he said and did Jesus showed awareness that he was describing something which was difficult to achieve in the here and now. It seems more than likely that in the beatitudes he was giving us his picture of God's kingdom in a more complete way than anywhere else in his recorded teaching. This is the kingdom as we will ultimately find it.

Nearly all of Jesus' other statements about the kingdom can be related to these six qualities of the life to come which are named in the beatitudes. There seems to be no question that these six beatitudes summarize the hundreds of references to another life which are scattered throughout the New Testament and give a direct description of what heaven is like. I know of no one better qualified to tell us about heaven than Jesus of Nazareth. His understanding carries weight even for people who do not accept the Christian belief that Jesus had a unique relationship with God and the kingdom of heaven. Men and women of spiritual discernment in nearly every religion and culture pay attention to his insights about spiritual reality as well as about matters of religious value and meaning.

We Shall Find Consolation

One of the biggest difficulties with our modern world is its ethic of success and the belief in many circles that the key to a happy and successful life is to keep up appearances and just whistle troubles away. This belief does not work very well, as one finds out by listening to people in depth. Behind the pretended gaiety one finds lives touched by agony, by fear and sorrow and pain. As Ian MacClaren once said, "Be kind, for everyone is bearing a heavy burden." In all my years of counseling I have never yet known anyone who did not bear some heavy burden of body or soul or mind. Few of us realize this fact because others show so little understanding of such problems. They even make fun of us for having them. There seems to be no one who can listen and accept everything, good, bad, and indifferent. And because of this, people fear that they are somehow different from others, and this burden is added to the rest of their burdens.

Behind the cheerful masks of college students one finds loneliness and fear and pain. In some ways the campus of a large university is one of the loneliest places in the world. My friend Kenneth

Johnson, the builder of the University of Massachusetts, confirmed what I experienced at Notre Dame.

Sickness, of course, plagues many, many lives, particularly as old age begins to drag our bodies down. But physical suffering is not the worst that we humans endure. Very few suicides are caused simply by physical suffering. It is rather mental, psychological, or spiritual anguish which makes people feel that they cannot go on any longer and drives them to suicide as a way out.

Sometimes one is so absorbed by the pain of losing a loved one that life seems empty and meaningless, filled only by an agony of loneliness. Boredom can become an intolerable burden, leaving us to face the prospect of hours dragging interminably on toward aging and helplessness. In other cases people are torn by the frustration of not being able to be what they wish to be, caught between choices which they do not know how to evaluate. Look deeply into almost any life and you will find there some tragedy which would make the plot of a real drama. One reason why tragedy played out upon a stage helps to relieve our burdens for a while is that it turns the spotlight away from us and shows that similar problems exist elsewhere, at least in imagination. It almost seems that someone has listened to us and heard.

The New Testament shows that Jesus often healed as he told people about the kingdom of God. The two seemed to go hand in hand, as in Matthew 4:23 and 9:35. These healings of mental and physical illness were clearly seen as one evidence of the nearness of the kingdom and the fact that it was breaking into people's lives. Gregory of Nyssa stated that the kingdom actually broke into the world in the resurrection of Jesus and that the healing ministry of the Church was a sort of first-fruits of that event.

In the beatitude about those who sorrow, Jesus suggested that in heaven one is healed of sorrow and comforted. According to the beatitudes, in the kingdom we will find these burdens of pain and fear washed away and new life will be given to us. This new life will be free from the downdrag of physical and psychological impediments. We have seen that something quite similar is described by people who come back from near-death experiences. Like Arthur Ford, who did not want to go back to "that beaten, diseased hulk" he had left behind in a hospital, people who have near-death experiences often resist returning to their bodies. We have also seen how often dying patients experience freedom from pain and almost joyous moods just before death. It is amazing to consider how close these descriptions are to the promise of *consolation* given in the beatitudes. It appears that we can expect even psychological pain to be cleansed from us, although this is more difficult because it seems to be built into the very structure of the soul.

The Greek word "to console" is *parakaleō*. It is the word from which "paraclete" or "comforter" is taken. In New Testament usage it means to encourage and strengthen by consolation or to comfort. The Latin equivalent is *advoco*, from which we get our word advocate. The comforter or advocate is the one who takes one's part and stands up for the individual. Although comfort and consolation are often seen as only release from pain, Jesus was speaking of more than a pain-killer or spiritual anesthetic. The person who is comforted is not just soothed and relieved of misery, but he or she is strengthened, reconstituted and re-established. Comfort and help which don't get at the root of the difficulty would be cheap indeed.

Our English word "comfort" carries something of this meaning. It comes from the Latin phrase *cum fortis*, meaning "with strength," and the later word *conforto*, "to strengthen." The paraclete, the comforter, is the one who not only takes away our pain, but also helps us through to rebirth, renewal and transformation. The "comfortable words" used in the Anglican Communion service following the people's confession of sin show this understanding. These are strengthening and renewing words spoken by Jesus and from the letters by Paul and John. They offer the real comfort which can help us to grow and find our place in the substantial life of the kingdom of heaven. This is what comfort is about. It is the help God gives us as we set out on new adventures toward his kingdom, ready to find the companionship of those who have already entered this dimension of life.

It is so hard for us to believe the real promise of consolation and comfort. Even when we realize that some people taste this promise in actual experience, we are not sure. We fear that the idea of life without pain and frustration may have been developed just in the hope of fulfilling human desires. But this is far from true. In fact we humans have trouble even imagining such a prospect until we are given a taste of it. Then we begin to see life more from God's perspective, from a more eternal stance. As we come to realize that our lives are ultimately in God's loving hands, we are able to see that much of our misery and inner agony are caused by our limited horizons. The destructiveness and death that are so evident in this life, that so often destroy parts of our very being, no longer seem to belong to the ultimate nature of things.

The promise of consolation is a guarantee that the forces which have caused havoc among human beings and disrupted spiritual reality will not always have power. "The years the locust have eaten will be restored," and therefore we will find the parts of ourselves that have been lost or damaged by evil given back to us. The kingdom of heaven is the place where evil loses its deadly power to destroy. It is the state of reality in which the victory of Jesus' resurrection is constantly reaffirmed and realized.

Heaven is also the place or state of reality in which our strength is renewed. We are comforted, in the sense of being built up and given a fresh start with new vigor and vision and drive. Many people, as they come to the end of life, grow tired and lose their courage and their desire to go on. In the kingdom of God they will find life renewed, charged with new energy and desire. Heaven is the place of rebirth. It provides the right conditions for creative new life to take place. As the Revelation of John suggests, those who reach heaven through difficulties and sorrow will never again feel hunger or thirst, or the sun's scorching heat. The Lamb who is at the heart of the kingdom, the new Jerusalem, will be their shepherd and will guide them to the water of life, and God "will wipe away every tear from their eyes" (Revelation 21:4). We can expect to enter this new reality filled with vigor that will never wear out and ready for transformation.

Possessors of the Earth

How can the gentle spirits gain possession of the earth? What sense does this make? Even if it is possible for them to inherit the earth, what does this have to do with heaven? In spite of some of the far-out ideas about that realm, both God and his kingdom seem to take a real interest in earth. Everywhere he went, Jesus let people know that the kingdom of God was reaching out to earth, trying to alter the state of things here. The idea of the incarnation—which is so basic to our Christian point of view—is that God seeks to have influence upon this earth. When men and women could not hear his teaching through the prophets, he brought his actual reality to earth to touch and mingle with them. Earth seems to be important and valuable to heaven, and God has gone to a lot of trouble to bring earth into the orbit of the kingdom. The meek, or the gentle in spirit, are those who are given the particular task of bringing this about. Perhaps this is why it happens so slowly. Evidently if people are to belong to the kingdom, they must be brought to it gently.

The Greek word translated as "possessors" or "inheritors" applied to the right to property and control over it. Heirs are those who will come into an estate, who will eventually control that estate and use it and enjoy it. They do not have it now, but the time will come when it will be theirs and they will make it their own. It is to become their province. In this sense the earth can be considered the inheritance of those in heaven. In God's good time they will possess the good qualities of earth as their own; they will have the fine and pleasing essence of the things of earth to use and enjoy. In the meantime they can help the owner of the estate by cultivating it, protecting it and encouraging it to grow and become what it is capable of becoming.

As heirs, then, the meek are those who help God provide the care he wants this earth to have. It makes little difference whether one believes in guardian angels or in some other kind of spirits. There seem to be beings in heaven who watch over people and care for those who die. They are apparently *carers* whose task is to help us achieve the good that we find. George Eliot concluded her novel *Middlemarch* in these magnificent words, "That all is not so ill with you and me as it might have been is largely due to those who lived faithfully a hidden life and rest in unvisited tombs." And that influence comes not only from the earthly actions of these individuals but from what they continue to do after they have died.

The deceased, particularly the gentle-spirited deceased, are the very ones who are given permission to exert a gentle and hardly perceptible influence upon those on earth who are open to it. Both Moody and Osis in their research and Billy Graham in his reports have found that the experience of being met at the point of death by a deceased friend or loved one is quite common. The other person is there to help one make the transition, and apparently has been keeping watch over the individual all the time.

The same truth that is expressed in this beatitude is also found in the Apostles' Creed in the words about the communion of saints. In repeating this belief we are affirming that even death cannot separate us entirely from those who follow Christ. In fact after their death these individuals may be closer to us than the next-door neighbors who are strangers to Christ. We have seen how St. Ambrose spoke of the continued relations he had with his deceased brother Satyrus. We have also considered the fact that many people have quite clear experiences of those who have died. Undoubtedly the deceased who are gentle spirits and have inherited the earth influence us in many other ways even though we hardly know it. Those in heaven are not so separated from us as we sometimes think. By becoming more conscious of the spiritual realm, we can often become more aware of the effects their lives in heaven have upon us.

True Satisfaction

It is perfectly obvious that those who hunger and thirst to see right prevail aren't always satisfied on earth. But in heaven they are filled and satisfied. They can see that earth will finally come to holiness and wholeness. For instance, Jesus spoke in his time about the equality of every individual, but it took nearly nineteen hundred years before *Christian* nations got the vision that slavery was a deep and abiding evil. It often takes a long time to realize heaven's reality on earth.

Real satisfaction almost always comes gradually. The word in Greek for "being filled" came from the word for hay and was used to describe cattle being filled and satisfied. This too is a gradual process. A cow does not get satisfied all at once. It goes on munching a bit at a time. The kind of satisfaction this beatitude speaks of is even more a gradual and growing state. It is the result of slowly munching away on eternal hay. Too much too fast could well choke us.

In Luke's version of the beatitudes it is the actual hunger and thirst of the unfortunate which will be filled. They will no longer suffer deprivation and poverty. The search for righteousness, of course, starts by trying to satisfy the physical needs of human beings. Martin Luther King was able to bring hope to the black people because he realized that Christian righteousness involved the way they were treated in buses and restaurants and job placement. In the Lord's Prayer Jesus told us to pray for our daily bread, and in various ways he showed how such needs will be satisfied in heaven.

There are other needs, however, besides physical ones. Some of the most miserable people I have known were individuals of wealth who lacked for nothing physically. They were free from the wanting and needing that keep most of us occupied, and so they were faced by the emptiness of their lives and the despair that comes unless something is found to fill the void. The psychological emptiness of human beings and their other psychological needs are much harder to fill than physical need. People must be cared for and loved if they are to be filled psychologically. And that means finding not only God who loves us, but a heaven with our Lord at the center of it where there is also care from other individuals like ourselves. This is why heaven, if it is truly meaningful, must be either a kingdom as Jesus described it, or oblivion as Buddha saw it.

Like John Stuart Mill, many of us cannot conceive of a world that would satisfy us. Our rational thinking fails when we try to picture how our deepest and most central needs can be satisfied. We have to rely on poetic visions to describe the reality of the kingdom of heaven. As Augustine put it in *The Confessions*, God made us for himself, and we cannot know rest or satisfaction until we find it in God.[2] While we have only the images of things we have known, we can allow them to be transfigured and seen in the light of this new level of reality. In *The Great Divorce* C. S. Lewis presents a superb picture of this transformation, although my personal intuition is that it will be easier to adjust to this reality than he suggests.

The images that Jesus used were often commonplace, and yet they showed that the kingdom of heaven is a treasure that exceeds our wildest imagination. He described it as a treasure hidden in a field (Matthew 13:44). It is like a pearl that is worth everything one owns (Matthew 13:45). It can be compared to a feast. The Galilean peasants cherished wedding feasts like the one at Cana where he did the first miracle described by John. But Jesus stretched people's imagination to taste a king's wedding feast, or a great man's feast with all the unfortunate people in the countryside seated with him (Matthew 22:1-14; Luke 14:15-24). Like a mustard seed or yeast (Matthew 13:31-33; Mark 4:30-33; Luke 13:18-21), the kingdom of heaven provides more than seems possible. It fills and satisfies us far more than we could expect. The kingdom meets needs we didn't even know we had.

Poets of almost every period, from the unknown creators of hero epics to Blake and Tennyson, have tried to give some picture of this reality. They have seemed to sense that without such a vision life goes flat. Virgil gave his vision of eternal things in *The Aeneid*, and Dante used Virgil as his guide through hell and purgatory. But it was Beatrice who then led Dante on to his final vision of heaven where his own wings could not carry him and phantasy lost its power. In a flash he knew where his desire came from, and found his will and his desire harmoniously turned by love. In this deepest vision of heaven Dante had tasted true and complete satisfaction.

In heaven we shall no longer be frustrated and incomplete because of our inability to be what we wish to be. On earth so much misery is caused by our failure to become the kind of people we want to be. We build prisons of guilt for ourselves by condemning and castigating ourselves for failing to hit the mark that we have set for ourselves. In heaven we shall at last be able to achieve our goals and become what we desire to be spiritually, psychically and morally. Neither defects of personality and mind nor weariness of body will get in the way.

Not only will the heavenly counterpart of physical need be filled, but also our intellectual, moral, creative, and artistic ambitions. We shall see clearly into the heart and center of things. To use Tennyson's image, we shall sit at a ten-league canvas and paint with brushes of comet's hair and be able to convey the visions of our hearts adequately. We shall be able to love and forgive, to understand and help others as we have wanted to do on earth and, yet, haven't quite made it. We shall be able to put off our pride and resentments, our hate and dislikes. Perhaps we shall even be able to play the kind of chess game we have never yet managed and share in the divine playfulness of heaven.

The best pictures we have of heaven suggest that we shall be slowly transformed until we become the kind of people we have always wanted to be. Then we shall find visions of new potentials and gradually move toward new goals. We shall be filled, satisfied, utterly and eternally, and each filling will be more complete than the last.

Mercy and Love

Christianity is the only major religion on this earth that promises free forgiveness and mercy to anyone who genuinely asks for it. Most of us have had just enough taste of the mercy which Christianity promises to be immunized against accepting and understanding it. I get so discouraged with Christian ministers who preach judgment, and more judgment, when the essential message of Christianity is mercy and forgiveness. Most people are already judging themselves far too much, and they cannot imagine being forgiven. Preaching judgment or acting it out only walls people off from us and shuts them up with their problems. It is very close to the essential idea of *karma* that individuals must pay for every sin and error they have committed. Reflecting on my own life, I hope and pray that this idea, which we shall consider later on, is not so. Over the years I have learned a great deal about retribution and self-hatred and being driven further and further from salvation, and I am very sure that judgment and punishment seldom redeem, very seldom.

God is not just; he is merciful. Heaven is not a place of retribution, but a place of forgiveness, mercy and love. Here, again, this idea is not just wish fulfillment, something we have made up out of whole cloth. On the contrary, it is beyond the fondest hopes of human beings on this earth until they are introduced to it. And that takes work, to open them up to any glimmering that this might be true.

We humans do not even begin to look for forgiveness for ourselves unless we are treated in this way by the people around us. Only as we are loved and forgiven in our ordinary lives do we begin to understand dimly that this is what God and his eternal kingdom are like. It is practically impossible to believe in the ultimate reality of the forgiveness of sins unless we have known it as proximate reality. There is probably no belief in the Apostles' Creed which is harder for us humans to accept than the forgiveness of sins.

In ordinary life we forget that the idea of mercy has been expressed in the Christian tradition from the beginning. One example is the Jesus prayer used in Christian devotion. For centuries this prayer, in one form or another, has been a central practice of Orthodox devotion. The person says over and over inwardly these few words: Lord Jesus Christ, Son of God, have mercy on me, a sinner. By constant, almost incessant repetition the reality of mercy becomes the foundation of the person's life. Both the *Philokalia*, a standard work of Eastern monasticism, and the story told in the little book *The Way of a Pilgrim* show how important this practice is in the Orthodox tradition. I find the simplest form—Jesus, mercy—of incredible help in dark and dangerous times. The *Kyrie eleison*—

Lord, have mercy, Christ, have mercy, Lord, have mercy—is said or sung in most Christian liturgies, often following the statement of the law. These practices suggest how central the idea of mercy is in real Christianity.

Hell, as someone has said, can be described as a state of eternal obsession with guilt so that one is unable to accept forgiveness. The flames of hell are then the rejected flames of God's love, as St. Catherine of Genoa held. By this definition we all have at least one foot in hell. I have known no one who did not need God's mercy, and love, and the few who *thought* they didn't have been the very ones who needed it most. Even Macbeth and his wife might have escaped their hell if they had been able to find forgiveness, but then Shakespeare would not have had his play about hell. The unique idea of Christianity is that humans do not need to suffer from guilt and self-condemnation. We can be forgiven any and every wrong-doing if we are truly sorry and truly try to remedy the situation so it won't occur again, and then sincerely seek mercy and forgiveness. Heaven is the state of being—the *place* in metaphorical language—in which we can be washed free of guilt and given a fresh start.

The Greeks had two sets of words relating to mercy. Those associated with the noun *oiktos* were used generally to speak of emotional reactions, feelings of pity or sorrow, and these words are found only a few times in the New Testament. The other noun for mercy or compassion was *eleos*, which indicated emotion that brought action and some kind of help for a pitiful situation. The Greeks even worshiped *Éleos* as a divine being embodying the qualities of mercy. This is the word found in the beatitudes and in many other places in the New Testament. When these passages are considered together, the meaning is quite clear. The person to whom mercy is shown is rescued and restored. This beatitude could be translated: "Blest are the merciful, for they shall be restored." And the merciful are those who will be able to give this kind of mercy freely without looking for it in return.

In the story of the prodigal son, this is the meaning of the ring which the father sends for, to place on the son's finger. Undoubtedly the ring was set with a signet which gave the son authority within the house once again. We have heard this story so often that we are no longer amazed by its wild extravagance, its incredible mercy. Often we do not even hear what Jesus was saying—that heaven is the place where prodigals are welcomed home if only they will get up from their pigsties and come. They are given not only authority but a joyous banquet and honor as well. Kenneth Bailey has called attention to the incredible mercy portrayed by this story in his remarkable little book *The Cross and the Prodigal.* It is important to remember that elder brothers can be forgiven also. All they have to do is relax and come to the party.

There are very few people who ever receive such mercy in this life, even from their families (in many cases particularly not from their families). This promise too is beyond the wildest hopes or expectations of most of us. Unless people are taught in one way or another to understand that this is the nature of God, they usually make God in the image of humans they have known. They then face the prospect of meeting him at death in fear of judgment and retribution.

Jesus tried to make God's mercy and the nature of the kingdom of heaven clear in parable after parable. But people very seldom ask and receive this kind of mercy and renewal unless they can imagine that God and heaven are like this. With my own children I often find it impossible to reach them with the kind of mercy I would like to give them unless they can come to me expecting it. As I have described in *The Other Side of Silence*, it takes a certain courage and humility to ask and receive mercy. Mercy is given to the poor in spirit described in the first beatitude. Their deepest needs are filled and their deepest sorrows removed. In heaven their lives are fulfilled in much the same way as the fulfillment promised to those who hunger and thirst after righteousness.

Persons who have received mercy know what it is to be loved by God and so they allow him to penetrate the deepest recesses of their hearts and lives. St. John of the Cross described this experience in his *Stanzas of the Soul*. In these lines he tried to put into images his experience of finding the Christ during a time of persecution. These images, I believe, give us a preview of the nature of heaven:

Oh, night that guided me.
Oh, night more lovely than the dawn,
Oh, night that joined Beloved with lover,
Lover transformed in the Beloved!
Upon my flowery breast,
Kept wholly for himself alone,
There he stayed sleeping, and I caressed him,
And the fanning of the cedars made a breeze.

The breeze blew from the turret
As I parted his locks;
With his gentle hand he wounded my neck
And caused all my senses to be suspended.
I remained, lost in oblivion;
My face I reclined on the Beloved.
All ceased and I abandoned myself,
Leaving my cares forgotten among the lilies.[3]

Austin Farrer has also written of a similar encounter with the Christ, describing his experience in these words:

God forgives me, for he takes my head between his hands and turns my face to his to make me smile at him. And though I struggle and hurt those hands—for they are human, though divine, human and scarred with nails—though I hurt them, they do not let go until he has smiled me into smiling; and that is the forgiveness of God.[4]

This is what it is like to be loved fully and to be given mercy. Experiences like these can be found in our deepest meditation. They give us a foretaste of the life which stretches beyond death. In this way we begin to realize that there is hope of encountering the same reality and finding just such love and mercy when we go through the dark night of death.

Few of us have ever been fully listened to, let alone truly loved with mercy. Those who are actually given this kind of compassion by some other human being know what it is to be reborn right in this present life. Very likely we will experience such rebirth again and again as new levels within us keep opening up and are transformed by mercy. Mercy is on-going and eternal.

The Vision of God

One by one the descriptions of heaven in the beatitudes touch our hearts like waves beating on the shore. One's heart jumps with joy at the promise that those who are pure in heart shall behold God. This is still another way of speaking of the fulfillment of our earthly striving, the satisfaction of our desires. There is nothing that a lover wishes more than to catch a glimpse of the beloved. This beatitude promises that we shall find ourselves before the One who sets our life on fire. We shall at last come face to face with the Love that lights our inner being.

Love is given to us to draw us toward God. Those who have never been head over heels in love cannot imagine the consummation which meeting the divine Lover can provide. Our human love is only a shadow of that Love which draws all that exists to itself with infinite tenderness, gentle patience. We humans celebrate our love in poems and stories. Few things arouse us as deeply as a really good love story. But none of our own can equal the divine love story. It is so good that most of the time we simply don't believe it. Only the greatest poets and storytellers can give a sense of it without maudlin sentimentality. C. S. Lewis had this ability. In the Narnia series, beginning with *The Lion, the Witch, and the Wardrobe*, he uses the image of the divine lion, Aslan, who guides and protects four children through daring adventures beyond this world. When Aslan is killed and raised again, the joy of the children at finding him alive points to the meaning of this beatitude.

Mystics in every period have spoken of the beatific vision, of seeing or experiencing God himself. This is one pole of the divine encounter, the one expressed in this beatitude, with the opposite pole represented by the next one. The essence of the beatific vision is an experience of ecstasy in which one's senses all cease and every care is forgotten. This experience is often imageless, or sometimes one becomes aware of a brilliant light, so intense that it normally would hurt one's eyes. This is the moment of coming to the center, finding the reality that is there, the source of all things, and knowing that one is accepted, desired, fulfilled.

Those who have this experience then come to themselves and realize that the reality they have encountered asks only one thing of them. They must go out and share with others the love and concern and strength which they have experienced, allowing the fabric of their being to radiate that love. On earth this means going out onto the highways and byways, into our families and churches, our offices and clubs, bearing this kind of love. In heaven it means taking our place as sons and daughters of God, brothers and sisters of Christ, ready to act as agents of the Holy Spirit.

There is a rhythm of the spirit. We need our moments of ecstasy and quiet adoration, and also times of action and reaching out. Unless we have both, we lack the balance and wholeness that is spiritual health. Those who emphasize only one aspect of the spiritual life, or of heaven, and look down on the other aspect do not contribute as much to people's spiritual wholeness and health. The spirit and heaven are both static and moving. We need both our moments of pure vision and rest and enjoyment and our moments of action, and we will experience both times of knowing and times of doing. We can be quite sure that the heaven-that-is will never be boring.

In his story of the rich man and the beggar Lazarus, Jesus gave a picture of the static nature of heaven. He described the rich man suffering eternal torment because of all the things he had not faced in this life, while Lazarus rested comfortably upon the breast of Abraham. Or, as the Greek reads, Lazarus lay in Abraham's bosom. This same freedom from care and sense of joyous contact that Jesus described are echoed in the experience of St. John of the Cross.

One of the most beautiful pictures of meeting and knowing God was written by a man who, for most of his life, was a professed agnostic, a man who died young. He had almost nothing to do with formal religion during his mature years, but just before his unexpected death the realization flooded in upon him that our lives have a future not bounded by this physical world in which we live. He was an honest man who had had the courage to deny what he did not believe. He now had the courage to affirm what he experienced. Thomas Wolfe had a genius with words and so his vision touches us all. He wrote:

> Dear Fox, old friend, thus we have come to the end of the road that we were to go together . . . and so farewell.
>
> But before I go, I have just one more thing to tell you:
>
> Something has spoken to me in the night, burning the tapers of the waning year; something has spoken in the night, and told me I shall die, I know not where. Saying:
>
> "To lose the earth you know, for greater knowing; to lose the life you have, for greater life; to leave the friends you loved, for greater loving; to find a land more kind than home, more large than earth—
>
> —Whereon the pillars of this earth are founded, toward which the conscience of the world is tending—a wind is rising, and the rivers flow."[5]

These were the last words of his last book, *You Can't Go Home Again*. They were almost the last words that he wrote for publication before his death in 1938. They have little relation to anything else that he wrote. It is as if they had poured out of the very heart of his innermost being, from the deep center of divine life that is within us all, from the powerful core of being from which most of us hide most of our lives. When something made him turn and look inward, he listened to this center. And out of its depths he heard these words and saw this vision.

Thomas Wolfe did not confront death very long. He was not quite thirty-eight years old when he wrote these words. He had not been feeling well for a few months. But when he wrote these words, he apparently did not yet suspect that life was ebbing away. As happens to others, the secret chambers of his heart understood things which his conscious mind did not yet know. People who are close to death are often given such visions, as Karlis Osis has shown so clearly. Stephen, as he was attacked by his persecutors and killed, saw the heavens open and beheld the glory of God and Jesus standing at God's right hand. These things happened not only in biblical times; they happen now, as the words of Thomas Wolfe show.

The Children of God

The peacemakers will be called the children of God (literally his sons, but, given Jesus' view of women, this unquestionably includes his daughters as well). There are moments when one enjoys lying on the breast of parents, simply enjoying their love. One of my richest memories of my own children goes back to the night before one of my sons was to leave for college. I often retire early and smoke a pipe. On that evening he came into my room quietly and lay down beside me with his head on my chest. There were no words, and after about half an hour he got up and went to his own room. The memory of those quiet moments together is priceless, and at the same time they remind me of other times when one of the children worked along with me at some task, with obvious delight. They knew that they could share with me and that they were loved.

Both of these experiences tell something about our relationship with God and how it will be in heaven. As children of God we will know quiet rest in him, and we will also be able to be fully active as his helpers. We will work beside him without becoming weary, helping him in his innumerable purposes. We will learn the meaning of the phrase in the ancient prayer for peace:* "whose service is perfect freedom." In heaven we can expect, as sons and daughters of God, that our work will be like the pure play of children, full of joy, fun, and excitement. In this way we will grow and develop, learning and serving, and then come to rest again on the breast of the Divine Lover.

Out of all his various stories and images and discussions about the nature of our life in heaven, there were two occasions when Jesus spoke directly, rather than in symbolic language, about heaven. One was the story of the rich man in Hades and Lazarus resting on Abraham's bosom in heaven. And the second was his answer to the Sadducees who were trying to catch him up with their questions and make his idea of life after death look ridiculous. They told the story of a woman whose husband was one of seven brothers. When the husband died leaving no children, the law required the second brother to marry her and raise up children in his stead, but the same thing happened to him. In turn each brother married her and died, and then the woman also died. At the resurrection, they asked, whose wife will the woman be?

Jesus, with his quick and penetrating mind, had no trouble answering. The vision of heaven he gave elaborates the idea presented in this beatitude. The men and women of this world marry, he said. But those who have been judged worthy of a place in the other world, in the resurrection from the dead, do not marry, for they are not subject to death any longer. They are like angels. They are sons of God, because they share in the resurrection. *The Jerusalem Bible* translates the central idea in these words: "For they are the same as the angels, and being children of the resurrection they are sons of God" (Luke 20:27-38; also Matthew 22:23-33 and Mark 12:18-27).

The angels are agents of God, his co-workers. The sons and daughters of God are also his co-workers, and this is what makes

---

*This prayer came originally from the Gelasian Sacramentary. As found in the former Episcopal service of Morning Prayer, it read: "O God, who art the author of peace and lover of concord, in knowledge of whom standeth our eternal life, whose service is perfect freedom: defend us thy humble servants in all assaults of our enemies; that we surely trusting in thy defence, may not fear the power of any adversaries, through the might of Jesus Christ our Lord. Amen."

them inheritors of earth. Each image speaks of a different aspect of the same truth. John told that the Pharisees were horrified to hear Jesus speak of himself as the Son of God. But Jesus pointed out to them:

> Is it not written in your own Law, "I said: You are gods"? Those are called gods to whom the word of God was delivered—and Scripture cannot be set aside (John 10:34-35).

The sons and daughters of God share in his very godliness with the angels whom he also created. This is the high destiny of heaven, which Jesus later emphasized to the disciples in a personal way. He told them,

> You are my friends, if you do what I command you. I call you servants no longer; a servant does not know what his master is about. I have called you friends, because I have disclosed to you everything that I heard from my Father (John 15:14-15).

Friends and adult children are in the same category. They share the confidence and life and work of the parent and friend.

One of the main ways that Jesus pictured heaven was in terms of a feast, and, even better, a princely wedding feast. He also spoke of feasting in heaven. In Matthew 8:11 and Luke 13:29 essentially the same words were recorded: "From east and west people will come, from north and south, for the feast in the kingdom of God." A feast is not only an occasion for filling oneself with food, but a time for exuberance and fun, for joy. Those who are not able to come to the party and celebrate because they are so hurt—like the elder brother in the story of the prodigal—may have to change and learn to enjoy others' good fortune before they can get into the kingdom. Jesus evidently did not expect us to be working or just resting with God all of the time. Times for playing with him are a necessary addition, because eternal anything, working, resting, *or* playing, would soon become dull.

The playfulness of God has been described in a delightful way by Alan Watts in *Behold the Spirit*. By visiting a good aquarium one can also observe that God must have a sense of humor to have created fish in all the colors and strange shapes that are found. A description of partying with God is given by Andrew Greeley, a vision patterned after a grand Irish drinking party. Greeley quotes from an anthology of Irish literature these words from the tenth century:

> I should like to have a great pool of ale for the King of Kings; I should like the Heavenly Host to be drinking it for all eternity.[6]

Children, sons and daughters, not only rest with their parents, they work and play with them; in a similar way in heaven we can expect joy and fulfillment as well as work in all of this activity.

Is Heaven Worthwhile?

Using the framework provided by the beatitudes, we can describe quite a bit of what heaven is like. It is that state of being in which we shall be comforted, made heirs of all of the earth's richest treasure, filled to the brim so that our deepest longings are satisfied. It is that eternal dwelling where we shall receive mercy, pardon, restoration, and rebirth. Then we shall behold God and work and play with him among those who love him. This is heaven. Boethius once summed it all up in one sentence: *Heaven is the simultaneous fruition of life without bounds.* It is like a bud bursting into eternal bloom, and a blossom ripening into eternal fruit. And then the process of bud and bloom and fruition starts over, again and again. Heaven is like emerging from a dark tunnel into the full light of day.

Is heaven worthwhile? There was a song we used to sing: "Heaven is my home; I'm just a pilgrim here below." Is the holy city worth the pilgrimage, the harbor worth the voyage?

You can tell much about a house by the way people have furnished and decorated it. You can tell much about a public place by the people who frequent it, and about a city by the people who come from it. We can tell much about heaven by the people we know must be there. Heaven is the place where we will find those kindly, fine, noble, courageous, self-effacing, humble, understanding, forgiving, striving spirits whom we have loved on earth. It is the place and state of being where they are happy and at home. Such a place certainly looks very worthwhile to me.

These are the people that we shall now look at. The beatitudes tell us that these people are in heaven. We shall ask how one achieves such a destiny. What are the qualifications for it?

X. Entering the Kingdom

The way to heaven is not what we ordinarily think. The world of Jesus Christ is certainly topsy-turvy by ordinary human standards. As Jesus saw it, the people who are powerful and intelligent and strong, who are able to live ascetic or religiously correct lives entirely on their own, are not the ones who are going to make it in God's kingdom. We do not get into heaven, he told us, because we are wise and know enough to get there on our own, but because we are childlike and seeking, aware that things are not so smooth. It is the dispossessed and unfortunate, the gentle and the merciful, who find a place in heaven. The words of the *Magnificat*, attributed to Mary by Luke, put it very clearly. These words became one of the great hymns of the early church:

> His name is Holy;
>> his mercy sure from generation to generation toward those who fear
>> him.
> the deeds his own right arm has done disclose his might:
>> the arrogant of heart and mind he has put to rout,
> he has torn imperial powers from their thrones,
>> but the humble have been lifted high.
> The hungry he has satisfied with good things,
>> the rich sent empty away (Luke 1:49-53).

The problems that these words present for human beings seem obvious. We find ourselves in a world that requires ego strength. God seems to expect us to use our own strength as far as we can to keep this earthly house in order, both inside and out. He even anticipates the mistakes we make in trying to develop our personalities and our relationships with other people, and he provides the forgiveness that allows us to make a fresh start and try again. But the idea of being able to fend for ourselves, even in limited ways, tends to give us a sense of power that can cut us off from God and his kingdom of heaven.

We seem to be on a tightrope or a narrow path. If we fail to use the ego power that is available to us and sidestep our responsibilities in this world, we may find ourselves turning away from heaven entirely. On the other hand, if we go ahead on our own and are successful in avoiding most wrongdoing and living up to the highest standards, it is all too easy to think we are headed for heaven when all we are doing is staying on a safe, well-traveled path that leads nowhere.

How then can ordinary individuals like you and me prepare for that other world which we call heaven, where we may finally meet God? The descriptions that Jesus gave in the beatitudes point the way. As I have tried to show, these statements were quite clearly intended to describe more than just the kind of people that may be found in heaven. They are also meant to show us the kind of attitudes and actions that will give us a taste of that kingdom in the here and now. And these are also the attitudes and actions that will allow us to share fully in that same kingdom after death.

These eight qualities or qualifications for heaven are not steps, however, which everyone must take one after another to reach this fortunate or blessed state. They are more like doors, any one of which will swing open and let a person enter the kingdom of heaven. The Father or Abba does not seem to require us to be totally integrated and to have all the virtues in order to find a place in his kingdom. He asks only that we are taking the right road and trying to find at least one of these entryways. These two ideas of how we find the kingdom can be pictured in a diagram (see next page).

Each of us has his or her own characteristic redeeming quality. It has been said that the person who experiences the world mainly through sensation, the sensing type, has the virtue of simplicity, while the intuitive person shows wisdom, and the thinking type is characterized by justice, the feeling person by joy. Each of us has a unique way of approaching the kingdom, and each of us must work toward the doorway that will let him or her in. Let us look at the eight ways that Jesus described in the beatitudes and see what pattern of life they suggest.

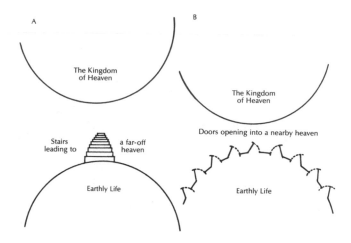

A, on the left, suggests how some people see the kingdom far off, separated from us by steep, difficult steps. The idea of the closeness of God's kingdom and our ability to step into it in any of several ways is pictured by B.

Beggars in the Spirit

Those who know their need of God, the poor in spirit, are literally "beggars." The Greek word used in the beatitudes is *ptōchós* which came from a verb meaning to skulk, to cringe or cower in fright. Originally it applied only to the indigent, those in actual economic want, and it had very negative connotations in the ancient Greek world. Until Christianity opened up a new attitude toward poverty, beggars were pictured as the refuse of society, wandering about in contemptible wretchedness. The story of Lazarus begging at the rich man's door (Luke 16:19-31) is striking for the way Jesus contrasted this ordinary image of the beggar with his own understanding of what lies in store for the poverty-stricken. Used in this way "beggar" had come to mean a person who was destitute or impoverished in any way, in wealth, influence, position, honor, or spirit.

In Luke's beatitudes the word for beggar stands alone, while in Matthew it is followed by "in the spirit." Beggar does not refer just to people who are poor in an outer way, but to those who are inwardly poor, whose spirits are not puffed up and arrogant. In most places Jesus made it very clear that he was talking about an inner quality. While physical poverty often leads to poverty of spirit, this is not always true. Unless that inner quality is present, lack of the good things of this life will seldom bring anyone closer to the eternal kingdom. People can become just as proud of poverty as they often are of their talents or powers or possessions, thus robbing poverty of any value. Wealthy individuals have also been known to refuse help to the poor for the hypocritical reason that their poverty will bring blessings. We humans find ways of distorting Jesus' meaning in opposite directions.

Among the very poor there is often a sense of detachment from life which opens them to another dimension of reality. They have so little to hang onto except life itself that they are not dominated by worldly attachments. The same thing is true of people who come to know real inner poverty and are forced to realize that they cannot stand by their own strength. These individuals have learned that they must have the help of some spiritual power greater than themselves in order to survive at all. They have come to know the complexity of the inner world, or dimension found within themselves. They know the incredible conflicts within their own psyches and realize that they cannot bring themselves together to cope with such a life without saving help. My own experience has shown me that I do not often turn to the risen Christ because I am virtuous, but because I cannot manage my life without him. This is what is meant by being "poor" or a "beggar" in spirit.

Few of us who will read these words have ever known actual poverty, even in religious communities. It is hard for us to imagine being completely dispossessed like the peasants of Jesus' time, at the mercy of both wealthy landlords and the petty officials of a foreign government. We have no comprehension of what it meant to be a beggar in that day, to be utterly dependent on other people's charity. Beggars knew that they had to have help if they were to survive, and that it had to come from beyond themselves as a pure gift or grace. Individuals who become lost in inner anxiety and turmoil and depression know something of the same quality of spirit. They know that they lack the resources to make it on their own.

Jesus had a great deal to say about what would happen to people who are at the bottom of the heap in this world. Several times he made the point that the first will be last and the last first.

This is the point of his story of the workmen in the vineyard who came late in the day and were still paid a full day's wages (Matthew 20:1-16). He illustrated the same idea to the disciples by taking a small child in his arms, showing how those who want to be first must become like servants to those who have the least (Mark 9:33-37). He told people not to take the places of honor at a wedding feast but to sit in the lowest seats, because those who humble themselves will be lifted up (Luke 14:8-11). In the parable of the last days when people will be separated like sheep from goats, he identified with the lowliest and the most downtrodden (Matthew 25:31-46).

When the Pharisees and scribes complained that he was friendly with sinners (Luke 15), Jesus told in parables how God seeks after the lost. He used the parables of the lost coin, the lost sheep, and especially the lost son, showing that those who know their lostness and despair are the very ones who can be found and restored. God seems to hanker after them because of their inner misery and need. This was apparently what Jesus recognized in Zacchaeus whom he sought out (Luke 19:2-10), and in Matthew whom he chose as a disciple (Matthew 9:9). As tax collectors they were both considered spiritually lost.

This idea is found again and again. The surest way to gain one's life or one's self-esteem is to lose it, while those who continue to put their own pride and self-conceit first will end up losers (Matthew 10:39; 16:25; 18:4; 23:12; Mark 8:35; Luke 9:24; 14:11; 17:33; 18:14; John 12:25). People who know that they are inferior and despised and outcast, the prostitutes and tax collectors, will enter the kingdom before those who have only scrupulously obeyed the law (Matthew 21:31).

John Sanford calls attention to the understanding of Gregory of Nyssa about the lost. He considered that they are individuals who have lost the divine image within, that image which the fashioner of each individual heart has stamped upon our inner being. When they recover that image, they then find the presence of the divine in their hearts and so taste the glory of the kingdom of heaven.

What does all of this mean for us today? It means that our most valiant efforts to hold the right beliefs and to do the right thing will come to naught if we become self-satisfied and arrogant. The moment we think we are worthy of God's favor, the door to spiritual development begins to close. Entry into the kingdom (or coming to wholeness or psychological maturity, which is this world's equivalent of the kingdom of heaven) is in part a pure gift. Only those who can accept it as a gift, unearned and unmerited, are able to receive it.

Jung emphasized this point again and again. One must seek growth in the spirit, and continue to search for it. But in the end it is never achieved by one's own efforts alone. The final coming together which opens the way to heaven is given from beyond the individual. It is given, as Jesus showed and as Jung found in the experience of his patients, to those who admit that they cannot make it on their own and become "beggars in the spirit."

In *The Great Divorce* C. S. Lewis tells a story which illustrates this fact superbly. A group from hell have been given an excursion into heaven, and among them is a man whose vices were minimal, and whose virtues were equally minimal. The first person he meets in heaven is a murderer. He is obviously upset and feels that things are mixed up, and after a bitter complaint he goes on:

> Look at me, now.... I gone straight all my life. I don't say I was a religious man and I don't say I had no faults, far from it. But I done my best all my life, see? I done my best by everyone, that's the sort of chap I was. I never asked for anything that wasn't mine by rights. If I wanted a drink I paid for it and if I took my wages I done my job, see? ... I'm asking for nothing but my rights.[1]

The murderer says that if it were a matter of rights, *he* would not be in heaven. People get something far better than they deserve, and he urges the other man just to be happy and come along with him. But the visitor answers, "I'm not asking for anybody's bleeding charity."[2] And he finally goes away grumbling, unable to comprehend what God offers.

God is so much more than we can imagine, so holy and pure and whole. We cannot rise to that level ourselves, but God is also more merciful than we can imagine. He longs to give us more than we can even think of asking. He wants to give us the kingdom, but the gift can be received only if we are willing to accept it. If we continuously look back at our familiar homeplace and refuse to give up our cherished possessions which are represented by rights and virtues and pride that seem so important to us in this world, then we often cannot recognize and move on to the better things as they are offered to us.

There was a time when many people felt that they could make themselves poor by excessive asceticism. Even St. John of the Cross wore a chain around his middle with spikes to dig into his flesh. Sleeping on nails and mortifying the flesh may make one feel poor in spirit, but these practices are more likely to express self-hate and self-punishment than poverty of spirit. They are often difficult to distinguish from symptoms of psychological illness. Something is wrong within individuals or with a culture where there is a need to abuse bodies by actions like these. If one will look deep within and face all the elements that go to make up our personalities, one will have little need to mortify the flesh in order to feel like a beggar in the spirit.

Being poor in spirit means facing one's inner shadowy side, and this is an unbelievably difficult task. Jung writes that accepting oneself in all of one's "wretchedness is the hardest of tasks, and one which it is almost impossible to fulfill. The very thought can make us livid with fear."[3] Anyone who wishes to fulfill this first condition for entrance into the kingdom need only look honestly within and bear the pain of finding there "the poorest of all the beggars, the most impudent of all the offenders, the very enemy himself."[4]

In the end facing death makes beggars of us all. As we come to death we enter the unknown. We may have had some experiences of the kingdom, but from the relative safety of physical existence and with at least some relation to life as we know it now. The final step of death strips us of all our pretensions and makes us truly poor. Only the most brash and unthinking individuals can face death without a sense of impoverishment and fear. Perhaps the reason that Moody so seldom finds judgment in near-death experiences is that death makes beggars of most of us.

The Sorrowful and Gentle of Spirit

The natural reaction to facing one's beggarliness is to mourn. Sorrow is the normal emotional response to the pain and loss we feel when we cannot avoid our brokenness and ugliness. The reactions we call emotions involve the whole human being, *body* as well as mind and psyche. Persons who truly mourn or grieve feel an inward

heaviness, but that is not all. Their sorrow is also expressed outwardly in their downcast expression, and often in their tone of voice
or by sighs and tears.

There are many things which can make us feel the emotion of
sorrow. The most common reason is bereavement, the loss of someone we love or watching that person suffer pain and illness. One
may grieve over loss of security or honor or position. There are
times when we are touched by the agony of other people and mourn
because there is so much suffering in this world and we can personally do so little to help. Evil so often seems victorious. Our mourning can result from the compassion we feel as we think of the
hungry, the mistreated, those who are dispossessed or imprisoned.
When we have compassion we suffer with and in the pain of others.

Some of us suffer inwardly as we look at how poorly we have
done with our lives. Different values often lay opposing claims
upon us, and the tension between them can keep us from accom-
plishing our goals and from finding peace and harmony. Sometimes
one is simply overwhelmed by a sense of inferiority and valuelessness. Or we may mourn because of the sinful and stupid things we
have done which we do not seem able to change. This attitude of
sorrow and grief is very similar to an attitude of contrition and
repentance. It is also our natural reaction when we become more
completely aware of ourselves, our inner nature and problems.

Jesus often spoke of repentance. In Matthew's Gospel his first
words about the kingdom were: "Repent, for the kingdom of
heaven is upon you" (Matthew 3:2). He asked people first to confront themselves, and then to react with regret and sorrow. This is
the way of the sorrowful whom Jesus called blest in the beatitudes.
The sorrowful are those who mourn over their inner and outer poverty and allow the suffering to permeate their whole being, both
physical and mental. As it does, something happens within the person. A new kind of life begins to emerge. When one really begins to
feel sorrow over one's inner condition, it is like being born from
above. Repentance and mourning open the way to new life.

The person who has never mourned is one who has never been
touched by the fullness of life. Those who go through life without
experiencing love for another may escape mourning. They escape
the devastating emotion that comes with any threat of losing the
other person, and they are usually protected from having to face
themselves head-on. They must pay a high price for this protection,

however. The price is isolation from the real world, a life without deep relationship with other human beings. Life on these terms is scarcely human. It is no wonder that these people are separated from the kingdom of heaven. They fail to develop the interdependence with others that makes us fully human and fully alive. When we lose someone really close to us, our lives simply collapse inside and we respond with grief, expressed both inwardly and outwardly.

Many people are afraid to let go and express their sorrow. The popular attitude in the Western world looks with distaste on expressions of grief. We are supposed to act like the captains of our souls at all times. When loss strikes, we are to bear up stoically without making a fuss. We must never talk about the agony of death, of watching someone we have loved suffer and die. Any show of emotion, tears or sobbing therefore should be avoided. Among men tears are often seen as a sign of weakness, an almost unpardonable social disgrace, while the tears of women have been considered an evidence of their inferiority.

This is not the Christian attitude toward grief and mourning. It is the attitude of a world which fears looking at loss and pain because it doubts that there is any power under the sun which can pull life together again if one gives in to grief and suffering. The Christian knows that Abba is there to strengthen us and that it is healthy and honest to express our anguish by crying. From the Christian point of view it is both religiously and psychologically sound for people to show grief by breaking down in tears.

There is no reason to be ashamed of grief or of letting it be seen. Jesus wept unashamedly at the tomb of Lazarus, real tears, tears which welled up from a sorrowing heart. He wept over Jerusalem when he saw how the people there were bent on destruction. Mary was weeping so hard at the grave of Jesus that she could not see through her tears and recognize her Lord when he appeared. David shed tears of real anguish over his beloved Jonathan. He was apparently not ashamed of his feelings since he set down the words of his magnificent lament, which we still treasure, to express them. These were real men and women whom we remember for their gallant deeds as well as for their religious heroism. As Unamuno once remarked, the chief sanctity of our temples is that they are places where people come to weep together.

Tears and emotion are given to us for a purpose. They serve to release tension. They soothe the wounded heart, allowing the accumulation of pain to pour out so that it doesn't corrode the heart that bears it. Those who do not mourn generally do not find healing of their loss. Tears even contain an agent which destroys germs and helps to protect us from disease. The Simontons, in their book, *Getting Well Again*, show that unfaced grief may result in physical illness and be a contributing factor in cancer.

Grief is cured only as we pass through the center of it, through the opaque darkness of pain and anguish. It can't be circumvented or skirted without causing damage to the human psyche and keeping one far from the kingdom. We need to face our inner pain and let it bubble up. This does not mean giving way to ostentatious grief, but it does mean avoiding stoical repression.

Bearing real sorrow and grief gives one a larger heart, and this is essential if one is to minister to other people who are suffering grief from either inner or outer causes. Only those who have passed through both kinds of sorrow and mourning can help others who face similar problems. In addition, passing through suffering provides an armor which strengthens us and gives us great power over calamity. Once we have faced grief we are better able to stand whatever life brings.

Those who have passed through the vale of grief know the meaning of infinite resignation, that quality which Kierkegaard has described in these words:

> Infinite resignation is that shirt we read about in the old fable. The thread is spun under tears, the cloth bleached with tears, the shirt sewn with tears; but then too it is a better protection than iron and steel. The imperfection in the fable is that a third party can manufacture this shirt. The secret in life is that everyone must sew it for himself, and the astonishing thing is that a man can sew it fully as well as a woman. In the infinite resignation there is peace and rest and comfort in sorrow—that is, if the movement is made normally.[5]

Considering that grief apparently has such value, it is not surprising that Jesus calls those who mourn blest and says that they are given entrance into the kingdom.

This does not mean, of course, that there is no place in life for joy and carefree abandon and happiness. When one's whole being is absorbed by mourning and sadness and sorrow, there is little room for creativity. One can distort life as much by avoiding joy and happiness as by ignoring suffering and grief. True living consists of both, and to ignore either the good things or our experiences of pain and loss can keep us from living in creative relation to the kingdom. By clinging to the notion that life must be all one thing, either all good or all bad, we avoid the pulsating alternation, the vital wave-like nature of human experience. It probably never occurred to Jesus that enough people would glorify sadness and grief to necessitate a warning against that idea. This attitude was rarely found in Jesus' time. It was developed by the Puritans and Jansenists who perverted the meaning of this beatitude.

One should rejoice when life goes well, and a sense of being enlightened, creative, or prosperous gives reason for rejoicing. When there is reason for sorrow, either inner or outer, one should mourn. But we must not allow these responses to keep us from sharing the feelings of others. Jesus told people to weep with those who weep, and to rejoice with those who are rejoicing. When one is experiencing darkness, nothing is worse than to have some well-intentioned person suggest that something must be very wrong to make one show so little joy. It is as destructive for the person who is truly rejoicing to be met by a recital of all the frightful tragedies in this world which should keep people from rejoicing. Many times it seems to be more difficult to find someone to laugh with us than to cry with us. We forget that making a creative adjustment to both the kingdom and our present life demands that we experience life's natural rhythms to the fullest. And this means that we must take the highs and lows when they come and not try to balance them out by feeling joy when we should be mourning, or the other way around.

Those who have mourned are among those that are called the gentle or the meek. They have faced the ugliness in life and have picked up their lives and gone on. Mourning is their emotional response to poverty of spirit, while meekness is their behavioral response, the life-style they have developed through facing the whole of life. Meekness is poverty of spirit in action. The meek or gentle are the unassuming, the humble, the considerate. They are not puffed up with pride or arrogance. They treat other people as equals, and they try to create conditions that will allow others to develop to the maximum of their capacities. They are facilitators, listeners, who try to help others become what they are capable of becoming. They do not force their own goals onto others, not even onto husbands or wives, children or employees. In one French New Testament the word *débonnaire* is used to translate "gentle" or "meek." It expresses this quality in a unique way. The meek are debonair about their lives. They take both the good and the bad equally well and go gently on, and they treat other people in the same way.

We sometimes confuse this virtue with the false and hypocritical humility portrayed so well in the character of Uriah Heep. Most virtues can be imitated through hypocrisy, as La Rochefoucauld suggested when he wrote that "hypocrisy is the homage which vice renders to virtue." A person with true gentleness of spirit can be distinguished, however, by the way he or she accepts human beings as they are, without hopelessness. The finest example of this unassuming meekness is the way Jesus took his arrest, the mocking, and being judged falsely and then tortured on the cross. This quality touches a secret latch that opens the gate to heaven.

Seeking and the Kingdom

Gentleness, however, is not weakness. This quality of life which results in true consideration for others is more like the tough resilience of a reed growing by a stream. The reed bends with the wind and survives. Even a gale cannot uproot it, while the mighty oak may be torn from its roots and left to die. The meek or gentle can withstand life's buffeting in a similar way. They have a real inner strength. They listen to the deepest longings of their hearts and continue on, exerting themselves and seeking. They hunger and thirst after righteousness.

The Greek words for hunger and thirst had far more meaning than these words have in modern English. As I poured over the lexicons, their meaning came alive to me. "Hunger" and "thirst" speak of the human desire to reach out and achieve, to seek fulfillment of the deep searching of the human heart. Love is essentially such a seeker. Love is that quality of life which is always reaching out, seeking to find the person who completes one's life or trying to complete the life of another.

Even in the early Greek usage these words implied a need for more than just food and water. To hunger meant to need or desire something strongly, to crave it ardently. The hungry are those in need. The word used in the beatitudes was also the one Luke used to warn people who are well-fed and satisfied that the time will come when they will go hungry (Luke 6:25). To thirst also indicated strong need or desire. When Jesus cried out from the cross, "I thirst," this was the same word that he used to speak to the Samaritan woman about the living water that one could drink and never thirst again (John 19:28; 4:14-15).

Hunger and thirst were sometimes linked together to suggest the most extreme privation, the greatest need to seek fulfillment. In John's account of the feeding of the five thousand, Jesus later spoke of bread from heaven and told the people, "I am the bread of life. Whoever comes to me shall never be hungry, and whoever believes in me shall never be thirsty" (John 6:35). In the Book of Revelation when John saw the first vision of the Lamb on his throne, he was told that people who had gone through their ordeal and come to the Lamb would never again feel hunger or thirst (Revelation 7:16). The early Church was convinced that those who knew their need were candidates for heaven and that in the kingdom they would find relationship with Christ which would meet their deepest needs. The hungry and thirsty, they realized, were in a better position than people who were wealthy in various ways. Those whose wants are already satisfied in one way or another are no longer pushed to keep on seeking. They lose sight of the kingdom and the place they might find in it.

What does it mean, then, to hunger and thirst for righteousness? There are few words in the New Testament that have been discussed so thoroughly, from the earliest time on. It is clear in the New Testament that there is more to righteousness than just the moral and legal aspects of right thinking and action. Paul suggested that people do not become righteous simply by following the law, but rather by accepting God's grace and mercy humbly, with meekness. The right is that which God approves. One becomes righteous by being drawn into fellowship with him. It is a state that is given to individuals as they hunger and thirst for the vision and presence and fellowship of God.

The seekers for this state, Jesus said, find their way into the kingdom of heaven. In the Sermon on the Mount he also told people, "Set your mind on God's kingdom and his justice before everything else, and all the rest will come to you as well" (Matthew 6:33; Luke 12:31). And he further instructed them, "Ask, and you will receive; seek, and you will find; knock, and the door will be opened" (Matthew 7:7; Luke 11:9). Those who ask and seek and knock find that doors are opened; they receive their requests and they find their treasure. They touch the reality of the kingdom now.

Two of Jesus' characteristic stories were told to emphasize the need to keep after God in prayer, even to nag him. Both stories suggest that God likes to be pestered by human beings about their needs. The first is the parable of the obstinate widow who pestered the judge until she was given justice, and the second tells about the man who got a neighbor out of bed in the middle of the night to borrow some bread (Luke 18:1-7; 11:5-9). God is a loving Father, but he does not pamper us. He wants us to seek him persistently, patiently, consistently. It is not enough to just ask once and then assume it will be granted. Persistent prayer often opens the door to the kingdom. It is important because it means in essence that we are seeking God's presence consistently, again and again.

Deep within us there is something vital and searching, something restless that sends us on strange quests and keeps us searching for deeper and deeper meaning. If one has not stifled it, there is an insatiable thirst within each of us for something that will be truly satisfying. Augustine suggested that God placed within us a hunger which only he can satisfy so that we must turn to him again and again. If we follow our inner hunger and thirst and do not give up, we are led inevitably and unerringly to God and his kingdom. We may be led through strange and difficult places, but in the end we arrive.

One can observe this hunger and thirst in normal children as they start out to explore and understand the world. Nothing has to be done to develop an inquisitive, seeking spirit in children. All that we need to do is to release their adventuring thirst. The trouble with much of the educational process is that it turns this torrent of desire and interest into a barely observable trickle. The average child is naturally a seeker, and through schooling becomes an average, unquestioning adult as society suppresses this questing spirit with its rigidity and rules and prohibitions. Few of us come to our full stature as adults because this spirit of childlike seeking is one of the elements of full adulthood and is difficult to regain once it is lost.

The source of our seeking is the reality, the energy or substance which we call love. Love is the mainspring, the font of all our searching, particularly of our search for meaning. Jung understood the power of love as few people in our time have been able to comprehend it. In his autobiography, near the end of his life, he wrote:

> In my medical experience as well as in my own life I have again and again been faced with the mystery of love, and have never been able to explain what it is. . . . Whatever one can say, no words express the whole. To speak of partial aspects is always too much or too little, for only the whole is meaningful. Love "bears all things" and "endures all things" (1 Cor. 13:7). These words say all there is to be said; nothing can be added to them. For we are in the deepest sense the victims and the instruments of cosmogonic "love" . . . . Being a part, man cannot grasp the whole. He is at its mercy. He may assent to it, or rebel against it; but he is always caught up by it and enclosed within it. He is dependent upon it and is sustained by it. Love is his light and his darkness, whose end he cannot see. "Love ceases not"—whether he speaks with the "tongues of angels," or with scientific exactitude traces the life of the cell down to its uttermost source.[6]

Laurens van der Post has also pointed out this seeking power of love, its power to lead, or even force us toward new life. In his novel *The Face Beside the Fire* van der Post writes:

> When the world and judgment say: "This is the end," love alone can see the way out. It is the aboriginal tracker, the African bushman on the faded desert spoor within us, and its unfailing quarry is always the light.[7]

If we want to find God and his kingdom, the surest way is to turn deep within and discover this insatiable desire, this passion of love, and follow it, never giving up. Science offers an example of this way of dedicated seeking. Scientists are seekers who follow their passion to discover and understand things wherever it leads.

Over the years I have known many, many people in depth. I have found this restless search for love in every one of them, even the most distorted or depraved. There have been none who did not, in the depth of their being, seek for something more than they felt life could offer. This hunger and thirst are deep within us and more persistent than most of us realize. They make us "dream the impossible dream."[8] As we seek for fulfillment, pursuing this passionate thirst for something better than we seem to have a right to imagine, we find the way to wholeness, to the fullness of life that shows one is close to the kingdom. Goethe apparently understood this and described how Faust, in spite of his sins, continued to search and finally was saved. His insatiable hunger and thirst saved him.

It is not so much what we actually accomplish in this life that counts, but our effort to keep on seeking, trusting that somehow, somewhere the dream of complete fulfillment will come true. God does not seem to reject people who seek in the wrong direction. The only ones who may find the door to the kingdom closed and locked are the lukewarm, those who will not leave the fireside and go out searching. The lukewarm are thrown out according to the Book of Revelation. The experience that turned Paul's life around is a case in point. Paul was seeking when it happened. But he was seeking to support the high priest and put Christianity out of business, and this led him straight into the hands of the Christ who started Paul out on a new life.

The Merciful and the Pure in Heart

Most of us find it difficult to be merciful. Mercy involves forgiveness, and it is not easy for us to forgive people when they hurt us. We each have some pet anger or resentment, a grudge, a bitterness that we hang onto even though we realize that there are real rewards for being merciful and forgiving. It is also very silly to risk the dangers of nursing anger and bitterness. As John Sanford has remarked, it is foolish to keep anger and resentment alive by failing to show mercy because this only ties us more and more firmly to the very people from whom we want to be free.

Jesus was clear about the importance of mercy and forgiveness. In the Lord's Prayer he included only one condition. We can expect God to give freely all that we need, including forgiveness, so long as we are able to forgive other human beings. People who cannot offer such mercy to others are caught by the dark forces which try so hard to corrupt and destroy us. When we will not forgive, we allow our angers to possess us. We are no longer masters in our own house; we let anger, pride, self-justification take charge. We are then shut out of the kingdom of heaven and may be consigned to hell where hate and anger reign.

What must I forgive? Sometimes in saying the Lord's Prayer I simply say: *Forgive us our unconsciousness, as we forgive the unconsciousness of others,* because this covers nearly everything. Charles Williams wrote in his book *The Forgiveness of Sins* that there are things which need not be forgiven, things which ought to be forgiven, and things which cannot be forgiven—and the Christian forgives them all.

Williams knew from experience what he was asking of Christians. At the time he was writing, the Germans were bombing London thinking that they were doing the right thing. He realized that their lives were caught up unconsciously in the darkness of Hitler. Like so many of us in our ordinary lives, the Germans were reacting to unconscious forces bent on destruction. Much the same understanding was found among the early Christians. When St. Perpetua, for instance, was about to be thrown to the wild beasts, a guard asked her why she did not curse her jailers. She told him that they were already under the power of darkness and she did not wish to add to it. This is the quality of mercy and compassion which is essential if we are to find the kingdom and relationship with God either now or in the next life.

The next question is a little harder to answer. How can we achieve this important quality of life, this spirit of forgiveness? The problem is that it cannot be done by an act of will alone. One can consciously decide, "I am going to show mercy to everyone." And then, in the midst of some difficulty, someone with an irritating manner and altogether different problems walks into the room. A biting remark slips out and the person goes away hurt. Or we may be simply angry at a situation, or secretly enjoying a juicy bit of gossip, when a person in need of compassion and forgiveness shows up. Often something unintentional and damaging spills over and spoils our effort to listen and help other people. There can even be times when things seem to hurt us so much that we turn our backs on other people's troubles and do not reach out a hand or give them the "kiss of peace" when they need it.

Of course we must keep on trying consciously to show mercy, directing our hearts and minds to follow through as far as we can. We must also reflect on the times when we have failed to be merciful and try to see how to change. However, our conscious determination is not enough. Mercy is part of a way of life. It flows naturally from a life marked by poverty of spirit. Those who truly mourn seldom spend time pointing out other people's faults. There is no better test of gentleness of spirit than to watch for the forgiving attitude of these individuals. Those who are seeking usually know how difficult it is to find one's goal, one's treasure or "the pearl of great price" and they are not likely to blame anyone who falls short or gets lost in the search. Mercy wells up out of a childlike spirit which knows that it is not prepared to deal with the adult world and that there must be gifts and growth in order to experience life as it potentially can be.

It is not a good idea for people who live in glass houses—as all of us really do—to throw stones. I am just as vulnerable as the person I might be preparing to attack or find fault with. Once we realize that we are all beggars in the spirit, unable to achieve our goal and yet continuing to seek, we know that we are in no position to judge any person. If we judge and are not merciful we are not consistent. We are not acting out of our own true condition. Either we are not aware of our condition, or else we think that by refusing to admit our human condition one can escape it and avoid the effort of searching for purity of heart.

In his book *Purity of Heart* Kierkegaard suggested that the pure in heart are those individuals whose wills are directed toward one goal. They act from one central motive, one center of being. They become one person as the many selves within them are joined together in seeking one common purpose. Like everyone else, I have many centers of being within me. As one or another of them comes to the fore, my personality changes. We are none of us simple unitary wills. I have described the complexity of the human spirit at some length in my book *Discernment: A Study in Ecstasy and Evil*. Within each of us there are many different powers and voices, many different desires struggling for control. Our task, as followers of Christ, is to try to bring this menagerie together into one, undivided personality. This seldom happens to any of us until we realize our poverty of spirit and try to open up all the parts of our being, asking that they be brought together into harmony by an act of grace.

The Greek words for "pure in heart" used in this beatitude are very revealing. We have a tendency to think of the heart only in medical or very materialistic terms. It is an organ that pumps blood through the body, or secondarily a source of courage or caring in the outer world. In Greek the heart was understood to mean only secondarily a physical organ. It was first of all considered the center and source of inner life. It gave rise to all that makes a human being—thinking, feeling, willing. It was the organ of natural and spiritual enlightenment, as well as the center of our passions and desires. "Heart" stood for the life within human beings on all fronts from physical and mental to moral and spiritual. In our materialistic time it is difficult to realize that the psyche or the whole inner being was as real to the Greeks as the physical body is to us.

Katharós, or "pure" in Greek, is a word rich with nuances of meaning. It was used to speak of substances that were clear, clean, free of admixture, especially water and metals. It could describe feelings that were unmixed, or a way that was open and clear, or something sound and undamaged. It also meant ceremonially and morally clean, free from offense or contamination. The person who was described as *katharós* in heart was sincere and single-minded, innocent, guiltless, blameless. Individuals like these have taken the trouble to learn about what is at the depth of their being. They seek to act as simple, unified beings, rather than as fragmented and scattered parts. They are trying to follow the teachings that Jesus gave about singleness of purpose and purity of heart.

In his parable comparing the eye to a lamp, Jesus taught that having a single eye, a sound eye, will give light to the whole body. And he went on to say that no one can serve two masters (Matthew 6:22-24). He warned that every kingdom divided against itself is headed for ruin and collapse. If the house of the soul is divided against itself, it cannot stand (Matthew 12:25). Only a good tree, he said, can bear good fruit, and a bad or corrupt tree will always be known by its bad fruit (Matthew 12:33). Jesus ridiculed the Pharisees for their concern about ritual cleanliness. He explained to the disciples that one is not defiled by what goes into the body, but by the things that come from the heart, by evil intentions, murder, adultery, fornication, theft, perjury, slander, and judgment (Matthew 15:1-20).

Purity of heart cannot be achieved, however, solely by our own will and effort. It is a gift which is given in the end to individuals who recognize their poverty and work at filling themselves from the one source which can satisfy the hunger and thirst of our souls. But our preparation to receive this gift is not exactly easy. As John Sanford points out so clearly in *The Kingdom Within*, the purity that Jesus was talking about does not originate alone from outer actions. It is purity of heart, and it comes to those who are growing in knowledge and acceptance of themselves so that the light of the kingdom will shine through every part of their being. For most people this requires a whole new attitude. As Mr. Sanford emphasizes:

> The ethic of the kingdom is a radically new ethic because it is based on the inner man and takes into account what is in the "heart" of man. It is founded upon the way of consciousness, for only the man who is conscious of his total self, and whose "heart" is not hidden to him, can reach a deeper morality than that of the scribes and Pharisees.[9]

When people take this way of consciousness, they come to know poverty of spirit and mourning. They find the meaning of mercy and gentleness of spirit and the need to keep on seeking. It is comforting to realize that the beggars in spirit are given an equal place in the kingdom beside the pure of heart. True purity of heart is more an attitude than a condition or state of life. It is the attitude which makes us willing to know ourselves, and to work at bringing each aspect into harmonious relation with the kingdom and its goals.

The Peacemakers and the Persecuted

People who bring mercy into concrete reality by bringing harmony and peace among men and women are called peacemakers. The Greek word for peace is *eirēnē*, from which we get the name Irene and also "irenic," or conducive to peace, harmony, moderation and conciliation. In a state of peace one is free from both inner and outer strife and war. One lives in harmony and health. A peaceful life is well ordered, secure and prosperous. The Hebrew word *shalom* expresses much the same meaning. This state of peace and contentment with life comes to people who are assured of God's love. Those who are given a taste of that love come to know the peace— this harmony and blessed joy—which is an essential quality of God's kingdom. But such a taste does not give them a place in the kingdom. That place is reserved for those who go on and try to bring harmony, joy and peace to others. They are called children of God.

In the Lord's Prayer we ask for God's will to be done and his kingdom to come on earth as it is in heaven. The peacemakers are the ones who try to help in bringing this about. They are instruments of the kingdom who help people taste this state of harmony in which all parts work together in joy and peace. In *The Divine Comedy* Dante's superb portrayal of paradise gives a picture of this state that appears real by the test of experience. In this state, Dante shows, each person abides in a place (or situation) which suits that individual best, and yet one shares in the reality found by all the others.

This state can come to only a few people on earth, however, as long as there is disharmony, war, strife, hatred, poverty, and want among human beings. As the peacemakers look out and see the world as it is, they cannot escape becoming beggars in spirit. They know how little is accomplished by their own efforts, but *they do not give up.* They go right on trying to make it easier for people to experience the peace of God's kingdom. This is probably why they are called children of God. As peacemakers, they share in the nature of God himself. They are growing in peace within themselves and they go on humbly seeking the kingdom. Those who have no peace within themselves can do little to help bring peace to others.

Martin Luther King was one of the great peacemakers of our time. He knew himself; he knew his anger and hatred. Before he could go on after being reviled or thrown into jail, he had to bring his inner violence to the Christ who lifted it from him. Jesus during the last days of his life became the archetype of the peacemaker. He took on himself the angers and hatred of the world and turned them into peace. As human peacemakers, we carry the burden of our own imperfections and poverty and share with others whatever peace we find. The first requirement of the peacemaker is a sincere desire to share the fine wine of the kingdom with all who would taste it. And the second requirement is to know our motives well enough to be sure that we do not offer peace with one hand and show a clenched fist with the other.

Unless I know myself well, I am always in danger of trying to promote good for violent reasons. A few years ago at the University of Notre Dame a series of courses was instituted to study the use of non-violent methods for achieving various purposes. It was discovered that the students often had violent motives for undertaking non-violence. We then added a course on personal perspectives in non-violence and found that as we looked at our own reactions within these groups we learned how much violence each of us has within us. We cannot hope to bring peace to people in this troubled world until we know ourselves and the violence that is within us and that is ready to boil over each time we are upset. We must realize once more our poverty of spirit and how much help we need to handle these destructive urges.

As I have listened to people trying to unscramble their lives, again and again I have realized that most people want to love. This means that they want to be peacemakers, for those who love are peacemakers. But most of us are afraid. We are afraid that if we let the power and peace of the kingdom really flow through us, the world will pass us by and we may be ground under its heel. We are afraid to give up our anxious, angry, bitter, cantankerous selves and become instruments of peace. It is so easy, we feel, to be deluded and to make mistakes.

We forget that peacemakers like St. Francis of Assisi made mistakes and did not give up. Few individuals have done as much as St. Francis to show Christians the way of peace. Yet even he could be deceived. He preached the Children's Crusade in which tens of thousands of innocent children were killed or made slaves. Even the greatest peacemakers are not perfect. If we want peace for ourselves and others we have to take the risk of trying and perhaps failing, and then try again. We can hardly do better than to follow the way described by St. Francis in these words:

Lord,
make me an instrument of thy peace.
Where there is hatred, let me sow love;
where there is doubt, faith;
where there is despair, hope;
where there is darkness, light;
and where there is sadness, joy.

O Divine Master,
grant that I may not so much seek
to be consoled as to console,
to be understood as to understand,
to be loved as to love.

For it is in giving that we receive,
it is in pardoning that we are pardoned,
and it is in dying that we are born to eternal life.

Obviously one cannot follow this way and put one's own peace and consolation and desire for love ahead of the need of others. To become peacemakers we have to try the way of unselfishness and aim at more than achieving peace just for ourselves. But this way is also a real investment in our own future. Even when our efforts are not very successful, they can bring us close to the kingdom by making us appreciate the value of peace and the danger of violence.

Honesty and sensitivity are essential qualities of the peacemaker. To find peace means being reconciled first with our human situation just as it is. Most of us would rather be lulled into a false sense of security by ignoring the less pleasant parts of being human. In Charles Williams' poetry about Arthur and the knights of the round table, he pictures Galahad asking his father Lancelot to pardon him for being as pure as he is, knowing that Lancelot will find this hard to bear. In this portrayal Williams suggests Galahad's acceptance of the human condition through an understanding of his father's humanness. We need this kind of sensitivity and honesty to start on the road toward peace.

These qualities, however, do not always bring appreciation and admiration from the world. Jesus did not offer us false promises that this way would be easy. Peacemakers often give people a glimpse of themselves. Since most people are frightened by their true condition and their need for help, they strike back in anger, and peacemakers are persecuted. In addition, those who are really trying to follow the way laid out by Christ are usually condemned whenever that way conflicts with the ideas and rules of society.

Jesus used strong words to speak of the persecution that is suffered for the sake of righteousness. He spoke of insults and every kind of lie, comparing it to the violent treatment of the prophets in former times. People who are persecuted are harassed, mistreated, pushed out of the way, even put to flight and pursued. They are reviled and upbraided, insulted and shamed. Individuals who are treated in this way have no choice but to bear their crosses if they go on following Christ. They cannot say that they did not know what they were getting into. Jesus warned that following him might lead to opposition, calumny and persecution. While the manners of society have become somewhat more polite in our time (with some notable exceptions), the world still has ways of showing its contempt for people who show a need for much more than conventional religion.

The suffering that can come to these individuals opens a door into God's kingdom. But this does not mean that we can find that doorway by inviting persecution, seeking it out either consciously or unconsciously. Persecution suffered for the cause of right is one thing. Any other kind is a form of self-destructiveness which the early Church took care to condemn. Efforts to seek martyrdom were considered a sign of sickness, not of holiness. It was understood that mistreating oneself or needlessly exposing oneself to persecution did not lead to the kingdom. Inner violence cuts us off from God just as effectively as outer violence.

We need to be peacemakers within ourselves just as much as in the outer world. Violence against ourselves can disrupt peace on many levels, far beyond its immediate effects. In his frightening book *Man Against Himself*, Karl Menninger has described the many complex ways in which we can turn our human self-destructiveness upon our bodies and minds and damage them. Consciousness is required of us in order to avoid self-persecution which leads away from the kingdom, and yet be willing to bear the pain of unavoidable persecution. We must be aware that violence, whether turned upon oneself or others, usually comes from the Evil One.

Courage is necessary if we are to bear the persecution the world brings us for trying to follow the way of consciousness, poverty, mercy and peacemaking. The way of the kingdom is never very popular in this world. When a prophetic role is involved, one is often misunderstood and harassed. In times like these the best example to follow is that given to us by Jesus as he bore the persecution in the days just before his crucifixion and resurrection. The way of the cross is a way of courage as well as of meekness. I doubt if anyone who does not have courage can maintain a truly humble attitude. Meekness that is not reinforced by courage can become weakness and sentimentality. In the beatitudes Jesus gave us fair warning that he was not offering us an easy way, and he demonstrated the courage that is required as he went up to Jerusalem to confront the powers of darkness. I have described this courage in my book *The Hinge*, which deals with universal meaning of Jesus' crucifixion.

There is a doorway of courage, steadfastness and forbearance opening into the kingdom. Those who may not be able to enter by way of peacemaking, humility, or even mourning can go in through this door. In Dante's vision he saw various circles of heaven, each appropriate for a different virtue. There was a special place for warriors of the spirit, for the courageous and the brave.

It must be remembered, however, that this virtue counts only if it is tied to suffering for the cause of right. It is foolhardy rather than courageous to court suffering needlessly or for an evil or vengeful reason. Such actions do not bring us closer to the kingdom, but take us in the wrong direction. If they are simply the result of being misguided or misinformed, I believe that our good intentions are taken into account. On the other hand, it is wise to become as conscious as possible.

Finding the Kingdom

Luke's account of the beatitudes includes a warning about the way which leads away from the kingdom (Luke 6:20-26). The rich, Jesus warned, have had their time of happiness. Those who are stuffed full will go hungry. Those who laugh now will mourn and weep hereafter. People who are admired, of whom everyone speaks well, will be treated like false prophets. Obviously Jesus felt that certain things should be avoided if people are to find their way into the kingdom.

Self-satisfaction and pride in what we have and what we are keep us tied to the values and short-lived satisfactions of this world. One is not free to seek and discover that only the kingdom can bring complete satisfaction. Pride can make people overbearing and keep them from knowing themselves. They judge others rather than stopping to realize that there is a listener within who sees them as they truly are. Thus they remain split so that purity of mind and singleness of heart are impossible for them. The world often thinks highly of them, and yet they are losing the lives they think they have gained. Then there is the careless attitude which lets people go along with whatever the world offers. Since they lack the seriousness to keep at a search, life usually leads them on a broad road away from the kingdom.

Some people, it is true, get their fill of living like this. They come to mourn their senseless boredom and begin to seek, and I am sure that it is never too late for anyone who honestly asks Abba to help them in need. But our task as Christians is to be ready to point the way. Our first job is to be aware of these attitudes in ourselves, to realize that we are all affected by them. Then we can do our best to make the attitude that Jesus suggested central in our lives.

Outside of the beatitudes the most specific direction that Jesus gave us about finding the kingdom of heaven was his instruction that the only way to the kingdom is to become like little children. Children, in their truly natural state, show most of the virtues which Jesus named as qualifications for the kingdom. Except for the intolerable few who are spoiled brats or prodigies, children are humble and self-effacing, poor in spirit. They give way easily to emotion, particularly joy. Because their inner and outer natures are in almost complete accord, they are single-minded and guileless. They are naturally direct, honest and unassuming.

Children also have a natural passion to learn and to become. They are striving to become, to fulfill what is in them. Few things are so sad as a child whose growth has been arrested. Real-life Peter Pans are not often very attractive. In addition most children are merciful and have a desire to bring harmony and peace among those they love. Adults do not very often realize how easily the child loses this spirit and learns another way from adults and older children who are disagreeable and angry, some of them abusive. Some children are like lambs led to slaughter.

The child by nature—the real child, before being pummeled into grown-up shapes and postures—is the paradigm of growing and becoming, and so a paradigm of the qualities that lead into the kingdom. Growth and becoming are the key words. And this is the pattern that Jesus gave us to follow. When one ceases to develop in this way, one steps into the rigidity of self-satisfied adulthood. The kingdom is so complete and perfect, and we human beings so imperfect and incomplete, that all of us who feel we have achieved have missed the basic message of eternal growth and development which makes the kingdom everlastingly attractive.

As each of us turns toward God's kingdom in this way, in the spirit of natural childhood, we must also remember that there are some questions which we can solve only as adults with mature experience and also with the imagination of unspoiled, natural children. Let us consider these final questions about our life to come and our ultimate destiny.

PART FOUR

Death and Eternal Life:
Some Unresolved Questions and Problems

The Issues

For many years discussion of death has been more or less taboo. There is a natural fear of death as simple and final extinction in the materialistic culture of which we are a part. Few of us want to be snuffed out. We avoid speaking to sick people about death, particularly if they are dying and do not know it. It is the worst breach of manners, even of morality, to let them know. It has seemed better to let them be extinguished into nothingness without the burden of fear. Ministry to the dying has been avoided, as Dr. Kübler-Ross showed very clearly in her first book, *On Death and Dying*. Now that the subject can be approached again, it is time to ask openly: How can we best minister to the dying?

In many circles there has been a growing interest in Eastern religions, and the idea of reincarnation has become very fashionable among these people. As I have mentioned, this point of view probably attracts more followers around the world than any other. Christian ministers like Leslie Weatherhead and Christian philosophers like Geddes MacGregor have openly espoused the idea of reincarnation. And so we need to ask: What is the evidence for reincarnation and how does it fit into the view of eternal life which I propose?

There is also a widespread fear of hell among many people today. For years certain branches of the Christian Church have tried to bludgeon people into living a good life by painting horrendous pictures of the torments of hell. I was amazed to discover that some of my most intelligent and sophisticated students at the University of Notre Dame claimed that they saw no reason to believe in life after death. They had all come from parochial schools and were attending a Catholic university. I was puzzled until I discovered that they had been so frightened about hell by fiery preachers and teachers that they felt safer in denying the entire idea of life after death. Where exactly does the idea of hell and eternal punishment fit into the ideas we are considering about life beyond death?

One could write a book on each of these subjects, but they need to be dealt with briefly in these pages in order to round out the understanding we have been developing.

XI. Ministering to the Dying

It is easy to forget that we all have a stake in the way the needs of the dying are met. Although this is one experience that none of us can escape, we have not given much thought to the effect which our attitudes and beliefs about death have on people who are dying. It seems only sensible to try to hide the fact that someone is dying and let him or her meet death as unconsciously as possible, if we are convinced that there is nothing but a void on the other side of death. We may even know and choose to ignore the findings of Dr. Kübler-Ross which show that awareness of impending death makes dying easier in the end in nearly every case.

If one believes that there is a life to come in which one's future depends on making a decision before one dies, then it may even seem sensible to frighten people into a deathbed decision. This is the way of many fundamentalist Christians, who sometimes appear to be more interested in releasing hostility than in saving souls. They forget that their job as Christians is not to hunt witches but to help human beings find the source of love. Some individuals are led by an opposite belief. This belief states that there is a future life in which nothing can go wrong and that their need is to know something of that life before entering it. They often emphasize the importance of psychic experiences before anything else. Those who believe in reincarnation sometimes put a similar stress on psychic experience, while others feel that their most important need is to improve the moral tone of their lives. By making amends for wrongdoing they can give their *karma* a boost.

There are other people, however, who believe that they enter a world beyond death in which they continue much the same struggle for consciousness and wholeness as in the present life. They stress the importance of patiently sticking with individuals in an effort to help them gain as much consciousness and awareness as possible before they step into the next world. This is the view which makes sense to me. It appears to fit with what we learn from the studies of near-death and other experiences surrounding death. In my opinion it agrees with the way Jesus spoke about God and his kingdom. And it also shows us ways of ministering to the dying and the bereaved that bring both hope and strength to dying individuals.

This understanding of what happens to us after death suggests that we come into the presence of the loving God who knows us better than we know ourselves. We find ourselves among others in the kingdom of heaven. There we shall continue the same growth process that we have known in this life, but without, I hope, the physical agony and the pain. We shall be able to seek help directly from the loving Abba and be given his guidance and encouragement.

We cannot expect the passage to this state to be easy, however. Death is the most major venture into the unknown that we can imagine. It changes our way of experiencing and seems to close the door on everything familiar. We are so immersed in the materialism of our time that few of us can escape the fear that the materialists might be right in denying the possibility of life after death. The evidence is simply not conclusive enough to answer all the questions without leaving some very reasonable doubts.

Ways of Preparing

Before one goes to visit the sick or dying, it is important to remember that people who are apparently unconscious can still perceive what we do and feel and say. The research with those who have come back from death or from a coma at the edge of death produces at least one significant fact: those who appear to be totally unconscious and impervious to any sense data usually report that they knew everything that went on at the time of their "death." The ancient Buddhist lamas apparently recognized this. *The Tibetan Book of the Dead*, which was written to instruct dying people about the dangers they would face and how to meet them, was read by a lama to the person immediately or very soon after death.

In *The Broken Heart* James Lynch discusses studies of unconscious persons which show that their heart rates tended to stabilize when they were touched, even when the touch was simply that of a nurse taking their pulse. Dr. Alan McGlashan has referred to several studies which indicate that patients with seemingly hopeless strokes sometimes recover when they are given the stimulation of various sounds for eight hours a day. He also tells in his book *Gravity and Levity* about certain patients who had suffered a bromide coma. When he was visiting these individuals, after asking everyone else to leave the room, he would take the unconscious patient in his arms and speak reassuring words to him or her. In each of these instances the patient got well and could tell him everything that he had done. These are vitally important facts for people to understand before they start to minister to the dying.

If we are to help individuals meet death and prepare to go on to another life, we must first of all admit that we have doubts and fears that make it difficult to face our own death. Our fears have a way of leaking out when we try to hide them. We can do very little for people who are already oppressed by facing death if we come to them bringing an undercurrent of doubt and fear. An honest confession of one's own worries about death allows the other person to express his or her own anxieties and fears. But this way of sharing the problem is only the *first* step in helping an individual meet death.

In order to get beyond this stage we need a view of the world which has room for some kind of existence beyond this life. We do not have to be professional philosophers to realize that today's materialism does not provide an adequate view of reality. Most people can easily see the gaps in materialism and realize that a more complete understanding of the world is needed to account for many facts right at hand. We cannot hope to work with the dying and answer the questions that death poses without such an understanding. Ministers who plan to spend much time with the dying need a firm and well-grounded conviction that there is a reality beyond the material world in which our lives can continue after death. They need good training in this thinking and also knowledge of the facts which give rise to this view.

There is no substitute for this kind of world-view. No matter how good our intentions are and how caring our bedside manner is, we still need some vision of another dimension of reality into which one steps at death. The lack of this vision will inevitably cast a pall on our relationship with the dying.

As I have tried to show, there are forces of darkness on the other side (in this other dimension) as well as forces of creativity and love. Individuals who minister to the dying need personal experiences of relationship with the loving God, some foretaste of actually meeting him and being transformed by him. There is no better way of coming to know God than through prayer and meditation. One Catholic religious order which puts most of its effort into preaching missions has started a retreat center where preachers can be trained in the spiritual life. A member of that order told me that his group had realized that good preaching rises only from a life of prayer. It comes only from a person who knows the love of God personally. The same thing is true in bringing comfort to the sick and dying. The only ones who can bring real comfort to the dying are those who, in spite of trouble and conflict and doubt, know the love of God from their own experience in prayer and meditation.

In order to bring this attitude of hope to the dying we need to let the knowledge of God's love permeate our entire lives. As we allow his love to flow through us, our words and actions become convincing to people on the verge of death. If we have known the experience of dying to our own desires and to all that seems central to our lives, and then rising again with new hope, we can share the fear and pain that come with the approach of death. Thus we can be aware that there can be resurrection on the other side of death. If one realizes that dying and being resurrected is an eternal process, one can then help the dying by bringing hope into their darkness.

It is futile and frivolous to chatter about God's love, or to tell someone who is dying that there is nothing to fear in death. Tactics like these keep dying people from expressing their real fears. They become even more isolated at this time when they need companionship most. In a class in which we were studying the best ways of working with the dying, the members were asked: How would you feel if you were about to face a firing squad? There were various answers, and the group came to the conclusion that only those who realized that they would be terribly frightened were really facing their fear of death. As individuals became more open to their true feelings, the group agreed that death is awesome and that people's inability to admit their fear leaves them without protection against the darkness and insecurity that threaten the human psyche.

Groups like this class are one way of preparing to work with the dying. With the support of other like-minded, normally healthy people, individuals can explore their fear of death and learn how to deal with the hopelessness that can engulf them. This can be a heavy trip, sometimes a shattering one, even for supposedly normal people. We have built a strong facade against facing death. When it crumbles, the experience of death is often agonizing. Even so, in this class many of the students, many of them preparing for medicine, felt that this group provided one of the most valuable learning experiences of their lives. In an article entitled "Facing Death and Suffering" I have described the procedures we followed and some of the results. The reading list which we used as a base for discussions is included as Appendix D.

Much the same preparation is helpful in dealing with people who have lost someone they love. These individuals are facing death in two ways. They know it both outwardly and within themselves. The terror and meaninglessness and loneliness of death has brought them into the presence of the actual destructive force that is working in us. As Edgar Herzog shows in *Psyche and Death*, the bereaved are sometimes more afraid than the dying. If they are to deal creatively with their situation, they must face the fact that they are usually as much concerned about themselves as about the person who has died. People in this situation are often more open to a genuine "search for meaning" than at any other time in their lives. True mourning is a death experience in itself. It can lead to a new understanding of life and bring one into the presence of God. Much of what I shall say about ministering to the dying also applies to ministering to the bereaved.

The Needs of the Dying

Nothing is more needed by the dying than constant, reliable companionship. They are already separated from the normal flow of life and they know the pain of loneliness. To have someone care enough to visit them is important. Even inept visiting is better than none at all. Simply coming again and again conveys understanding, consolation and love. It conveys more than words one says or does not say. What is really important is to keep coming regularly and not break off the contact. It is almost better not to come at all than to start visiting a dying person and then find that one is too busy to continue the visits. The dying are sensitive, and one thing they don't need is further rejection at this time when life already seems to be rejecting them. We take on a real responsibility when we start

ministering to the dying. One can never know how long a person
will go on living, and anyone who really feels responsibility is
locked into caring about the person as long as it takes.

Few of us have known what it means to be listened to adequately. We hunger for the listening that expresses real love. The
need of the dying is even greater. If someone will only sit quietly
with hands outstretched in a gesture of openness, and listen to
them, just listen, the dying person soon understands that one is
there just because one cares, that one is not trying to entertain them,
or ask them to perk up, or make any other demands on them.

Shortly before she died my mother spoke to me about the way
some people had treated her during the long months of her illness.
There had been friends and family, she said, who came just to be
with her quietly, and they had helped her to carry on simply by
listening openly, with acceptance. But there were others who
seemed to demand and take something from her. They seemed to
come needing to be reassured, almost asking to be entertained so as
to forget their own troubles. The hours I spent quietly with my
mother during those last months taught me much about the value of
quiet listening.

There can even be periods of complete silence. One story is told
which illustrates this possibility. A man who was being counseled
arrived one day for his regular session. The counselor welcomed him
and sat down across from him, arms outstretched, open and ready.
But the man sat there and said nothing. Five minutes, ten minutes
went by. Half an hour passed in complete silence. Finally the hour
came to an end. The counselor stood up, and the man reached over
and shook the counselor's hand and said, "You will never know
what this hour has meant to me. I didn't believe that anyone could
stand me for a whole hour without talking." People who are dying
can't help feeling much the same way a lot of the time. Ministering
to them is not very different from ministering to any of us who are
not too sure of ourselves, except that the dying are more sensitive,
and we may not have a chance to correct our mistakes.

Anyone can learn to listen. This is something which can be
learned through teaching techniques of quiet, responsive, non-judg-
ing, non-evaluating types of listening. Before practicing it on the
dying one should learn to listen to people who are hale and hearty.
It is amazing how often we think we are listening to someone, when
the truth is that if we were to ask the other person if he or she has

felt listened to, we would learn that he or she has not felt listened to at all. The other person to whom one is listening is the only person who can tell us whether we are hearing him or her or not. It is not our job to set such a person straight or to express our opinions, but it is our job to warmly and openly listen. Few people have ever been listened to enough.

Love depends upon listening. One cannot love another without knowing that person, and we have no real way of knowing people until we listen to them. Listening is so important for love that training in it should be a part of the education of all Christians. But listening can be learned only in interaction with other human beings. Reading about it can be helpful,[1] but the ability to listen comes from working with people, particularly with those who know how to listen. They can be found and are usually glad to help others learn this ability.

The dying have even more need than most of us for the simple human contact expressed by touching them. This is a natural way of letting a dying person know our feelings for him or her.* Sitting at the bedside of someone who is dying and simply holding his or her hand may convey more than all the words that could be said. A touch conveys the feeling that one is with the person sharing the pain and fear that have to be borne. It is like the kiss of peace among close friends in a eucharistic celebration.

Visiting the dying can be a truly sacrificial ministry. People who are facing death often make things difficult for everyone around them. They generally go through stages of denial and bargaining, of despair and depression, of anger and hopelessness. Anyone who spends much time with a dying person will sometimes feel that he or she has become the target of the person's anger. One must be very secure in order to listen and not react to the anger expressed. It is like listening creatively to people with any kind of depression.

---

*While everyone has this need to be touched and sense human care in this direct way, we are usually afraid to touch individuals whom we are counseling or ministering to. There is good reason for most of us to avoid such a suggestion of intimacy. One can become caught in the psychological process known as transference. This process can weave a web of either mutual attraction or mutual repulsion and hatred, and in either case one becomes involved in situations that are beyond individual control.[2]

The situation of the dying, of course, is different. One does not have to worry about transference in working with the dying. We can allow our natural human feelings to guide us.

We can help them only if we have dealt with the things within ourselves that can drag people into depression. We can offer nothing that will really change the situation until we know the way darkness and fear and anger work within each of us. This is not easy. But it is necessary if one is to recognize the fear that lurks behind most anger. If we can bear the anger, then we can find the crying child within the other person and be able to pick it up and give comfort.

Before we even think about visiting the dying, it is important to know how to keep our own fears and hurts and angers from being projected out upon other people. The best way is to look deeply within and acknowledge our emotional needs, and then lay them aside for the moment. One can then approach the dying to fulfill the needs that St. Francis stressed—to console and love and understand them, rather than to ask for consolation, love, and understanding. It is always difficult for us to give in this way without any strings attached, but giving of ourselves to the dying is probably easier than giving in this way to most other people. As one succeeds in reaching out to the dying, one dies and rises again and the reality of the Gospel comes alive. The kingdom of heaven may not be so far away if we will take the next step and treat all human beings in the way that we try to treat the dying.

Prayer, of course, has a special place in meeting the needs of the dying. Over the years I have learned that praying silently within myself as well as aloud helps to bring me in touch with the person and also makes the realm into which that person is entering more real. Most people have expressed a need for prayers spoken aloud, and I usually ask that God's perfect will might be accomplished in the individual, that pain might be diminished and that the person will be relieved of fear and given peace. Many people have thanked me for the comfort this simple prayer has brought them. Saying the Lord's Prayer is also helpful. This prayer touches people's religious roots, particularly if they share in saying it.

The Eucharist gives great consolation to many people with a sacramental background, so long as they do not consider it a rite administered to sick people only at the point of death. The dying often experience real peace as the final words of blessing are spoken, even when these words are used by themselves and not as a part of the Communion rite. For some people it is important to use the familiar form of Communion that they have used all their life rather than the form given specifically for the sick. The familiar form often carries a meaning for them that the shortened or more modern forms do not. One can simply ask the person which form he or she prefers and use the one that is asked for.

The meaning of these ways of prayer, however, will depend largely on one's life and practice. If prayer is like a costume put on just for certain occasions, it generally doesn't fit too well. Our best preparation for ministering to the dying is to have a real and vivid relationship with the Lord of love, and to experience this sense of care for us no matter what we are or what we have been. We will then realize that the Divine Lover wants to give love to us whenever we open ourselves to this reality.

When we are truly sensitive to the needs of the dying, we realize that there comes a time when the dying do not wish to get well and should be prepared to move on into the next life. It is difficult to perform this act of love and release the individual, unless we believe that there is another dimension of reality into which we can move. How does one relate to a person who has come to this point? The best suggestions that I have seen on this subject were written by Carl and Stephanie Simonton in their book *Getting Well Again*. As doctors they want to do everything they can to help patients get well. But there comes a time when it is their task to help a person release his or her hold on life and move on, and they have described how they approach this step.

There is also a real place for intercessory prayer for the dying and the deceased. It seems very likely that in the next life we come to a place of transformation and growth, rather than a final separation of the sheep from the goats. Some of us may need the prayers of the living to give us the courage and strength to go on trying to grow and be brought to our full potential. If there is any truth to the Church's doctrine of the communion of saints, then we do have a channel of communication with the world beyond. We are not fair either to ourselves or to those on the other side when we ignore this possibility. By dropping all connection with people once they have died, we say more about our real belief about the chance of a world to come than our best phrased statements of faith.

The dying need us human beings. This is an important ministry in which many people can give of themselves. It is a selfless ministry in which there seem to be few visible returns. Some of the greatest saints found their most complete satisfaction in visiting and ministering to the dying. St. Catherine of Genoa and her followers ministered not only to people dying of disease, but to those condemned to death. The prospect of death faces us with human need in its most extreme form. In the dying we find the needs of the poor and hungry, and prisoners, the naked and the thirsty combined. This ministry demands that we share the love which is given to us as we encounter the Christ who met death and conquered it in order to lift us out of that dark pit.

We can meet the needs of the dying by the same kind of loving action that is generally effective in helping human beings grow toward maturity and wholeness. Death is a natural stage of life. It is one more step in human development which requires our last loving action for the person in this life.

XII. What About Reincarnation?

In recent years the interest in reincarnation among Western Christians has grown by leaps and bounds. This has come at a time when most Westerners have lost their belief in any significant spiritual reality, and reincarnation seems to provide materialists with an acceptable way of imagining how we humans can hope for a future life. It gives them a way of believing that we will get a second chance and can hope for continued growth without having to look beyond the material world.

Reincarnation is probably the most widely held view of the afterlife known to human beings. It is the point of view of nearly all Hindus and most Buddhists, both in India and in China and Japan. The increasing influence of these religions on Western Christians has brought more and more acceptance of their basic thinking, particularly about the nature of life after death. People seem to have a real need for some way of picturing eternal life and they look for whatever belief they are able to accept.

In addition many psychics come to an apparently independent belief in the reality of reincarnation. Edgar Cayce is probably the best known and the most convincing of this group. He not only healed the sick through his amazing psychic powers, but he also gave life readings which seemed to reveal people's former incarnations. There are also some interesting cases of people who claim to know who they were in a former life. Sometimes they give accurate descriptions of a person who actually lived and reveal intimate details of that person's life. Occasionally there is even a physical resemblance between the two individuals.

A lot has been written about reincarnation for popular consumption. The books of Gina Cerminara, *Many Mansions* and *The World Within*, have sold hundreds of thousands of copies. *The Seth Material* and *Seth Speaks* by Jane Roberts and *Many Lifetimes* by Joan Grant and Denys Kelsey (who is not related to me as far as I know) also speak of this subject and are also widely read. While some of this current material consists mainly of anecdotes without much effort to understand them critically, I have found works by two men that show careful and serious study. These are Leslie D. Weatherhead's *The Case for Reincarnation* and Ian Stevenson's *Twenty Cases Suggestive of Reincarnation* and *The Evidence for Survival from Claimed Memories of Former Incarnations*. Weatherhead is a well-known Christian minister, while Stevenson is a professor of psychiatry at the University of Virginia Medical School. They each present a balanced and thoughtful case for reincarnation.

Reasons for Believing in Reincarnation

A variety of reasons are given by various people for expecting to return to life as we know it now. Let us look at these ideas in some detail and try to see how they can best be understood.

1. The oldest, most traditional idea sees reincarnation as the necessary way in which justice is established in this universe. According to this point of view in this present life we humans are given very different lots. But through the invariable law of *karma* everyone has the chance to change and become something more (or less). Earth is our learning ground. As we go from incarnation to incarnation, we learn more and more. If we do well we are rewarded by going on to a more desirable state. But when we don't make something of what we are given, we are punished by starting life over from a worse beginning. By means of *karma* and reincarnation one gets exactly what one deserves. There is no need to worry about the apparent inequities in life. One can be sure of the just nature of God and the universe. In the long run everything will work out with perfect justice.

2. Weatherhead feels that reincarnation not only assures the justice of the universe, but it helps to make sense of life. It shows us how we can grow and become. He believes that the universe operates purely on cause and effect and that transmigration of souls is

one good example of how the universe works. When people suffer now, one can see that it is because they did so badly in their previous incarnations. We need only look for the psychic cause and effect to understand their suffering. Weatherhead seems to need some such understanding of the universe in order to feel comfortable in it.

3. In addition he considers that reincarnation explains our ability to progress and develop in this life. The individual, he feels, starts with the abilities that were developed in the previous existence. Mozart, for instance, showed incredible musical ability as a child. Weatherhead believes that Mozart brought this ability with him from a former incarnation.

4. Some individuals who deal with emotionally disturbed people find evidence that reincarnation may account for the problems of these people. They are troubled by fears and desires that make no sense in the context of their present lives. But they can sometimes be helped, as Morris Netherton and Nancy Shiffrin suggest in *Past Lives Therapy*, by seeing their condition in a former existence. In this way, by believing that the fears and compulsions came from another lifetime, they may find that these problems are resolved.

5. The voices that mediums hear apparently have a good deal to say about reincarnation, and these discarnate spirits seem to convince quite a few people that this is the reality they will find after death.

6. The readings of former lives which Edgar Cayce and perhaps a handful of other sensitives have been able to give people seem to be in some ways even more convincing. The readings apparently tell the individuals so much about themselves that they find it hard to disbelieve.

7. Finally, there are the alleged memories of people who describe details of a former existence which turns out to be the life of someone who actually lived. Sometimes they describe an individual who lived in the recent past so that most of what they say can be checked out, and yet there is no way the facts could have come to them through sensory means. Dr. Stevenson's study is the most careful analysis of this kind of occurrence available. In it he tells of several children who began spontaneously to talk about their "other family," whom they had no way of knowing, and to pinpoint details of life in that family with amazing accuracy.

Understanding the Experiences

These last experiences seem to offer the best evidence for reincarnation. Do they prove it as a fact, or are there other ways to account for these apparent memories of another life? In his painstaking cross-cultural study Dr. Stevenson has considered eight different ways in which this evidence might be explained. Let us first look at these possible explanations.

1. Obviously there may be fraud. Men and women often go to great lengths to convince themselves and others of certain ideas, and they may do deceptive things either consciously or unconsciously. It does not seem likely, however, that the people who report these experiences are very often involved in fraud.

2. A second possibility is that people learned the facts about their supposedly former existence through perfectly normal means. They then forgot all about it until something happened in their lives which brought the dead person to mind and made them feel closely identified with the facts they had learned about that person. Something quite similar happened to me when I was looking for a title for my book on meditation. *The Other Side of Silence* came to me. I thought it was entirely my own creation. Then I went to visit my stepmother in Pennsylvania and she remarked that it was interesting where I had come up with the title for my new book. She went to the shelf and took down Sir Hugh Clifford's *The Further Side of Silence,* which had been one of my father's favorite stories. It had been forty years since I had read it, and I had completely forgotten the story, title and all. I opened it and started to read, and soon realized that faint memories of the story were beginning to come back. This mine of buried memory, popping up from the past, can certainly account for some instances of feeling identity with a dead individual, but not for all of them.

3. The fact of "racial memory" as pointed out by Jung and others can definitely explain many experiences that suggest knowledge of a former life. This is the understanding that there is a vast psychic pool available to all of us in which everything which has ever happened to human beings still exists and can be recalled. A whole realm of experience from beyond the physical world, or sometimes in the distant past, can be tapped in dreams. It can be brought to consciousness through meditation or other spiritual practices, or by certain individuals who are simply sensitive to it. Dr.

Stevenson who wrote *Twenty Cases Suggestive of Reincarnation* obviously does not understand this important kind of experience.* We shall come back to it after we look at the other possible explanations of these intimations of another existence.

4. It is possible to account for nearly any "memory" from the life of an individual who has died through the capacity for extrasensory perception known as telepathy. Recollections of a dead person can be picked up from the minds of living people through telepathy, and one can even acquire feelings which might place the memories as one's own. But this explanation fits only some of the experiences that are described.

5. Just as precognition allows one to see into the future, there is also an extrasensory ability to see the unknown past, which is known as retrocognition. This ability undoubtedly explains some of the facts and even some of the feelings about a previous life that come to people. (This argument is closely related to the idea discussed in section 3 above.)

6. Communications from a surviving personality in another kind of existence, or from a split-off part of a personality, can also account for information about another life, which an individual might feel was his or her former life.

7. Some of the experiences which seem to support the idea of reincarnation may actually result from some kind of possession. The person is sometimes described as being possessed by a discarnate spirit.

8. Then there is the possibility that these "memories" and other experiences actually show that our personalities survive in a reincarnated form. After an exhaustive analysis of this wide range of alternatives, Dr. Stevenson seems to be clearly convinced that the hypothesis of reincarnation offers the best explanation for the various stories and data he presents. He suggests no way in which our lives and personalities might continue on after death other than through reincarnation.

My own conclusion is different. It seems to me that a thinker like Dr. Stevenson would see further possibilities if the Church were doing its job and trying to provide an adequate view of reality. The problem is that Dr. Stevenson is trying to deal with a puzzle that

---

*Stevenson speaks only of "genetic memory" which may be passed from father to son or others in a direct blood line.

God himself could not solve if he did not have a bigger view of the facts than the materialism accepted by most churches today. This view of reality cannot help making people uncomfortable with the whole idea of an afterlife, and so most churches have simply copped out. They use some pleasant rhetoric and soothing, poetic words about heaven, but that is about all. While poetry can touch some people deeply, it is seldom convincing when its message runs counter to the dominant world-view. *Reincarnation has filled the vacuum left when the Church stopped believing in eternal life and ceased to speak of the victory won by Jesus Christ.*

Another View

Once we realize that there is good reason to stand behind the world-view proposed by Jesus, then the Church can begin to show with conviction that there is a realm apart from the material world in which our lives will continue after death. There is more and more support for this understanding of a non-physical or spiritual realm in modern thought.

This is Jung's basic understanding of "racial memories." It is supported by thinkers like C. D. Broad, Henri Bergson and Aldous Huxley, who realize that all that has ever happened and much of what is to come exist side by side in a vast realm which is so similar to the human soul that it is described as "psychoid" or spiritual. As long as we live in this world, however, we are protected by the brain and nervous system from being bombarded by information from this realm and distracted from daily living. This is apparently why it is usually known only in dreams, as I have mentioned, or through practices like meditation. This point of view has been developed by Robert Ornstein in his book *The Psychology of Consciousness*. It is also supported by Einstein's view of the world and by the theory, described in an earlier chapter, that the universe is a unified field in which nothing totally passes away.

Once this view is understood, the facts that seem to support reincarnation begin to fall into place. There is no time or space in this realm, or in the depth of the human soul which Jung called the collective unconscious. Memories can be received, particularly in dreams, from people beyond the grave. Communications can come, apparently from various sources, about either the past or the future. Precognition as well as retrocognition and communication with surviving personalities can be understood within this point of view. Once we realize that human beings can be in touch with many beings in another realm of existence, then people's "memories" of their previous existence can be understood as simply present experiences of another time or place or realm of experience.

This is my main reason for doubting that reincarnation should be considered as a general theory of survival. It is not needed to account for the various facts that are cited. Unexpected, intimate knowledge about the life of someone who has died may come from an actual psychic encounter with the person, or with someone else from the same time and place. The idea of participation in a spiritual or psychoid realm is a simpler theory than reincarnation, and it explains more phenomena. In that non-physical world events and people both continue to exist in a real sense. One can be in touch with any element from any time or place in this realm that sometimes seems like a vast bank of non-physical data.

Although Weatherhead tries to show that the idea of reincarnation is found in the Bible and in Christian tradition, I am not convinced by the references which he presents.* It is quite possible that there have been Christian groups at certain times who believed in this idea, just as some Hebrews did. But there is little evidence for reincarnation in either the Old Testament or the teachings of Jesus, and the Church Fathers certainly did not present it as a *general theory* of what happens to human beings after death. There is good reason why they avoided any such theory.

In the first place, one of the main reasons for believing in transmigration of souls is that it provides for justice in an unjust world. The proponents of this theory do not feel that it is possible for God to be merciful and for human beings to be transformed through his mercy. Some people believe in the torments of hell for the same reason. It is the only way they can bolster their idea of God's perfect justice. The New Testament and the Church Fathers, however, stressed God's mercy, not his justice. If mercy is more the essence of God than justice, then there is no need to propose the

---

*Geddes MacGregor, emeritus professor of philosophy at the University of Southern California, also supports the idea of a Christian belief in reincarnation. His book *Reincarnation in Christianity* was published in 1978 by the Theosophical Publishing House in Wheaton, Illinois.

Weatherhead refers to the following passages of Scripture to support his belief; Job 1:21, Ecclesiastes 6:6, Psalm 126:6, Matthew 11:14, 16:13, 17:12, Mark 9:11, Luke 9:18, John 9:2.

unvarying and rigid system of rewards and punishments which reincarnation involves.

Second, many people believe that reincarnation alone provides the milieu in which growth can occur, and they do not believe that spiritual reality can offer any such medium of growth. On the other hand, when people break out of the materialistic framework, they generally seem to find that the non-physical spiritual world is just as real as the physical one and that it provides just as much opportunity for growth and transformation as our life in the physical world. In fact, the New Testament writers and the Church Fathers seemed to believe that the world of the soul, the non-physical or psychoid world, is a better place in which to learn and grow and be transformed because it is more open to God and his powers of mercy and light than the physical one. Reincarnation does not give a very deep or adequate view of spiritual reality and its infinite depth and variety.

There was probably one more reason that the early Christians avoided the theory of reincarnation. This idea does not give much impetus to an active life of moral action. If everyone is actually getting what he or she deserves, there is little point in trying to improve the lot of people who are in miserable circumstances. As I have mentioned elsewhere, the Hare Krishna people made this apparent to some of my classes at Notre Dame. When they met with us to present their chanting and their views, they insisted that one should not try to help the miserable because it might mess up their *karma* and force them to come through this world of toil and sin still another time. The idea of reincarnation may encourage people to improve their own lives and their relation with God, but it does nothing to arouse them to reach out to the miserable and poverty-stricken all over the world. Yet this was one main emphasis of Jesus' message.

Dr. Jung has suggested that too much concern with reincarnation, or any other question about life after death, can involve people in so much speculation that they sometimes turn away from the central business of life and may even be swallowed by the unconscious. He wrote:

> We are dependent for our myth of life after death upon the meager hints of dreams and similar spontaneous revelations from the unconscious. . . . We cannot attribute to these allusions the value of knowl-

edge, let alone proof. They can, however, serve as suitable bases for mythic amplifications; they give the probing intellect the raw material which is indispensable for its vitality. Cut off the intermediary world of mythic imagination, and the mind falls prey to doctrinaire rigidities. On the other hand, too much traffic with these germs of myth is dangerous for weak and suggestible minds, for they are led to mistake vague intimations for substantial knowledge, and to hypostatize mere phantasms.[1]

He then went on to a wise discussion of the idea of reincarnation and *karma*, concluding with these words:

> I know no answer to the question of whether the karma which I live is the outcome of my past lives, or whether it is not rather the achievement of my ancestors, whose heritage comes together in me. Am I a combination of the lives of these ancestors and do I embody these lives again? Have I lived before in the past as a specific personality, and did I progress so far in that life that I am now able to seek a solution? I do not know. Buddha left the question open, and I like to assume that he himself did not know with certainty.

> I could well imagine that I might have lived in former centuries and there encountered questions I was not yet able to answer; that I had to be born again because I had not fulfilled the task that was given to me. When I die, my deeds will follow along with me—that is how I imagine it. I will bring with me what I have done. In the meantime it is important to insure that I do not stand at the end with empty hands. Buddha, too, seems to have had this thought when he tried to keep his disciples from wasting time on useless speculation.[2]

For my own part, I have one prejudice which makes it difficult for me to believe in reincarnation, although I recognize that this is not a good reason. The doctrinaire and poorly reasoned arguments of most believers turn me away from the idea. I strongly doubt the final truth of any easy, doctrinaire belief.

My conclusion about reincarnation is that it is a possible occurrence. No one knows what God allows in certain situations. Perhaps God in his infinite mercy allows certain people to return to earth who are totally attached to it. This idea was suggested by Arthur Ford in *The Life Beyond Death*. Those who are completely bound to earth and earth's pleasures may be allowed to try it through another time. As a general principle, however, either of justice in the universe or to explain what happens to everyone at death until they are ready to enter *Nirvana,* reincarnation does not seem to me an adequate theory. Most of the data produced in support of this idea can be accounted for more adequately and simply by the hypothesis of the collective unconscious or the reality of a vibrantly real spiritual world. If God is as loving and merciful as most of the Christian saints have claimed, and as I have found him to be, it does not seem likely that he wants us to go through the same kind of tasks all over again.

My own hope is that I won't have to go through this life again. Once is enough for me. And knowing my many transgressions and faults and failings, I certainly hope that I don't have to pay for them in full. When I say the words of the Apostles' Creed—"I believe in . . . the forgiveness of sins"—I mean them. I do not expect to have all the sin wiped away, but I have suffered a good deal of pain and torment for these wrong-doings and I believe that I can be received by my Lord with mercy and forgiveness. Reincarnation without more memory of one's past life than most people would appear to be given seems an almost intolerable destiny. Eternal life looks much, much more attractive to me.

XIII. The Problem of Hell

The idea of hell is certainly not popular among most modern Christians. There are good reasons why so many people have abandoned this idea. As belief in the spiritual world began to fade, the less attractive parts of it quite naturally disappeared first. For a long time preachers in most branches of the Christian Church did their best to frighten people into being religious and good by giving them large doses of hell-fire and damnation. Even into this century many a sermon was patterned on Jonathan Edwards' famous preaching of *Sinners in the Hands of an Angry God*. Hell was seen as a reality of flaming fire just below the earth's crust. Those whose actions did not please God would be plunged into it to burn until the end of time.

It is easier to use fear as a persuader than to try to draw people toward God and goodness by loving action. But fear of retribution and punishment does not often change people, except momentarily. Ultimately they reacted against this kind of religion and its idea of a God who treats human beings worse than they treat each other. The traditional hell sounds more like a torture chamber concocted by demons than the way a loving and caring father would treat his children, no matter how bad they were. Why bother if the stories of God's love are so completely false?

Christians who make up their minds that it is good for humans to be judged and frightened by visions of hell know little about the struggle that goes on in the depth of most of us. Most people are already judging themselves too much and for the wrong things. The task in counseling, as I have indicated, is usually to help individuals accept more of themselves and not judge and reject so much. Anyone who is brought to a halt by an anxiety neurosis or depression knows the agony that is caused by coming face to face with the whole of our humanness. When there is no busy-ness or human contact that can screen off the rejected parts, the unacceptable elements, hell is no longer a theory but a stark reality. The punishment of a violent, agitated depression is real enough without dreaming up Jonathan Edwards' hell. There are times, in fact, when ordinary flames might even be a welcome relief.

The Reality of Hell

In times of quiet and self-examination people find much the same suffering. This is one reason so few individuals go very far into prayer and meditation. The quiet that is required brings us into direct confrontation with the hidden, rejected parts of our being. I know how hard it is to face these elements—my indolence and stupidity, the pride, lust, cruelty and senseless destructiveness that I try to hide even from myself. The suffering involved in having to deal with the whole of one's being is more than most of us can stand. One can imagine people in hell sitting on a meaningless plain where nothing grows, haunted by their worst fears and guilts, and being stuck there forever, depressed and castigating themselves for it all. This would certainly be hell.

Since heaven and hell are both experiences either *in* or *of* (coming from) the spiritual realm, there is no reason to believe that one has to die to experience either one. Heaven and hell can both be found here and now as well as in the hereafter. People who experience the blackest depressions do not speak of entering a void. Far from it, they describe being pursued by fearful terrors and experiencing a destructive, tormenting reality that makes every moment intense agony. Their descriptions often fit the classic picture of hell. While they do not have to stay in this condition, as I shall suggest, the hell they describe is no less real.

Grof and Halifax in their book which I have referred to earlier describe an experience like hell or purgatory in their LSD therapy with patients dying with cancer. They found that most of their subjects experienced a violent and traumatic confrontation with constriction and pain at one stage of their treatment. The authors see this experience as a kind of rebirth experience in which the pains of rebirth are a natural prelude for the later stage of transcendence which is experienced by many of those who underwent LSD therapy. They show how nearly universal such experiences of rebirth as a stage of religious development are in the religions of humankind. Strangely, however, they never mention the Christian conviction about death and rebirth which is so central to the Christian liturgy of baptism and to Christian devotion.

It seems quite superficial to think that people will jump from this kind of suffering, or from the other agonizing problems and pain of this life, straight into perfect bliss. The idea that in the twinkling of an eye we will all be transformed into perfectly happy and secure individuals suggests that the problems and suffering we face in this life are not really important. This does not seem to be the idea of the New Testament. There is no indication in it that our present experiences are considered trivial, either in this world or in the world beyond. On the contrary, there are many suggestions, especially in the Gospels, that our experiences, our suffering and the way we react have a real effect on what happens to us after death.

There does not seem to be much question that there is an actual hell which may keep some people from stepping directly into eternal bliss. But there are three specific questions about that hell: Will it last forever? Is there any possibility of changing the direction of one's life after leaving this earth? Is there a part of the spiritual world which is subject only to the Evil One? The thing that bothers thinking people the most is how to reconcile the idea of eternal punishment with our experiences of a loving and merciful God. It is probably true that God does not want to force growth or bliss on anyone who really prefers the torment of his or her own pride. But if God is actually merciful, how could he leave any individual with no options whatever? And if he really is all-powerful, how can he keep from using his power to close down the establishment run by Satan?

On many occasions Jesus let people know that living this life and preparing for the next one is serious business. He warned them against mistreating anyone or refusing to take the way of God seriously. Jesus did not promise people a Pollyannaish afterlife any more than he suggested that his followers in this life would find their path strewn with roses and approval. The way of the cross which he demonstrated is hard, but it is the way of transformation, of finding the lost parts of ourselves, as well as the lost souls in this world.

Jesus stressed the woes of the lost (Matthew 5:22, 29; 10:28;

18:9; 23:15; Mark 9:43-48; Luke 12:5), but he did not promise to make their problems any easier. I have sometimes complained strenuously that he could have made the way easier, that it does not have to be nearly so difficult to renounce evil and seek God. But I do not really expect an answer when it is given so clearly in the Gospels.*

I am not so sure, however, about the various statements of unending time that Jesus was reported to have made. I question whether he was expressing a final philosophical statement about things that could never change in all eternity. Such an idea of perpetual, unending time is almost impossible to express in either Aramaic or Hebrew. I am inclined to believe that he was presenting a picture, a poetic image in a way that people would not be able to forget, and that the idea of human beings left in a permanent condition that would never change was not intended to be taken literally.

Salvation and Growth

The literal interpretation of eternal punishment is very difficult to support in the light of Jesus' mission on earth. If we understand that Jesus was the Christ who was here on earth for the purpose of freeing human beings from the powers of hell, then it is hard to imagine him consigning anyone to everlasting punishment with no chance of changing or being rescued. After all, this is what salvation is all about. Anyone who will really try to follow Jesus' way of love (for oneself as well as for others and for God) can be freed from the destructive reality of hell, either now or in the hereafter. Jesus came to destroy the power of that kingdom, and the lost who are caught in it are the very ones that he is offering to save.

Salvation begins right here on earth among people who suffer mental anguish that is just as bad as anything we can imagine in a hell hereafter. Some of them have been very holy people. Thomas Merton, for instance, endured almost intolerable depressions during certain periods of his life. In addition, *growth itself is not an easy process, and it does not occur without pain.* Pain of all kinds, physical, mental and

---

*Jesus told us that he came not to bring peace but a sword (Matthew 10:34-39; Luke 12:51-53), and he challenged us to split from our conventional attitudes and try the difficult road toward wholeness, toward fulfilling all the human potential of which we are capable. He asked us not just to take actions, but to *become* fully human, fully ourselves.

spiritual, seems to be part of the fabric of life and an inevitable element of growth or individuation.

Individuation, or the process of spiritual and psychic growth of the individual, involves a kind of death. One's ego must die to make room for a new center of being which is given. The worst thing about death is the utter giving up of oneself to the unknown. In this process of giving up the ego people usually experience negative realities from the unconscious like the terrifying encounters described by Jung in Chapter 6 of *Memories, Dreams, Reflections* and by Carlos Castaneda in *The Teachings of Don Juan*. People who go this way must endure suffering as intense as the agony of actual death. They often wonder if it can be endured. There are times, in fact, when one would gladly exchange it for simple dissolution into meaningless molecules. To invite such experience, Jung wrote in his "Psychological Commentary on 'The Tibetan Book of the Dead,'" is like "meddling with fate, which strikes at the very roots of human existence and can let loose a flood of sufferings of which no sane person ever dreamed."[1]

Yet, as Jung acknowledged, anyone who goes through the individuation process must pass through this kind of experience. One of the real insights of *The Tibetan Book of the Dead* is that there is no avoiding the growth process. Those who do not make the confrontation during this earthly life will be faced with making it in the next world. But most of us go right on avoiding the way of growth. For many people the nihilism of modern thought provides an easy out. If one simply believes that there is not going to be any future life, there are not so many demands on the individual at present. Very likely this attitude is motivated by unconscious fear of life. Then there are people who are not aware of the depth of the psyche and have a sentimental idea of death as an easy transition to a life of bliss, harping on the clouds. Existential thinkers are right to ridicule this naiveté. It debases not only death but life itself, as a simple, unconscious process, basically without direction.

On the other hand, people who confront the negative contents of the unconscious lose their fear of physical death for a different reason. They have met realities that are even *more* terrifying, and they have found the possibility of rebirth. Dreams of death do not frighten them because they realize that these productions of the unconscious generally point the way to rebirth, giving specific hints for the dreamer's own life. Usually dreams of death do not mean one is going to die physically. Rather, they mean that a part of the individual will die, has died, or should die. When such dreams are understood, people often find new awareness and understanding, a wider and more developed consciousness. New developments in the person's outer life often come at the same time.

In the past, various cultures have had initiation rites (such as the Eleusian mysteries in ancient Greece) which provided some experience of death and rebirth. Baptism has this meaning, and it can also be found in the Eucharist. The Church, however, does little to make this meaning available to people. Few clergy seem to have the confidence to stand by suffering individuals and try to help them pass through psychic death or neurosis. Instead these individuals are generally referred to an analyst. Yet, as Jung has complained, sometimes forcefully, the Church is the one place where such sufferers should be able to look for help and for a way out of their experience of death and hell.

If we can reconcile our opposing ideas about heaven and hell (both now and hereafter), and thus understand human experience a little better, the Church could draw many more people who need the help that it could offer. Let us look at the idea of hell in relation to the Church's understanding of purgatory,* which comes from the Jewish belief a century or more before Christ.

Hell and Purgatory

If we take seriously what Jesus said about heaven, then we certainly should be consistent and take what he said about hell seriously. According to Jesus there is a kingdom in which the Evil One reigns over the fallen angels and any humans who persistently rebel against following God's way. From here evil reaches out into the world to try in various ways to cut people off from God, from other human beings, and from the reality of their own being.

Jesus did not specify how this kingdom came into being, but he

---

*The need for a shift in emphasis is suggested by sales of Dante's *Divine Comedy*, in the translation by Dorothy Sayers and Barbara Reynolds. By 1976 *Hell* had gone through twenty-five printings, practically one a year. There has been some interest in heaven. In 1977 *Paradise* had been reprinted four times, or about once every three years. But *Purgatory* was still in the first printing after twenty-two years.

Are people not interested in a chance for continued growth after this present life? Or is the idea of purgatory as a place where individuals go on developing toward their greatest potential simply not understood by people today?

made it very clear that it was not God's idea. It was not created by him as a way of punishing disobedient humans or other offending spirits. There is clearly no basis for the idea that the Evil One is God's agent, responsible for tormenting anyone who fails to meet certain standards of holiness or does not take care to keep from being caught by evil.

Instead, as the Book of Revelation shows, the kingdom of hell was created when rebellion broke out in heaven (Revelation 12:7ff.). Satan, whom the Church Fathers knew as Lucifer or son of the morning,* was apparently the brightest and best of God's angels. But Lucifer evidently felt that he could run heaven better than God. He wanted to tidy things up and make heaven more efficient and rational and understandable. But when he rejected the incredible love that is the essence of God, Michael marshaled his angels and threw Lucifer out of heaven. He then created his own kingdom of hell.

Many people, of course, laugh at this ancient myth of good and evil. They are sure that it was only a foolish tale invented by human beings who had not learned enough. These people are generally convinced that there is no reality to evil. They see no reason why it should be found in our world except for the stupidity or stubborn perversity that keeps humans from doing the right thing. This explanation for evil is known in some religious circles as the idea of the *privatio boni*, or the theory that evil is caused simply by a deprivation or absence of good.

This theory makes little sense to people who have plumbed the depth of the human heart and have come to know the most profound aspects of our souls.** These individuals have dealt with human emotion. They know how our behavior is shaped by hope and joy, or anger, fear and depression, and how difficult it can be to understand and influence our ways of behaving. It my book, *Discernment: A Study in Ecstasy and Evil*, I have shown that it is next to impossible to work with the deepest emotions except by using the language of images and stories. Anyone who makes a real effort to

*The name Lucifer or "light-bearer" comes from Isaiah 14:9-20 where the Evil One was called the shining star, bright enough to be seen in the daylight. When he used his light to despoil the earth and take people prisoner, he fell or was thrown down from heaven into Sheol.

**The Church in its wisdom has never pronounced on the subject of evil and never ratified the idea that evil is only a privation or diminution of good.

get at the roots of the evil that influences people's actions must sooner or later realize that it comes from some source that is very real. The idea that evil results just from an absence of good is not adequate to explain our experiences of it.

As Jung remarked more than once, one can hardly explain the German concentration camps as merely an absence of good. The same thing is true of the Soviet labor camps. Evil of this kind seems to originate in a destructive kingdom of its own. This is the reality expressed in the myth in the Book of Revelation, and the same understanding is found in the world's greatest literature. In the West it was expressed by Dante, Shakespeare, Goethe, and now in the works of Tolkien. It was Charles Williams who first brought home to me the reality of the kingdom of evil in his seven powerful novels.[2] This was certainly the understanding of Jesus and the early Church.

The early Church made it very clear that God does not want anyone to be in hell. Over and over the belief was expressed that Jesus had come to take as many people out of hell as possible. This is the whole point of the incarnation and atonement, of God's being present in Jesus, of his death and resurrection. When people no longer believe in the reality of hell, the incredible mercy of God's sacrifice loses much of its meaning. God becomes almost a monster who sacrifices his Son simply to satisfy his own honor by ensuring that human beings would have to live up to his particular standards of holiness. When hell is eliminated as the kingdom from which Satan or Lucifer can reach out and enslave human beings, the whole understanding of the birth and life and death of Jesus as a rescue operation is lost.[*]

The idea of hell as an independent and powerful monarchy in communication with this present world is a central element of the belief that has come down to us from the apostles. The Apostles' Creed even holds that Jesus descended into hell, and not just on a sightseeing tour. As the early writings clearly show, Christians from the beginning understood that Jesus went down into hell in order to set free the dead who were caught there.[3] And this belief in the atonement was meant for everyone. Jesus would keep right on

---

[*]Gustaf Aulén has shown in his book *Christus Victor* that nearly the whole early Church accepted the ransom theory of the atonement. My suggestion is that it still makes sense when we learn to think in symbols, when we can understand and use mythology.

reaching out to both the living and the dead who became trapped by the powers of hell. This is just as true today as it was for those Christians who were closer to the actual life of Jesus.

There is nothing creative or valuable about hell. It is a pocket of destructive guerrilla resistance against God's kingdom and his love. It is an active, continuing resistance, a struggle to separate human beings from God. If we will give up our resistance and let God's love filter into us, even those who seem hopelessly caught in hell can be rescued. In the last chapter of my book on meditation, *The Other Side of Silence*, I have shared some of my own experiences of being delivered from the power of evil. In the section called "Three Violent Meditations" I describe the pain and fear of feeling oneself trapped in hell and suggest how one can be delivered out of that condition.

Even more recently I have known a time of inner darkness so great that I seemed to be buried in the very pit of hell. As I turned inward in meditation, I saw myself standing before the tribunal of hell, being condemned and mocked and tortured. I was stranded there, powerless to move, until I began to realize that, bad as I am, I did not deserve this. *As long as I feel that I really deserve the worst that hell can do, there is no way to get out of the agony.* But if I will stop to realize that I do not need to suffer like this, then the way opens up. This was the reason that Christ died, in order to release people like me from the pain of such imprisonment. As soon as this realization broke through, I felt the gates of hell collapsing, and there before me stood the bright figure of the transfigured one. The judges and persecutors fled in horror from the radiant light. Then the risen Christ took me in his arms and healed me and led me out of that place.

So often I am dragged into this place of agony, and each time the Christ graciously comes to rescue me once I wake up to the fact that I do not belong there in hell. Each time I am made aware once more that this is the central meaning of the atonement. It was never intended that we humans should wait to become free of this world before we begin the struggle against hell. We are supposed to seek rescue right now in order to open up our own way toward God's kingdom and help others find their way.

The first moments of release are perfect bliss. Then I realize that release is only a first step. Hell is static in that there is no place to go. Heaven, on the other hand, is a place of growth, and if I do not actively pursue that growth, I will almost certainly fall back into hell. Once I am released I must start the search for greater maturity and development. Since this process involves dying and rising again and again, it is not an easy way. Some people insist that it is given by God and so it must be easy. These are usually individuals who have not yet experienced the transforming effects of Love and the effort and humility and adaptation it demands of us.

In *The Great Divorce* C. S. Lewis uses the symbol of light to picture the transforming effect of heaven. People who are newly arrived in heaven find the place uncomfortable. They have been in the dark so long that they lack substance and the light is even painful to their eyes. Much the same thing can happen in this life to people who try, consciously or unconsciously, to keep their shadows (their negative sides) from showing. If a brand-new experience suddenly lights up their lives, they are often unable to handle it and go off the deep end because they have neglected the development that comes from knowing and working with the shadow side of our personalities. This may be just the difficulty of so many psychics who offer such a namby-pamby view of heaven. They may never have had a chance to discover that light can penetrate and burn as well as relax and illuminate.

These sentimental ideas about heaven should be taken with a grain of salt. The accounts of most psychics, such as Dr. Hans Holzer's *Beyond This Life*, are quite inadequate. This point is underscored by John Weldon and Zola Levitt in their fundamentalistic treatment of ideas about the afterlife, *Is There Life After Death?* While the original reports presented by Dr. Raymond Moody may seem to suggest an over-optimistic view of the next life in some ways, in his second book he shows that there are spirits who seem to be in a dark and uncomfortable place. In both books he also shows that the dead are apparently almost always asked to review the *whole of their lives*. The experiences described by Dr. Maurice Rawlings among his patients also indicate that encounters of a frightening nature may be more frequent than the first investigations showed.

These reports, of course, do not go beyond the first things that happen to people after death. For obvious reasons they do not deal with the possibility that we will continue to grow and develop, and that we may face as many problems trying to grow up in the next life as we do in this one.

The prospect of trying to continue the growth that we have

started here on earth is not entirely a pleasant one. As I have said and will undoubtedly say many more times, Jesus was not offering seductive promises of an easy way. His view of eternal life makes our task as Christians serious business. Personally I get very tired of keeping on trying to grow and mature. But the alternative seems far less palatable. Being left as one is, with no chance to develop or change, could be real imprisonment. In the end it may be actual hell. But if we can work along and try to grow and develop, it may be more like purgatory than hell. For most people it is easier to face the prospect of difficulty and hard work than the stagnation of hell.

Perhaps in purgatory one may be given a fresh start. St. Catherine of Genoa wrote that people in purgatory leap into their labors of purification and redemption because they have tasted and felt the reality of God's love and they hunger for more of it. The idea of such a place of growth and purification avoids the absurdity of seeing every one of us consigned to either a static hell or a static heaven, to either perpetual boredom (or some other torture) or perpetual ecstasy. The God whom I have known does not seem to have ideas like that. My experience indicates that he is a God of love who is really trying to lead us to become his sons and daughters and share with him more and more as instruments of his creation and peace.

The difference between hell and purgatory is not so much a matter of how long one will be there, whether temporarily or perhaps forever. Hell is a place where we are caught, often by our own sense of valuelessness which is created in us by one of the cleverest, most compelling techniques of the Evil One. Purgatory, on the other hand, is a place of redemption and renewal where we are transformed and grow more and more into children of God, closer and closer to the love of Abba. The real difference is that in hell I feel caught and do not know that I can get out, while in purgatory I know that I am free to work toward a destiny far more magnificent than we in this world can imagine.

Dr. George Ritchie describes the element of choice involved in life after death. In *Return from Tomorrow* he suggests that people seem to be in hell only because they cannot imagine or see the light, and so they continue in their meaningless obsessions and bickering. One of the finest descriptions of the optional nature of heaven and hell in modern literature is found in the novels of Charles Williams, particularly in *Descent into Hell* and *All Hallows' Eve.* Williams provides an unsurpassed vision of the afterlife. He sees life continuing the same essential quality after death that it had before, but he also sees a possibility for choice in the next life which can reverse the process. In *Descent into Hell* he describes the transformation of a workingman who committed suicide to avoid an ugly, unpleasant life. Faced with the alternatives in the next life, the man goes back to the point of his suicide to deal with life rather than avoiding it.*

In spite of this possibility for change people do become caught in hell. Let us look at the ways in which this can happen, and then ask whether there are people who may remain in hell forever and if we may have a chance to change our minds and our ways of reacting after we enter the next life.

Ways To Remain in Hell

There seem to be several ways to remain in hell. The surest way, of course, is to align oneself with evil, with hatred, destructiveness and pride. One of the problems with hell is that it is no longer painful once people are actively serving the devil and his purposes. Some souls in hell are like the humans that Aldous Huxley called "adrenaline addicts," who are not really happy unless they are angry and in a snit. These souls may actually relish their vindictive and destructive ways. Sometimes they even convince themselves that love is silly and weak and that they have chosen the stronger and better way.

There are at least a few who actively worship Satan. They are more interested in power and esteem than anything else, and they value elegance and self-expression. Their attitude is exactly opposite to the ideas expressed in the beatitudes. Such personalities are portrayed by C. S. Lewis in *That Hideous Strength* and by Charles Williams in *Shadows of Ecstasy*. While these individuals do exist, there are probably not many of them because acting in this way usually takes even more effort than serving God.

Another way of falling into hell and remaining there is to believe that we humans are entirely on our own and have to work out our own salvation for ourselves. Some people have tasted the bitter power of the Evil One in depression and raging anxiety and

---

*For those who find Williams' novels difficult to fathom, Helen Luke has provided an exposition of his seven novels in a privately printed booklet, *Through Defeat to Joy*, which can be obtained from her at Apple Farm, Three Rivers, Michigan.

have been rescued from this unconscious state. They have learned that none of us can manage entirely on our own. This is the real problem of individuals who take their own lives, either by the conscious act of suicide or by allowing illness or an accident to do it unconsciously. For one reason or another they have not found the help that is available, and they see only despair ahead by depending on themselves or other fallible human beings. And so they take the gift of life into their own hands as if it were theirs to dispose of. Much the same arrogance or assumption of power over life and death is involved in both murder and suicide. As the beatitudes show, this attitude does not open the way toward heaven, and other sources say the same thing. Suicide is a dangerous way to enter the other side of human existence.

The cause of most suicides is not physical pain, but the hope of escaping from inner agony, agony of the soul. In many cases the person is also tormented by a voice that screams within that one is valueless and deserves death, eternal death. But death does not seem to bring release from either the agony or the screaming, derogatory voice. The tragedy is that the person apparently leaps directly into the kingdom where the annihilating, insulting, belittling voice reigns supreme. Does this mean, however, that one must remain there forever? Or could the shock of finding oneself in hell bring people to themselves and make them humble enough to seek the help they need?

One can also risk remaining in hell by steadfastly refusing to believe that there is any heaven of grace or love, and then taking care to live and act in accordance with this belief. If the individual sees life only as cyclical variations of yin and yang with no possibility of reaching into eternity to encounter the Divine Lover, one can shut this reality out as if it did not exist. *What we will not or cannot imagine can seldom be encountered and realized in our lives.* This is one of the most important reasons for prayer and meditation. These practices open us up to the infinite reaches of heaven and divine love. We must first take the idea of divine love seriously in our heads, and then meditate on it, before we can translate it into reality in our lives and begin to act on that reality. Unless we will follow these steps in thought, imagination and action, realizing that our lives depend upon them, we may well find ourselves drawn into hell.

In addition we can be trapped in hell by a resolute decision not to face death and the prospect of rising again. The denial of death can keep us from living at all. When people refuse to acknowledge

the natural process of dying and rising again, they become caught in
death and may never graduate from the kingdom of the Evil One.
This point is well made by Ernest Becker in *The Denial of Death* and
by Edgar Herzog in *Psyche and Death*. Herzog in particular shows how
much agony is caused in this life by people's refusal to deal with
death.

One of the main tasks of effective psychotherapy is to help
people gain enough faith in the process of living so that they are
willing to face death and dissolution, trusting in resurrection. A
great deal of neurosis and psychosis arise from the resolute desires
of individuals to avoid the unpleasantness of death and the effort of
preparing for rebirth. Nothing binds one more firmly to emotional
illness and immaturity than this childish requirement that life be
pleasant at all times. Dying and rising are part of the eternal process.
If we insist on wasting our lives hoping in vain for some other way
out, we never get down to the real business of seeking and finding
life and light and the kingdom of love. I often wish reality were
different, but this seems to be what life is like.

Will Hell Last Forever?

Must we conclude, then, that this will always be true, and that
the kingdom of hell will last forever, keeping its victims hopeless
prisoners of the choices they made during their lives on earth? C. S.
Lewis has written wisely on this subject. In *The Problem of Pain* he
says:

> If a game is played, it must be possible to lose it. If the happiness of a
> creature lies in self-surrender, no one can make that surrender but
> himself (though many can help him to make it) and he may refuse. I
> would pay any price to be able to say truthfully "All will be saved".
> But my reason retorts, "Without their will, or with it?" If I say "With-
> out their will" I at once perceive a contradiction; how can the supreme
> voluntary act of self-surrender be involuntary? If I say "With their
> will", my reason replies "How if they *will not* give in?"[4]

This is a clear statement of the mystery of the human will in its
relation to hell. I doubt, however, if such things in God's universe
can ever be understood precisely in terms of human either/or logic.
This is very much like the problem of understanding the nature of

light. The physicist is left with no way of deciding once and for all whether light is actually a ray or a series of particles. How can we expect to understand the ways of God even as well?

How can we even guess at the unflagging love and mercy of God, the love that Jesus described in the story of the prodigal son? Will he ever stop reaching out for the lost who have been flung out on the cosmic dumpheaps of the universe? I can imagine him rummaging there forever among the debris until he finds some response. To say that men and women after death will be able to resist the love of God forever seems to suggest that the human soul is stronger than God.

In stories like the one of the prodigal son, it is so easy for us to forget that Jesus was telling about several different levels of reality. For one thing I don't think that the prodigal had the easiest time at the feast as the neighbors came up to ask where he had been and how he was. I doubt if he always slept well on the nights that followed. But he was welcomed and given the chance to grow back into fellowship by a father who made no attempt to hide his delight. The way Jesus described the father in this story left little question that the prodigal would have found a royal welcome whenever he returned home, no matter how long it took him to ask for his father's love and mercy.

There is certainly general agreement among Christians that any of us can decide that we need God and heaven right up to the moment of death. But the idea that some people must suffer ever-lasting punishment is very strong among many groups. E. J. Fortman, for instance, discusses this question in the book I have mentioned, *Everlasting Life After Death*. He gives all the traditional reasons for believing that we are stuck forever with the choices we make here on earth. This idea does not seem to fit the picture of God's love given to us in the New Testament. I feel quite sure that if people awaken to themselves after death and desire heaven, God will be waiting to open the door for them.

Since Jesus has already confronted the forces of hell and risen victorious over them, that kingdom of evil no longer seems to be impregnable. When we need help against the depredations of that kingdom in this world, the powers of heaven are able to reach directly into our present hell and rescue us. There seems to be no reason to believe that this is not just as true in the afterlife. My own deepest and most prayerful intimation is that God will always be able and ready to reach out and rescue us whenever we turn to him. It is certainly foolish, however, for us to suffer now and wait until the next life to discover the power of God and heaven.

Will the kingdom of darkness last forever? Or will there one day be an end to it? Julian of Norwich gave an answer in these words: "All will be well. All manner of things will be well." The same hope has been expressed by nearly all of those whom we call saints, those who have known and loved God and have been loved by him the best. It is difficult for me to imagine that the God who sought me out and lifted me out of the darkness and turmoil will not ultimately seek out all who are lost. He knows, even better than the best criminologists, that punishment rarely changes human beings for the better. He wants to save them from needless suffering, and as he helps one individual after another turn to him, I feel sure that even hell itself will finally be eliminated at the end of time. Hell is, however, still a stark and horrible reality which we can encounter both in this life and the next. Christ seems to be continually recruiting followers to help themselves and others out of hell. This seems to be what salvation is essentially about.

XIV. A Conclusion of Hope

We have seen the evidence that has been accumulating about the human soul, both in ordinary living and in experiences at death's door. These varied experiences point more and more clearly to the possibility that our lives continue after death. We have also seen that death can apparently bring at least some people an encounter with a divine being, a "being of light" who may be a representative of God or even God himself. In addition we have considered a number of hints that life itself is a preparation for growth toward God and his kingdom. I cannot imagine Love resting until all who need his love are touched and have turned to him. This is certainly not inevitable or easy. The way that he took to win so many of us cost dearly. There will undoubtedly be further cost, and he will probably ask our help in seeking to bring all reality to him. But I believe that in the end nothing will prevail against him. It is at this point that I have little evidence to go on other than my own experience and faith. I have known the unfailing love and mercy and the victory of the risen Christ, and I can no longer doubt that his victory, even over hell, will one day be complete.

Much that I have learned about souls and their growth toward God has come through the broad knowledge and deep understanding of Dr. Carl Jung. Few thinkers—with the exception of Plato in ancient times—have dealt with the problem of death as fully and directly as Jung. He struggled to give an understanding of the human psyche or soul, including the inevitable problem of facing death. And he also wrestled with the possibility that the individual psyche may persist after this life. He did not approach this question as a classical philosopher or theologian, but as a psychiatrist, a doctor of the soul. His task was the practical one of helping people who were torn by psychic pain and by the loss of meaning in their lives.

Dr. Jung attempted to share something of his own experience and understanding with patients who were often overwhelmed by the thought of death, and so by a sense of meaninglessness. Since these people had found little or no help in the usual religious circles, he realized that the problem was up to him. As a physician, he had to do his best to offer them the understanding and confidence that could bring relief. "Meaninglessness," he wrote, "inhibits fullness of life and is therefore equivalent to illness."[1] His job was to get at the roots of this illness, and so he tackled the question of life after death.

He realized that our psyches are in contact with a reality beyond the world of space and time. Experience of this non-physical reality, such as dreams, visions, and intuitions, could sometimes bring amazing knowledge about people who had died or were close to death. Jung also realized that religious beliefs are in no sense conscious creations. They come from a continuing encounter with a reality beyond the known world. He made it very clear that we become sick when we ignore these hints of another world and another life. Our task is to develop them so as to enrich our lives and prepare for the future. He wrote:

> A man should be able to say he has done his best to form a conception of life after death, or to create some image of it—even if he must confess his failure. Not to have done so is a vital loss. For the question that is posed to him is the age-old heritage of humanity ... which seeks to add itself to our own individual life in order to make it whole.[2]

He expressed his knowledge that our lives find fulfillment in a non-physical dimension and that we must prepare now for the steps to come. Death, he suggested, is actually a goal toward which we can strive, and "shrinking away from it is something unhealthy and abnormal which robs the second half of life of its purpose."[3]

In the last pages of his memoirs, when he had lived out a full life, Jung gave the clue to the way life is to be lived in order to participate in the most meaningful and lasting reality of the universe. At the end of the chapter "Late Thoughts" he set down a paean of praise to Eros. He described Eros as the *daimon* of Greek genius, the same reality of love which Paul praised in 1 Corinthians 13. The person who loves in this way does not just satisfy his own wishes or desires. By *loving*, one shares in the very creative force of the universe, the source of all our ideas and understanding, particularly our understanding of the essence of God. In his words:

> For we are in the deepest sense the victims and the instruments of cosmogonic "love." . . . [Man] is at its mercy. He may assent to it, or rebel against it; but he is always caught up by it and enclosed within it. He is dependent upon it and is sustained by it. . . . "Love ceases not"— whether he speaks with the "tongues of angels," or with scientific exactitude traces the life of the cell down to its uttermost source. Man can try to name love, showering upon it all the names at his command, and still he will involve himself in endless self-deceptions. If he possesses a grain of wisdom, he will lay down his arms and name the unknown by the more unknown . . . that is, by the name of God. That is a confession of his subjection, his imperfection, and his dependence; but at the same time a testimony to his freedom to choose between truth and error.[4]

Jung believed that people who build this reality into their lives build permanently, and that the chances of realizing on it are as good as the probabilities of quantum mechanics.

It does not take much imagination to see the implications of his conclusions for Christianity. His understanding is not very different from the theology of the Fathers of the Church. If one translates the terminology, it is easy to see that they are saying the same thing. There may be a change of key, but the tune is still the same.

Jung's critical thought and detailed presentation of experience give modern and much needed support to the early Christian view of the afterlife. The most demanding modern thinkers can affirm the basic Christian belief with confidence if it is stated in terms like this: When men and women live in Christ who is Love incarnate, they allow the reality which Christ incarnated to operate in and through their lives. Those who live in this way build a kind of permanence into their lives which extends into a mysterious and continued growth in a life to come.

I shall always be grateful to Jung for helping me to rediscover the reality of our Christian point of view, and for his specific reflections on life after death. While I do not agree with all that he wrote, he gave me a launching pad to get back into the ideas of Jesus and the early Church. I have found only one other modern thinker who tried to show the importance of love to human beings and their future with anything like the force of Jung's statements. This is Karl Jaspers who also studied medicine and practiced psychiatry before his interest turned to philosophy. In a book *Death to Life* he wrote these words, which are reminiscent of Plato:

> The consciousness of immortality needs no knowledge, no guarantee, no threat. It lies in love, in this marvelous reality in which we are given to ourselves. We are mortal when we are without love, and immortal when we love. . . . I achieve immortality to the extent that I love. . . . I dissipate into nothingness as long as I live without love, and therefore in chaos. As a lover I can see the immortality of those who are united to me in love.[5]

This is the way that opens up to Christians who will try it.

One Encounter with Death

Some years ago my only brother died. We had never been close and there were unresolved conflicts between us. I did not realize that he was as near death as he was, and I was out of town when he died. The news did not even reach me in time to get to the funeral. There were harsh words and recriminations from others in the family because I had not kept myself available and ready to come. Added to this was my own guilt and self-recrimination for not having made the effort to visit him while he was still living. I found myself drawn down into deep depression.

I still had to fulfill obligations, however, and two weeks later I got on the plane to Minnesota to address a conference on the subject of meditation. Alone and able to be quiet, I realized that if I were to be of any value to people at the conference, I had to deal with my own darkness. I turned inward. I realized that not only had I been touched by my brother's death and my grief and guilt, but I was afraid of my own death. I realized that I was now the oldest member of my branch of the family. As I turned inward into the darkness, I found that death was a palpable personality and reality. The follow-ing words flowed through and out of me. They are also included at the end of my book on meditation, and I offer them here as my final statement of hope and faith.

I Met Death Face to Face

There you stand glaring. No one could doubt
Your identity, ancient foe of man and me.
Face to face we stare at one another.
"When does your bony index finger
Reach out and touch me, chill me?
You are not pretty, Death.
I cannot stand against you; I have
No power, no talisman to fight you off.
I stand alone. So many times you've tried
To finish me—sickness, rejection,
Folly, guilt and fear. Have you some trick,
Some new trick to undo me
And so collect my rotting bones?
When will you have your prey?
Am I the next, the next in line?"
I stand naked on the wild moor . . .
The wind is howling and the sea
Screams against the crumbling cliffs—
"Why don't you take me, do your deed?
A silver filament is all that holds you back . . .
You do not move. You cannot move?
Oh, you can't cross over? It frightens you?
You, Death, are afraid and tremble?
You have died, have been defeated?"
My eyes become accustomed to the gloom.
The silver thread is more. It is a net,
Let down from heaven. And I look up—
There is a brightness and out of it flow images . . .
Comforting arms, tears like rain,
A dazzling perfect youth, father, mother,
Brother, lover, friend, ransom, guide.
A boundless jewel turning one face
And then another. From this there hangs
A net of silver and of gold which stands
Between me and the grinning skull,
Surrounds him as a silken pouch.
A voice like thunder shakes the net.
Shakes heaven, earth and even hell.

"He cannot have you long, this one.
His victory is for the moment only.
And he cannot even have his day
Until the time is ripe and full.
Death has died and so has lost his power.
He risked all and lost. His power's fear.
Only as you fear him can he control.
Only as you're drawn into the net,
Having given up in fear,
As rabbits move toward the snake's hypnotic eye.
Stare him down. Laugh in his face.
I am with you until the end,
With those you love whom death has touched.
They are not lost because they disappear.
Remember me, my child, my beloved.
I am here, always, and with love!"
The thunder rolls away. The rain falls.
I look Death in the face, straight on. I laugh.
He turns and slinks away.
Something deep within me speaks
And tells me that the day will come
When the voice of thunder will touch death's heart
And he will be one of us, the chosen, the redeemed, the loved.
Strange world, where death brings life,
If only, if only I don't give up,
But struggle on in spite of dark and pain.
O death, where is your sting?
O grave, where is your victory?[6]

APPENDICES

A. The Aristotelio-Mediaeval World-Scheme*

The conception of man can no more be separated from the conception of the cosmos than man himself can be separated from the world. Hence it is not altogether possible to follow the transformations which the conception of man underwent, unless we also take account of the modifications undergone by the conception of the world. The two conceptions act and react upon one another continuously. Thus Boehme's religious speculations are, to a certain extent, manifestly conditioned by the new cosmology (especially by the ideas of Paracelsus and Copernicus), and only become really comprehensive when taken in connection with it, and this notwithstanding that he puts religio-psychological considerations in the first place. On the other hand, we find in several of the thinkers whom we should now regard as founders of the new world-conception, valuable ideas and discussions with regard to psychology and ethics, which, in and for themselves, entitle them to a place among the thinkers who discovered Man. Nevertheless it may perhaps be admissible to assign them their place under the point of view which constitutes their chief importance in the history of thought.

In order to understand the magnitude of the change in the conception of the world which ranks, together with its art and its discovery of man, among the greatest feats of the Renaissance, we must first get a clear idea of the main features of the world-scheme, which, as late as the fifteenth century, was regarded by learned and lay alike as beyond all question. It was descended from the Aristotelian physics and the Ptolemaic astronomy, and was interwoven with Biblical images; a conjunction easily effected, since the whole world-scheme was based entirely on immediate sense data, merely giving these a more exact determination and a systematic carrying-out.

Even according to the current view, it was evident that there is a great

*Dr. Harald Höffding, *A History of Modern Philosophy*, London, Macmillan and Co., 1935, Chapter IX.

difference between the motions in the heavens and those that take place on this earth. Here continual change seems to prevail. Phenomena increase and decrease, arise and pass away. Motions arise which, after a longer or shorter time, cease again. Very different is it up there: the stars continue in their regular course without any appreciable change, and that course leads them ever back again along the same path in eternal, ceaseless, circular motion. ARISTOTLE founded his conception of the world on this antithesis between the heavenly and the earthly or sublunary regions. He relies on that which perception appears to teach, pointing at the same time to the old faith of Greeks and barbarians alike, i.e. that the heavens are the seat of the eternal gods. The heavenly region is eternal; the motion which takes place in it is likewise eternal, and absolutely regular. The sublunary region, on the contrary, is the home of transitoriness, where motion and rest, arising and passing away, alternate with each other.

These two regions, then, cannot consist of the same matter. The heavenly bodies must consist of matter which has its home in no one definite place, and which can therefore continue in motion throughout eternity. This matter, the "first body," Aristotle calls Aether. It fills the heavens, and in it the eternal circular motion takes place. Only circular motion can be eternal, since it alone always returns into itself, and goes from every point in the circle to every other point. In the sublunary region every motion stops at a certain point, i.e. when the body has reached its natural place. Here rectilinear motion prevails, which proceeds either outwards and upwards from the central point of the world, or else inwards and downwards towards this central point. That which has its natural place in or near the central point of the world is called heavy; while that of which the natural place is situated above or near the upper regions of the sublunary world is called light. The constant changes in the earthly regions arise because the elements are not always in their natural places. The heavy element is earth, the light fire; between these two lie water and air. For fire mounts ever aloft, while the stone that has been thrown into the air falls earthwards again. Every element strives after its appointed place in the universe. The four elements may pass into one another reciprocally, but they cannot be resolved into simpler component parts; all bodies, on the other hand, consist of combinations of them.

There can only be one single world. If we were to suppose for a moment that there were several, we should see that the heavy elements must finally collect around one single central point, and thus we should again be reduced to one world. The earth, as perception shows us, is situated at the centre of the world, and from this, if we go outwards and upwards, we come first to the other three sublunary strata, and above these again to the region of the aether, the matter of which is purer the farther it is from the earth. The heavenly bodies, first the moon, the sun, and the other planets, then the fixed stars, are situated in solid but transparent spheres which turn on their axes. Aristotle adopted this belief from the astronomer Eudoxus. The ancients could not conceive the heavenly bodies moving freely in the heavens. All spheres revolve round the earth as the central point; the moon, the sun, and the other planets have each their sphere; all these spheres, consequently the whole world-system, are enclosed by the "first heaven," the sphere of the fixed stars, which is itself moved directly by the Deity, while subordinate principles or spirits guide the motions of the other spheres. The highest is that which encompasses and limits. The upper or outer part of the world is the most perfect.

The Aristotelian world-scheme presented a frame which apparently not only corresponded with the teaching of sensuous perception, but was able to take up into itself the observations made by the astronomers of later antiquity. In order, it is true, to take account of the motions to and fro of the planets, it was found necessary to ascribe very complicated motions to the planetary spheres; but this difficulty was met by conceiving every single planet as bound to several spheres at once, of which each has its own motion. Or else it was thought that the motions did not take place in simple circles, but in smaller circles, or epicycles, whose central points moved in larger circles. And with the progress of inquiry this system of epicycles became more and more complicated. Ptolemy of Alexandria (in the second century A.D.) gave an exposition of the world-system which, like Aristotle's system in philosophy, was regarded as authoritative within the sphere of astronomy throughout the Middle Ages.

Since, like the Biblical cosmology, the Aristotelio-Ptolemaic system adopted the standpoint of sensuous perception, according to which the earth stands still while the sun and stars move, it readily lent itself to combination with the religious notions prevalent in the Middle Ages. It harmonized also, as Aristotle had perceived, with the old belief that the heavens are the seat of the Deity. An essential difference emerges, however, between the antique and the mediaeval conception of the world. Aristotle, it is true, placed the earth at the central point of the world; but this was not because he thought that everything else in the world existed for the sake of the earth or its inhabitants. On the contrary, for him that which surrounds and limits was the highest; while he regarded the earth as the place of the lowest matter. But in the mediaeval view of the world, it is precisely on this earth and the events which take place upon it that everything hangs. Nevertheless this view was able to avail itself of the Aristotelian schema and of the notion of the imperfection of the sublunary world, since, according to it, the heavenly powers descend in order to intervene in mundane affairs and lead them towards the right goal.

Apart from the difficulties involved in the combined spheres or epicycles, this method of conception was, as a whole, clear and comprehensible.

It rested on the supposition that sensuous space is absolute space, and that within this space there are absolute places. The philosopher or astronomer took—as the practical man does to this day—the terrestrial ball on which he found himself to be the absolute center of the world. And the world which forms itself out of the different spheres around this central point had its limits in the outermost sphere—on the other side of which nothing existed. It was an essential part of the antique conception of Nature to think of everything as formed and limited. The unlimited was the dark and unformed, if not the evil. Here, too, the schema found a support in sensuous perception and imagination, which stop at some definite point and never feel the necessity of asking what lies beyond.

Such a world-scheme as this was open to attack on two sides. Firstly, when observations and calculations should be brought forward conflicting with it or, at least, making another conception possible or probable. Secondly—and this is perhaps more interesting to us here—whenever the naive confidence in the absolute validity of sensuous space should be disputed. When it has become evident that every determination of place is dependent on the place of the observer, there is no longer any absolute distinction between the heavenly and the earthly regions, nor between the natural places within the earthly region. In both these ways the Aristotelio-mediaeval world-scheme was attacked by the inquiries of the Renaissance period. And, as we shall see, the latter way was the one first adopted.

B. Two Modern Visions In Near-Death Experiences

Two personal accounts of visions during near-death experiences follow. The first of them was written by the well-known psychic, Arthur Ford, in a book published after his death, *The Life Beyond Death*. His story was recorded by Jerome Ellison and was published in 1971. The second was told by Carl G. Jung to his secretary Aniela Jaffé and was included as part of a book published after Jung's death, first in German, and then in English as *Memories, Dreams, Reflections* in 1963. I have selected these accounts rather than some of those described by Moody because they are personal published accounts of this experience. These experiences contain much similar material and together embody most of the elements detailed by Moody.

*Arthur Ford's Story**

I was critically ill. The doctors said I could not live, but as the good doctors they were, they continued doing what they could. I was in a hospital, and my friends had been told that I could not live through the night. As from a distance, with no feeling except a mild curiosity, I heard a doctor say to a nurse, "Give him the needle; he might as well be comfortable." This, I seemed to sense, was "it," but I was not afraid. I was simply wondering how long it would take to die.

Next, I was floating in the air above my bed. I could see my body but had no interest in it. There was a feeling of peace, a sense that all was well. Now I lapsed into a timeless blank. When I recovered consciousness, I found myself floating through space, without effort, without any sense that I possessed a body as I had known my body. Yet I was I *myself*.

Now there appeared a green valley with mountains on all sides, illumi-

---

*Arthur Ford, as told to Jerome Ellison, *The Life Beyond Death*. New York: G. P. Putnam's Sons, 1971, pp. 201-205.

nated everywhere by a brilliance of light and color impossible to describe. People were coming toward me from all around, people I had known and thought of as "dead." I knew them all. Many I had not thought of for years, but it seemed that everyone I had ever cared about was there to greet me. Recognition was more by personality than by physical attributes. They had changed ages. Some who had passed on in old age were now young, and some who had passed on while children had now matured.

I have often had the experience of traveling to a foreign country, being met by friends and introduced to the local customs and taken to places of interest any visitor to the country would want to see. It was like that now. Never have I been so royally greeted. I was shown all the things they seemed to think I should see. My memory of these places is as clear as my impression of the countries I have visited in this life: The beauty of a sunrise viewed from a peak in the Swiss Alps, the Blue Grotto of Capri, the hot, dusty roads of India are no more powerfully etched in my memory than the spirit world in which I knew myself to be. Time has never dimmed the memory of it. It is as vivid and real as anything I have ever known.

There was one surprise: Some people I would have expected to see here were not present. I asked about them. In the instant of asking a thin transparent film seemed to fall over my eyes. The light grew dimmer, and colors lost their brilliance. I could no longer see those to whom I had been speaking, but through a haze I saw those for whom I had asked. They, too, were real, but as I looked at them, I felt my own body become heavy; earthly thoughts crowded into my mind. It was evident to me that I was being shown a lower sphere. I called to them; they seemed to hear me, but I could not hear a reply. Then it was over. A gentle being who looked like a symbol of eternal youth, but radiated power and wisdom, stood by me. "Don't worry about them," he said. "They can come here whenever they want to if they desire it more than anything else."

Everyone here was busy. They were continually occupied with mysterious errands and seemed to be very happy. Several of those to whom I had been bound by close ties in the past did not seem to be much interested in me. Others I had known only slightly became my companions. I understood that this was right and natural. The law of affinity determined our relationships here.

At some point—I had no awareness of time—I found myself standing before a dazzling white building. Entering, I was told to wait in an enormous anteroom. They said I was to remain here until some sort of disposition had been made of my case. Through wide doors I could glimpse two long tables with people sitting at them and talking—about me. Guiltily I began an inventory of my life. It did not make a pretty picture. The people at the long tables were also reviewing the record, but the things that worried me did not seem to have much interest for them. The conventional sins I was warned about as a child were hardly mentioned. But there was sober concern over such matters as selfishness, egotism, stupidity. The word "dissipation" occurred over and over—not in the usual sense of intemperance but as waste of energies, gifts, and opportunities. On the other side of the scale were some simple, kindly things such as we all do from time to time without thinking them of much consequence. The "judges" were trying to make out the main *trend* of my life. They mentioned my having failed to accomplish "what he *knew* he had to finish." There was a purpose for me, it seemed, and I had not fulfilled it. There was a plan for my life, and I had misread the blueprint. "They're going to send me back," I thought, and I didn't like it. Never did I discover who these people were. They repeatedly used the word "record"; perhaps the Akashic Record of the ancient mystery schools—the great universal spiritual sound track on which all events are recorded.

When I was told I had to return to my body, I fought having to get back into that beaten, diseased hulk I had left behind in a Coral Gables hospital. I was standing before a door. I knew if I passed through it, I would be back where I had been. I decided I wouldn't go. Like a spoiled child in a tantrum, I pushed my feet against the wall and fought. There was a sudden sense of hurtling through space. I opened my eyes and looked into the face of a nurse. I had been in a coma for more than two weeks.

Several things occurred to me as factors which have inhibited our ability to apprehend the realities of the beta body and of the expanded universe available to it. Perhaps the most formidable is the misconception that our five senses—sight, hearing, taste, smell, and touch—are the only means of knowing that we have. It is obvious, if we would only stop to think, that we have many more senses than these. Nobody has ever seen a person. We see the physical body of the person and some of the kinetic effects it produces, but the person himself is invisible. Our consciousness resides even now in the same beta body it will inhabit in its further journeys. We know people not through the gross five senses but through subtler awarenesses of the beta bodies.

In this sense, speaking from the point of view of the workaday world, we are already invisible and should not be surprised if the actualities of deeply experienced life are not available to our outer eyes and ears. The beta body can be prepared for its further journey beginning here and now. Character is developed not in the act of dying but in the act of living. Spiritual illumination is no more reached in a single step than is physical perfection or intellectual attainment. One cannot convince another of the truth of immortality by intellectual arguments or external evidence. It must be known by that inward awareness which is part of every human psyche. It is that awareness which, as Wordsworth put it, comes as "A sense sublime/Of something far more deeply interfused ... /A motion and a spirit, that impels/All thinking things, all objects of all thought,/And rolls through all things."

Carl Jung's Vision *

At the beginning of 1944 I broke my foot, and this misadventure was followed by a heart attack. In a state of unconsciousness I experienced deliriums and visions which must have begun when I hung on the edge of death and was being given oxygen and camphor injections. The images were so tremendous that I myself concluded that I was close to death. My nurse afterward told me, "It was as if you were surrounded by a bright glow." That was a phenomenon she had sometimes observed in the dying, she added. I had reached the outermost limit, and do not know whether I was in a dream or an ecstasy. At any rate, extremely strange things began to happen to me.

It seemed to me that I was high up in space. Far below I saw the globe of the earth, bathed in a gloriously blue light. I saw the deep blue sea and the continents. Far below my feet lay Ceylon, and in the distance ahead of me the subcontinent of India. My field of vision did not include the whole earth, but its global shape was plainly distinguishable and its outlines shone with a silvery gleam through that wonderful blue light. In many places the globe seemed colored, or spotted dark green like oxydized silver. Far away to the left lay a broad expanse—the reddish-yellow desert of Arabia; it was as though the silver of the earth had there assumed a reddish-gold hue. Then came the Red Sea, and far, far back—as if in the upper left of a map— I could just make out a bit of the Mediterranean. My gaze was directed chiefly toward that. Everything else appeared indistinct. I could also see the snow-covered Himalayas, but in that direction it was foggy or cloudy. I did not look to the right at all. I knew that I was on the point of departing from the earth.

Later I discovered how high in space one would have to be to have so extensive a view—approximately a thousand miles! The sight of the earth from this height was the most glorious thing I had ever seen.

After contemplating it for a while, I turned around. I had been standing with my back to the Indian Ocean, as it were, and my face to the north. Then it seemed to me that I made a turn to the south. Something new entered my field of vision. A short distance away I saw in space a tremendous dark block of stone, like a meteorite. It was about the size of my house, or even bigger. It was floating in space, and I myself was floating in space.

I had seen similar stones on the coast of the Gulf of Bengal. They were

*C. G. Jung, *Memories, Dreams, Reflections*, recorded and edited by Aniela Jaffé, New York, Pantheon Books, 1963, pp. 289-296.

blocks of tawny granite, and some of them had been hollowed out into temples. My stone was one such gigantic dark block. An entrance led into a small antechamber. To the right of the entrance, a black Hindu sat silently in lotus posture upon a stone bench. He wore a white gown, and I knew that he expected me. Two steps led up to this antechamber, and inside, on the left, was the gate to the temple. Innumerable tiny niches, each with a saucer-like concavity filled with coconut oil and small burning wicks, surrounded the door with a wreath of bright flames. I had once actually seen this when I visited the Temple of the Holy Tooth at Kandy in Ceylon; the gate had been framed by several rows of burning oil lamps of this sort.

As I approached the steps leading up to the entrance into the rock, a strange thing happened: I had the feeling that everything was being sloughed away; everything I aimed at or wished for or thought, the whole phantasmagoria of earthly existence, fell away or was stripped from me—an extremely painful process. Nevertheless something remained; it was as if I now carried along with me everything I had ever experienced or done, everything that had happened around me. I might also say: it was with me, and I was it. I consisted of all that, so to speak. I consisted of my own history, and I felt with great certainty: this is what I am. "I am this bundle of what has been, and what has been accomplished."

This experience gave me a feeling of extreme poverty, but at the same time of great fullness. There was no longer anything I wanted or desired. I existed in an objective form; I was what I had been and lived. At first the sense of annihilation predominated, of having been stripped or pillaged; but suddenly that became of no consequence. Everything seemed to be past; what remained was a *fait accompli*, without any reference back to what had been. There was no longer any regret that something had dropped away or been taken away. On the contrary: I had everything that I was, and that was everything.

Something else engaged my attention: as I approached the temple I had the certainty that I was about to enter an illuminated room and would meet there all those people to whom I belong in reality. There I would at last understand—this too was a certainty—what historical nexus I or my life fitted into. I would know what had been before me, why I had come into being, and where my life was flowing. My life as I lived it had often seemed to me like a story that has no beginning and no end. I had the feeling that I was a historical fragment, an excerpt for which the preceding and succeeding text was missing. My life seemed to have been snipped out of a long chain of events, and many questions had remained unanswered. Why had it taken this course? Why had I brought these particular assumptions with me? What had I made of them? What will follow? I felt sure that I would receive an answer to all these questions as soon as I entered the rock temple. There I would learn why everything had been thus and not otherwise.

There I would meet the people who knew the answer to my question about what had been before and what would come after.

While I was thinking over these matters, something happened that caught my attention. From below, from the direction of Europe, an image floated up. It was my doctor, Dr. H.—or, rather, his likeness—framed by a golden chain or a golden laurel wreath. I knew at once: "Aha, this is my doctor, of course, the one who has been treating me. But now he is coming in his primal form, as a *basileus* of Kos.* In life he was an avatar of this *basileus*, the temporal embodiment of the primal form, which has existed from the beginning. Now he is appearing in that primal form."

Presumably I too was in my primal form, though this was something I did not observe but simply took for granted. As he stood before me, a mute exchange of thought took place between us. Dr. H. had been delegated by the earth to deliver a message to me, to tell me that there was a protest against my going away. I had no right to leave the earth and must return. The moment I heard that, the vision ceased.

I was profoundly disappointed, for now it all seemed to have been for nothing. The painful process of defoliation had been in vain, and I was not to be allowed to enter the temple, to join the people in whose company I belonged.

In reality, a good three weeks were still to pass before I could truly make up my mind to live again. I could not eat because all food repelled me. The view of city and mountains from my sick-bed seemed to me like a painted curtain with black holes in it, or a tattered sheet of newspaper full of photographs that meant nothing. Disappointed, I thought, "Now I must return to the 'box system' again." For it seemed to me as if behind the horizon of the cosmos a three-dimensional world had been artificially built up, in which each person sat by himself in a little box. And now I should have to convince myself all over again that this was important! Life and the whole world struck me as a prison, and it bothered me beyond measure that I should again be finding all that quite in order. I had been so glad to shed it all, and now it had come about that I—along with everyone else—would again be hung up in a box by a thread. While I floated in space, I had been weightless, and there had been nothing tugging at me. And now all that was to be a thing of the past!

I felt violent resistance to my doctor because he had brought me back to life. At the same time, I was worried about him. "His life is in danger, for heaven's sake! He has appeared to me in his primal form! When anybody attains this form it means he is going to die, for already he belongs to the

Basileus = King. Kos was famous in antiquity as the site of the temple of Asklepios [the healing god], and was the birthplace of [the great Greek physician] Hippocrates.—A. J.

'greater company'!" Suddenly the terrifying thought came to me that Dr. H. would have to die in my stead. I tried my best to talk to him about it, but he did not understand me. Then I became angry with him. "Why does he always pretend he doesn't know he is a *basileus* of Kos? And that he has already assumed his primal form? He wants to make me believe that he doesn't know!" That irritated me. My wife reproved me for being so unfriendly to him. She was right; but at the time I was angry with him for stubbornly refusing to speak of all that had passed between us in my vision. "Damn it all, he ought to watch his step. He has no right to be so reckless! I want to tell him to take care of himself." I was firmly convinced that his life was in jeopardy.

In actual fact I was his last patient. On April 4, 1944—I still remember the exact date—I was allowed to sit up on the edge of my bed for the first time since the beginning of my illness, and on this same day Dr. H. took to his bed and did not leave it again. I heard that he was having intermittent attacks of fever. Soon afterward he died of septicemia. He was a good doctor; there was something of the genius about him. Otherwise he would not have appeared to me as a prince of Kos.

During those weeks I lived in a strange rhythm. By day I was usually depressed. I felt weak and wretched, and scarcely dared to stir. Gloomily, I thought, "Now I must go back to this drab world." Toward evening I would fall asleep, and my sleep would last until about midnight. Then I would come to myself and lie awake for about an hour, but in an utterly transformed state. It was as if I were in an ecstasy. I felt as though I were floating in space, as though I were safe in the womb of the universe—in a tremendous void, but filled with the highest possible feeling of happiness. "This is eternal bliss," I thought. "This cannot be described; it is far too wonderful!"

Everything around me seemed enchanted. At this hour of the night the nurse brought me some food she had warmed—for only then was I able to take any, and I ate with appetite. For a time it seemed to me that she was an old Jewish woman, much older than she actually was, and that she was preparing ritual kosher dishes for me. When I looked at her, she seemed to have a blue halo around her head. I myself was, so it seemed, in the Pardes Rimmonim, the garden of pomegranates, and the wedding of Tifereth with Malchuth was taking place. Or else I was Rabbi Simon ben Jochai, whose wedding in the afterlife was being celebrated. It was the mystic marriage as it appears in the Cabbalistic tradition. I cannot tell you how wonderful it was. I could only think continually, "Now this is the garden of pomegranates! Now this is the marriage of Malchuth with Tifereth!" I do not know exactly what part I played in it. At bottom it was I myself: I was the marriage. And my beatitude was that of a blissful wedding.

Gradually the garden of pomegranates faded away and changed. There followed the Marriage of the Lamb, in a Jerusalem festively bedecked. I cannot describe what it was like in detail. These were ineffable states of joy. Angels were present, and light. I myself was the "Marriage of the Lamb."

That, too, vanished, and there came a new image, the last vision. I walked up a wide valley to the end, where a gentle chain of hills began. The valley ended in a classical amphitheater. It was magnificently situated in the green landscape. And there, in this theater, the *hierosgamos* was being celebrated. Men and women dancers came onstage, and upon a flower-decked couch All-father Zeus and Hera consummated the mystic marriage, as it is described in the *Iliad*.

All these experiences were glorious. Night after night I floated in a state of purest bliss, "thronged round with images of all creation." Gradually, the motifs mingled and paled. Usually the visions lasted for about an hour; then I would fall asleep again. By the time morning drew near, I would feel: Now gray morning is coming again; now comes the gray world with its boxes! What idiocy, what hideous nonsense! Those inner states were so fantastically beautiful that by comparison this world appeared downright ridiculous. As I approached closer to life again, they grew fainter, and scarcely three weeks after the first vision they ceased altogether.

It is impossible to convey the beauty and intensity of emotion during those visions. They were the most tremendous things I have ever experienced. And what a contrast the day was: I was tormented and on edge; everything irritated me; everything was too material, too crude and clumsy, terribly limited both spatially and spiritually. It was all an imprisonment, for reasons impossible to divine, and yet it had a kind of hypnotic power, a cogency, as if it were reality itself, for all that I had clearly perceived its emptiness. Although my belief in the world returned to me, I have never since entirely freed myself of the impression that this life is a segment of existence which is enacted in a three-dimensional boxlike universe especially set up for it.

There is something else I quite distinctly remember. At the beginning, when I was having the vision of the garden of pomegranates, I asked the nurse to forgive me if she were harmed. There was such sanctity in the room, I said, that it might be harmful to her. Of course she did not understand me. For me the presence of sanctity had a magical atmosphere; I feared it might be unendurable to others. I understood then why one speaks of the odor of sanctity, of the "sweet smell" of the Holy Ghost. This was it. There was a *pneuma* of inexpressible sanctity in the room, whose manifestation was the *mysterium coniunctionis*.*

I would never have imagined that any such experience was possible. It was not a product of imagination. The visions and experiences were utterly

---

*Another term for the mystic marriage or joining of the opposites, as Isaiah pictured in his prediction of the coming of Christ. He described the wolf and leopard and lion at peace with the lamb, the kid, and the calf, led by a little child (Isaiah 11:6).

real; there was nothing subjective about them; they all had a quality of absolute objectivity.

We shy away from the word "eternal," but I can describe the experience only as the ecstasy of a non-temporal state in which present, past, and future are one. Everything that happens in time had been brought together into a concrete whole. Nothing was distributed over time, nothing could be measured by temporal concepts. The experience might best be defined as a state of feeling, but one which cannot be produced by imagination. How can I imagine that I exist simultaneously the day before yesterday, today, and the day after tomorrow? There would be things which would not yet have begun, other things which would be indubitably present, and others again which would already be finished—and yet all this would be one. The only thing that feeling could grasp would be a sum, an iridescent whole, containing all at once expectation of a beginning, surprise at what is now happening, and satisfaction or disappointment with the result of what has happened. One is interwoven into an indescribable whole and yet observes it with complete objectivity.

I experienced this objectivity once again later on. That was after the death of my wife. I saw her in a dream which was like a vision. She stood at some distance from me, looking at me squarely. She was in her prime, perhaps about thirty, and wearing the dress which had been made for her many years before by my cousin the medium. It was perhaps the most beautiful thing she had ever worn. Her expression was neither joyful nor sad, but, rather, objectively wise and understanding, without the slightest emotional reaction, as though she were beyond the mist of affects. I knew that it was not she, but a portrait she had made or commissioned for me. It contained the beginning of our relationship, the events of fifty-three years of marriage, and the end of her life also. Face to face with such wholeness one remains speechless, for it can scarcely be comprehended.

C. The Puzzle of the Kingdom of God

The following discussion of the meaning of the kingdom of God or the kingdom of heaven was writen by John Sanford as part of an introduction to his book, *The Kingdom Within*. It has never been published and he has given me permission to present this material. The reader who wishes to see the implications of this study for the actual understanding of the parables of the kingdom of God is referred to his unique and practical book, *The Kingdom Within*.

The Role of the Kingdom of God in the Teachings of Jesus

In a Gothic cathedral the central architectural feature is the arch. Remove the arches from a Gothic building and the entire structure will collapse, for they are central to the entire design. With the teachings of Jesus there is also such a central arch: the kingdom of God.

The teaching of Jesus regarding the kingdom of God, or the kingdom of heaven as Matthew calls it (apparently to avoid the direct use of the sacred word "God"), is central to his entire message. The expression occurs in Mark's Gospel thirteen times, in Luke's Gospel twenty-eight times, and in Matthew's Gospel thirty-eight times. In John's Gospel it occurs only once, although here in a very significant passage, but John does frequently use the equivalent expression "eternal life." Fifteen of the parables of Jesus are directly concerned with this kingdom of God. In Matthew alone twelve of his parables are introduced with the expression, "The kingdom of heaven is like. . . ."

In addition, a second aspect of Jesus' teaching is certainly directly connected to the idea of the kingdom of God. The expression Jesus uses to describe himself is the "Son of Man," and we are on solid ground if we suppose that the kingdom of God and the Son of Man are closely related to each other in Jesus' thinking. The term "Son of Man" is used only by Jesus as a self-appellation; used in this way it occurs twenty-one times in Matthew's Gospel alone.

It is apparent that if we knew what Jesus meant by the kingdom of God and the Son of Man, we would know a great deal, for we would be in possession of the key to his entire teachings, since everything else he had to say is in some way related to his understanding of the kingdom. Unfortunately, however, it is not immediately clear what Jesus had in mind when he spoke of the kingdom. The student is likely to be confused by the scholarly opinions on the subject, which differ considerably from each other, while the lay reader is likely to be confused by the diverse and seemingly enigmatic ways in which Jesus talks of the kingdom. Before we can proceed further we must try to understand what Jesus meant by the kingdom, and to do this we must begin by looking at the historical background.

The Jewish Background

The exact expression "the kingdom of God" is not found in Jewish writing before the Christian era. It does occur in Jewish prayers of the Tannaic Period, which covers the first two centuries A.D. in Palestine, and also in the Targum, an Aramaic translation of the Old Testament done almost entirely in the early centuries A.D. We do not find the expression in the language of the Pharisees, the Rabbinic teaching of Jesus' day, the Apocrypha, or in the Old Testament. On the other hand we do find in the Old Testament that the general idea of the kingship of God is widespread and important. Out of this idea of God's kingship over the world comes the Jewish hope and expectation for an end to the world, an understanding of which is very important for an evaluation of Christ's message.

In the Old Testament it is asserted that God was and is king over his creation; the world was created by him and is still, in spite of unruly men, under his authority. The message is particularly clearly developed by the prophets, especially by First and Second Isaiah, Jeremiah, and Ezekiel, that Yahweh is king over all peoples and all nations and is in ultimate control of history. Out of this idea of God's kingship comes the Jewish hope for the future. It is true that at the present time, the prophets declared, many men are disobedient to God so that his will for the world is not being accomplished and his rule is not now perfect on earth. Only when men are perfectly obedient to him can his kingly rule be truly and completely present. But though men now serve the powers of evil because of their wayward will, the time will come when God will act decisively and his plans for the world will be consummated. This time is known in the Old Testament as "the Day of the Lord," or simply as "the Day," or "that Day."

The Day of the Lord was variously conceived. Amos pointed out that, while the Jews generally looked forward to the Day of the Lord as a triumph for them, it will in fact be a Day of gloom for many as God will bring fire and punishment for those who have disobeyed him (Amos 5:18-

20); nevertheless, in that Day Yahweh will rebuild Israel in her own country and there will be a restoration of the faithful (Amos 9:11-15). Hosea declared that the Day of the Lord will be like a betrothal of Israel to Yahweh which will bring about integrity, justice, and love, so that virtue will reign once more over men (Hosea 2:18-24). Zephaniah declares that on the Day of the Lord Yahweh will repeal the sentence of judgment he has now passed over Israel; her punishment will be over and the faithful remnant, those who have endured to the end, will shout with joy (Zephaniah 3:11-18). Isaiah declares that on the Day Yahweh will take revenge over Israel's enemies and the unfaithful; the remnant of Israel who have remained loyal to him will become a holy people (Isaiah 2:4). Second Isaiah declares that on the Day Yahweh will gather his faithful offspring from all the corners of the world; all shall rejoice at that time, enmity shall cease, and even the wolf and the lamb shall feed together (Isaiah 43:5-7, 65:19-25) as the nations of every language shall at that time be gathered together to acknowledge his glory (Isaiah 66:18-24).

To summarize: The Day of the Lord would be a conclusion to history as ruled by man and the beginning of a supernatural rule by God. The wicked would find it a Day of doom, but the remnant who were faithful would constitute a new people and the beginning of a new kingdom under God. For them it would be a Day of joy.

The exact nature of the kingdom which God would establish when the Day of the Lord finally came was not clearly defined. Sometimes it appears that earthly things and institutions would remain in existence but would be transformed into their ideal condition, with all injustice removed. Others suggested that Israel at that time would become the first nation on earth and would lead the entire world into a new order. But the most important conception was of the establishment of a supernatural reign of God. According to this "apocalyptic" conception, history, as we understand it, would come to an end, and a heavenly reign would begin.

This supernatural conception of the Day of the Lord was bound up with the idea of the Messiah, the One who would come to act in God's name. There is neither clarity nor uniformity of belief in the Old Testament regarding the person or nature of the Messiah in the debate of biblical scholars. Scholars to this day debate many passages which refer to the Messiah and are not sure whether prophets, such as Isaiah, have in mind one single person when they are referring to the Messiah or conceive of the Messiah collectively as being the nation of Israel itself, acting as the people of God. What is clear, however, is that the Day of the Lord will be brought in by a special act of God, that he will act through some divinely appointed agency, and that this messianic agency might be a particular being or person.

This conception of how the Day of the Lord would be ushered in led to the so-called "double hope" eschatology. According to this, the first act of God would be the appearance of the Messiah. Then would follow a time of tribulation or struggle, a period of great cosmic conflict. Finally would come the victory of God and the final judgment of all men. The "in between days," when the Messiah had come but the final power of God was not yet established, would be days of great crisis and tribulation, featured by many apocalyptic struggles. We have many examples of this kind of literature in both the Old Testament and in the inter-testamental writings. Some of the more important passages are found in Daniel, the Book of Baruch, 2 Esdras, the Psalms of Solomon, and Fourth Ezra.

By Jesus' time there was no uniform interpretation of all these ideas in the minds of the Jewish people. Nevertheless it is certain that the general idea of the kingship of God over creation, of the need for a Messiah, and of the final action of God was part of every Jew's thinking. What was not certain in the minds of the Jewish people was how all this would come about, what the rule of God would be like, and when his kingship would be established. The Zealots apparently believed that men would have to act first before God would act, so they urged active revolt, and envisioned the coming rule of God at a time of political supremacy by the Jews. (This was the activist party whose revolt against the Romans in 66 A.D. led to the destruction of Jerusalem by Titus in 70 A.D.) The Pharisees felt that God was waiting for men to act righteously before he acted. Some asserted that if only all Jews would observe two sabbaths perfectly God would act to bring in his rule. Sadly, there was always some Jew somewhere who fell short of this perfection. But generally most Jews thought that God would have to take the initiative and act through a Messiah, an intermediary of some kind.

When we look at the New Testament writings which come from the period of the early Church, it is clear that many of these Jewish ideas are still very much in existence. The Book of Revelation, for instance, is more like a book of Jewish apocalyptic literature than a Christian document. Here the double hope theory and the old Jewish apocalyptic hopes reappear in all of their hoary detail, and the Christ of Love of the Gospels becomes the avenging cosmic Messiah who will usher in the final conflict. This raises questions: To what extent were the Christians of the early Church still influenced by the Jewish apocalyptic thinking, and did they possibly alter many of Jesus' ideas to fit into this old scheme of things? Or did Jesus himself have in mind much the same things as the Jews before him, so that his ideas of the kingdom of God, and of the Son of Man as the Messiah, were only new versions of the old theme? This is what we must now consider in more detail.

Contemporary Attempts To Reconstruct
Jesus' Idea of the Kingdom of God

Naturally the importance of the concept of the kingdom of God has not gone unnoticed by scholars and commentators, and there are many and varying theories of what Jesus meant by the kingdom. One of the favorite ideas of a century or so ago was the social concept. According to this Jesus had in mind a perfect social order, an ideal society where justice and Christian concepts of brotherhood would completely prevail. Says one of the representatives of this point of view, "The kingdom of God is humanity organized according to the will of God. . . . It is the Christian transfiguration of the social order" (Walter Rauschenbusch, as quoted in Vol. VII of *The Interpreter's Bible*, p. 152). The German philosopher Immanuel Kant also conceived of the kingdom in somewhat this way, likening it to the supreme ethical state when the rule of God is complete over the lives of men, because men are now obedient to God. The difficulty with this interpretation of the kingdom of God is that Jesus nowhere said that this was what he meant, and if this had been what he meant, he would have declared so. There is nothing strange or hard to conceive about the social conception of the kingdom; anyone can understand what this means. If this is what Jesus had in mind he could have easily said so in plain language. The fact that he did *not* say so argues against this interpretation.

More profound scholarly thinkers on the subject also recognize that the social interpretation of the kingdom is not adequate to the facts of the Gospel message, so that the prevailing contemporary interpretation of what Jesus meant by the kingdom in scholarly circles has shifted to a very different ground. According to most scholarly thought today, everything Jesus said about the kingdom of God must be understood *eschatologically*.

Eschatology, from the Greek word "eschaton," the final thing or end, is the study or science of the final things. When applied to New Testament writings it is the study of the end of the world, the final goal toward which God is moving. The "Day of the Lord" of the Old Testament, for instance, comprised the main eschatological idea of the Hebrews. When applied to Jesus' sayings it means that Jesus had in mind by the kingdom of God a final state, an end to the historical process to be brought about by God. This, of course, makes Jesus' concept of the kingdom an extension of the apocalyptic thinking of the Jews of his time, who, as we have seen, likewise looked for God to come and establish his kingdom.

The scholar chiefly responsible in our time for this interpretation is the German scholar Johannes Weiss, who first clearly stated this hypothesis in a highly influential little volume entitled (in English) *The Preaching of Jesus on the Kingdom of God*. According to Weiss we cannot attach any modern ideas to Jesus' teaching on the kingdom. For Weiss, the kingdom of God was something wholly in the future, as was the Day of the Lord in the Old

Testament, and it was thought of as a supra-worldly state to be established by God. Hence Jesus prays in the Lord's Prayer, "Thy kingdom come." The kingdom is visible here on earth now only as a kind of shadow, just as an approaching cloud might cast a shadow on earth before it actually arrives overhead.

Jesus himself, says Weiss, does not establish the kingdom; he only proclaims its coming. "Repent, for the kingdom of heaven is drawing near" is his proclamation. He has no special messianic function with regard to bringing about the kingdom but, like John the Baptist and others before him, he waits for God's supernatural actions to bring it about. Jesus did, however, at the beginning of his ministry, think that the kingdom was not approaching as rapidly as he had thought. He realized that he had miscalculated the nearness of God's action, and came to believe that he must do something to prepare the way and hasten the kingdom's arrival. This was to be done by his death, a sacrificial death by means of which he would relieve the guilt of his people and enable God to act.

Once the kingdom did come, says Weiss, Jesus felt he would return as the Messiah. At that time his true and proper messianic function would begin and he would be revealed as the Son of Man. Weiss felt that this was an apocalyptic title referring to the Messiah as he would come to initiate the kingdom, and that it was derived from the use of the term in this way in the Book of Daniel and the Similitudes of Enoch. In Daniel 7:13 we read, "I gazed into the visions of the night, and I saw, coming on the clouds of heaven, one like a son of man." When the kingdom came there would be an end to earthly institutions and to history as men conceive of it, for God's rule would now be complete, and life would be guided by supernatural edict.

Jesus' ideas on the kingdom of God thus differed little, if at all, from those of John the Baptist, and were essentially the same ideas as had been, and still were, current in Jewish eschatology. The only major difference was that Jesus believed in the imminence of the kingdom and in his own special forthcoming messianic role when the kingdom finally arrived. But everything Jesus had to say, said Weiss, must be understood in the light of ideas on the kingdom of God. His teaching was throughout an "eschatological teaching."

Another modern scholar who wrote on the subject was Albert Schweitzer, who did much to popularize, among scholars at least, the eschatological interpretation of the kingdom of God in his comprehensive book *The Quest of the Historical Jesus*. Schweitzer differs from Weiss only in extending Weiss' ideas still further. Not only is everything Jesus said to be understood in the light of his eschatology, but also everything which he did is to be understood in this light. This view Schweitzer calls "thorough-going eschatology."

Schweitzer felt that Jesus had a messianic consciousness but kept it a deliberate secret, for he was not to be revealed as the Messiah until the kingdom should arrive. This Jesus expected would soon happen. He sent out his disciples throughout Israel on the famous mission described in Matthew 10:1-16 (and its parallels in Luke 9:1-6 and Mark 6:7-13) because he expected the kingdom to arrive at any minute. When the kingdom did not come as expected, he changed his mind and realized that only his death could hasten its approach.

This messianic consciousness of Jesus was known to the disciples since the time of the transfiguration, when it was revealed to Peter, James and John. This story, Schweitzer feels, occurred prior to Peter's famous confession on the road to Caesarea Philippi: "You are the Christ, the Son of the living God" (Matthew 16:16). What Judas betrayed to the high priests was this messianic consciousness of Jesus, this closely guarded secret which only the disciples knew. But even with Judas' betrayal the high priest in the trial of Jesus is helpless to condemn him until Jesus himself openly admits his messiahship: "Moreover, I tell you that from this time onward you will see the *Son of Man seated at the right hand of the Power and coming on the clouds of heaven*" (Matthew 26:64).*

In all of this there is little difference from Weiss' essential position. What Jesus had in mind by the kingdom of God was the final, end state of things to be soon brought about by God's action. Jesus was the Messiah, but his messiahship would be realized in the future when he would return as the apocalyptic "Son of Man." Now his only mission was to proclaim the kingdom and prepare for its arrival. Everything Jesus said, and everything which he did, is to be understood in the light of this eschatology, according to Schweitzer.

A typical passage of the kind which Schweitzer says refers to the kingdom as an eschatological reality is Matthew 16:27-28: "For the Son of Man is going to come in the glory of his Father with his angels, and when he does, he will reward each one according to his behavior. I tell you solemnly, there are some of these standing here who will not taste death before they see the Son of Man coming with his kingdom." Here, so it is asserted, we have a passage filled with typically Jewish apocalyptic ideas. The Son of Man is the Messianic title for the forthcoming agent of God who will usher in the future kingdom.

Other examples which seem to support the eschatological theory are found in Matthew 24—for instance, where the disciples ask Jesus, after he foretells the destruction of Jerusalem: "Tell us, when is this going to happen, and what will be the sign of your coming and of the end of the world?" (Matthew 24:3). And after giving a sketch of the events which will precede the coming of himself as the Son of Man he adds, "This good news

*The biblical quotations in this discussion are all taken from *The Jerusalem Bible.*

of the kingdom will be proclaimed to the whole world as a witness to all the nations. And then the end will come" (Matthew 24:14). Later he continues in what appears as typical Jewish apocalyptic fashion: "And then the sign of the Son of Man will appear in heaven; then too all the peoples of the earth will beat their breasts; and they will see the Son of Man coming on the clouds of heaven with power and great glory. And he will send his angels with a loud trumpet to gather his chosen from the four winds, from one end of heaven to the other" (Matthew 24:30-31). However, the passages from Matthew 24 are somewhat suspect due to the suspicion many scholars have that this chapter is heavily influenced by the early Church so that we may not be hearing Jesus at this point, but utterances from an early Christian community reacting under persecutions.

The most recent scholar to consider with regard to the eschatological interpretation of the meaning of the kingdom of God is the English scholar, C. H. Dodd. Dodd also interprets the kingdom of God eschatologically, but he differs from Weiss and Schweitzer in his thesis that the kingdom for Jesus was an already present reality, not a future state yet to come. The kingdom of God *had* arrived, in Jesus' thinking, says Dodd—hence the term "realized eschatology." So for Dodd the kingdom is not to be considered a final state still coming in future history, something ultimate in time, but is ultimate in point of value, for the time has already been fulfilled and the kingdom has arrived. This was Dodd's original position. Later, under the impact of criticism, he acknowledged that the kingdom must be thought of as in a state of *being realized* rather than as complete in a final sense. The shift is from "realized eschatology" to "being realized eschatology." The realization of the ultimately valuable reality called the kingdom takes place in the whole course of Jesus' life, culminating in the crucifixion and resurrection.

Among the passages which Dodd cites in support of his view is Mark 1:15 (and its parallels in Matthew 4:12-17; Luke 4:14-15; Matthew 3:2 and 8:10), where we read that Jesus first proclaimed the message: "The time has come, and the kingdom of God is close at hand. Repent, and believe the good news." Dodd feels that the Greek verb here translated "is close at hand" has the force of "has now drawn near." He points out that in another place, after Jesus has cast out a demon, he says: "But if it is through the Spirit of God that I cast devils out, then know that the kingdom of God has overtaken you" (Matthew 12:28; Luke 11:20). Here the Greek verb is a different one which, Dodd says, certainly means "has arrived."

Dodd differs from his predecessors in the great sophistication of his application of his understanding of the kingdom to the various parts of the New Testament. With regard to the Fourth Gospel he points out that the "eternal life" of which the Fourth Gospel speaks is the equivalent of the kingdom of God and is to be understood as a present reality in which men can now participate. In the Epistle to the Hebrews, Dodd sees the idea of the kingdom linked up to Platonic concepts of reality. Here we find there is an "eternal order of reality," an archetypal spiritual dimension to life, the realm of being to which Christ passes at his resurrection. It is this world of unalterable spiritual truth beyond the world of phenomena where true reality is to be found, and this is the kingdom of God. In most of the later New Testament writings, however, Dodd sees a regression to a more primitive Jewish attitude. It seemed to the early Church as though the kingdom had not come after all, in spite of the resurrection of Christ, and so the early Church looked forward to a second coming of Christ when the kingdom would finally be ushered in once and for all. In this they differed little from previous Jewish hopes for the forthcoming Day of the Lord. For St. Paul this coming kingdom, and this second return of Christ, were beginning already in the hearts of the believers—hence his "Christ-mysticism." For the Book of Revelation, however, it was pictured entirely as a future cosmic conflict.

Dodd's ideas go considerably beyond the other eschatologists. He has, however, been widely criticized and not generally accepted. Some scholars attack him on theological grounds, and others quarrel with him on linguistic grounds, claiming that the passages he cites in support of his realized eschatology involve Greek verbs which do not necessarily imply a present reality. For our purpose it suffices to state that the prevailing scholarly interpretation of the kingdom is the narrower eschatological theory. Before we can proceed further, then, we must look at this theory and make an evaluation. But we will have occasion to allude to Dodd's theory later.

*Evaluation of the Eschatological
Interpretation of the Kingdom of God*

The eschatological theory is impressive because it can point to many sayings of Jesus regarding the kingdom of God and the Son of Man which can readily be claimed to point to Jesus' belief in a future kingdom yet to come. On the other hand, there are many facts which the eschatological theory does not adequately explain.

1. If Jesus had an eschatological interpretation of the kingdom of God, it must at least be granted that it differed in many important ways from the older Jewish ideas. For instance, in Jewish documents such as the Book of Daniel the interpretation of the coming Day of the Lord is very involved with the events of history. The act of God is called into being by historical events, even necessitated by them, but there is nothing in the teachings of Jesus to indicate that he felt the kingdom was coming because of the historical movements or political situation of his time. To the contrary, the kingdom's approach is described as a purely spiritual movement.

2. In Jewish thinking those who belonged to the kingdom would be the

people of Israel, or all those who were faithful to the Law, or some other clearly defined group. In Jesus' thinking we find a radically different conception of who shall belong to the kingdom, for according to Jesus entrance into the kingdom of God depends entirely upon one's inner credentials. It does not even matter if one is not a Jew so long as one has the right inner life and a spiritual orientation involving a new consciousness.

3. In Jewish thinking the final act of God comes because of extreme pessimism concerning the world. The world is so bad and hopeless that God *must* act. There is no such pessimism in Jesus, and the kingdom is pictured as coming in the fullness of time, out of the bounty of God and his care for his creation.

4. In current Jewish thinking the Day of the Lord will be initiated by God's own mighty acts from without. Supernatural intervention will bring in the kingship of God. In the bulk of Jesus' thinking God's rule over men will be established from within. God will act in men's hearts, and not impose his will and rule on history from outside of man.

5. Undeniably Jesus had a messianic consciousness, an awareness of his own unique relationship to the kingdom of God. But his conception of his messiahship differed markedly from current Jewish ideas. Only in the picture of Isaiah's suffering servant, as we find it in Isaiah 53, do we find an idea in Jewish thought analogous to the messiahship of Jesus.

6. Although there are many passages in which the expressions kingdom of God and Son of Man can conveniently be interpreted along the lines of the eschatological hypothesis, there are other passages where such an interpretation is much more difficult, even impossible. We will be looking at some of these passages later.

7. One cornerstone of the eschatological hypothesis is that the expression "Son of Man," which Jesus used of himself, is identical with the meaning of that expression in Daniel 7:13 and is a special messianic title used to refer to the Messiah when he comes on the final day. However, this expression may also mean simply "Man," or the "Essence of Man." Hans Lietzmann, another well-known scholar in the field, has gone to great lengths to show that the expression "Son of Man" may be a way of denoting "general mankind." In this case it would be analogous, in Platonic thought, to the Archetype of Man. It is, as we shall see later, used in this way in many places in the Old Testament—for instance, in the Book of Ezekiel where the prophet, as the representative of mankind, is referred to as "Son of Man," or in Psalm 8:4, "What is man that you should spare a thought for him, the son of man that you should care for him?"

8. Finally, the idea that the kingdom of God was, in Jesus' mind, a future supernatural state yet to come bears all the mark of an invention. Had Jesus conceived of the kingdom in this way, it would not have been difficult for him to make quite clear what he thought the kingdom was and

when it would come. In fact, Jesus' sayings about the kingdom have, at first glance, an enigmatic, puzzling quality, because he refers to the kingdom primarily by using images and figures. He was not being deliberately obscure in referring to the kingdom by this means. Rather, he was attempting in this way to convey to his listeners a reality which they had not yet contemplated.

The fact is that Jesus' ideas regarding the kingdom of God are different from the collective ideas of those around him. If in the matters we have discussed above he has such a unique point of view, it is unlikely that his concept of the kingdom would be identical with prevailing Jewish conceptions. His uniqueness calls for us to look for something unique in his conception of the kingdom as well.

The Spiritual Hypothesis

In science, if any hypothesis accounts for some of the facts, but not all of them, it is not regarded as adequate. It is the facts which a hypothesis does not account for which turn out to be all-important in framing a new and more creative theory. For instance, Newton's concepts in physics accounted for almost all of the then known facts, but it failed to account for certain minor but discernible discrepancies in the movement of the planet Mercury. Einstein's theory of relativity was found to explain not only the facts which could be interpreted by Newton's concepts but also could interpret precisely the movements of Mercury. Clearly Einstein's hypothesis was to be preferred to Newton's, and the one hitherto unexplainable detail turned out to be vitally important.

Since the eschatological theory does not explain satisfactorily all of the facts regarding the kingdom of God we must look elsewhere for another, and perhaps more satisfactory, hypothesis. There is in fact another explanation of what Jesus had in mind by the kingdom of God which comes primarily from the early Church Fathers rather than from modern scholars, and which might be called "the spiritual hypothesis." According to the spiritual hypothesis Jesus meant by the kingdom of God a non-physical, invisible reality, which was most clearly discovered in one's own soul. We might therefore also call it the "psychological hypothesis" since it was a reality personally discoverable by an individual in his own life and being. From the point of view of this hypothesis the kingdom is not something coming upon man from outside of himself, initiated supernaturally by God, but is a reality within himself, already present in him, as the archetypal foundation of his life, yet waiting to be recognized and entered into by the individual believer.

This is the theory of the kingdom accepted by all the major Fathers of the early Church after the first half of the second century. It was also the cornerstone of a unique method of interpreting Scripture. The famous early Christian scholar Origen, of Alexandria in Egypt, is a good example of this. According to Origen a passage of Scripture might be understood on three levels. On the first level is its historical sense; here we understand a story or incident to tell something which actually happened. Second is the moral sense; here we find in the story moral instruction for the leading of our lives. Third is the spiritual sense; here we find that the story, or incident, or saying, conveys by means of its symbolism, or its "hidden" meaning, an insight into the spiritual world. With the third level of meaning the details of the stories are very significant. Thus, for example, the details of the construction of the tabernacle in the Old Testament are to be understood as all-important, for the numbers, lengths, proportions, and decorations of the building all refer, in a symbolic way, to the spiritual edifice of the kingdom of God. Similarly the Song of Solomon with its beautiful love story is to be understood as a figure, hidden within which is the mysterious conjunction of Christ with the Church, or Christ with the soul of the individual believer. Similarly the story of Adam and Eve is intended to have a "secret meaning," "a philosophic meaning in a secret covering" (*Against Celsus*, IV, xxxviii). Especially with regard to the Gospels he says, "What do we find when we come to the Gospels? Is not hidden there also an inner, namely a divine sense?" (*De Principiis*, IV, 1. 9). For in the Bible generally "those words which are written are the forms of certain mysteries and the images of divine things" (*De Principiis*, Preface), so that virtually all the passages in the Bible are to be understood, at their spiritual level, in this way. "But all the narrative portion, relating either to the marriages, or the begetting of the children or to battles of different kinds, or to any other histories whatever, what else can they be supposed to be, save the forms and figures of hidden and sacred things?" (Origen, *De Principiis*, IV, 1. 9. Cf. *ibid*, 11. 2; Origen *Contra Celsus*, III. xlvi; IV, xxxvii; IV, 1).

The spiritual hypothesis has been attacked by modern thinkers on a variety of scores. The most important criticisms launched against this theory are the following.

1. It is said that this hypothesis goes counter to the entire Jewish thinking of the age. It is asserted that the spiritual hypothesis of the kingdom is an example of Greek thought and mysticism and is foreign to Jewish thinking, and that no Jewish precedent can be found for this theory.

2. The point is made that the spiritual hypothesis is based upon Luke 17:21, "The kingdom of God is within you." However, modern scholars say the correct rendering of this verse should probably be "among you" and not "within you."

3. It is said that this theory lays the field of biblical criticism open to hopeless subjectivity. The Fathers of the Church fell prey to this fault in their spiritual interpretation of the Bible since according to this view

anything can be made out to mean anything. Such a theory can only lead to variant forms of gnosticism, subjective interpretations which please the individual inventor of them but have no basis in historical fact.

4. Finally it is pointed out that the spiritual hypothesis is based upon outmoded concepts of reality which are no longer tenable today. Today we believe in science, in the reliability of the physical world. There is no room in our thinking for an hypothesis of a non-physical dimension to reality which man can know and in which he can participate.

We will now meet these objections in order.

1. The argument that Jesus could not have had a unique spiritual conception of the kingdom of God because it was foreign to the Jewish tradition is valid only if we assume that Jesus was an ordinary man. The truth is that occasionally, though very rarely, a unique man does come up with a perfectly unique thought, for which little if any historical precedent can be found. One such example is Einstein, whose theory of relativity is so unique that it is almost impossible to find antecedents to his concepts. There is no reason why Jesus could not have also been this unique in spiritual matters. His person was unique in its wholeness and its freedom from historical conditioning. It is not only possible, therefore, but likely, that his basic idea of the kingdom of God should be one without precedent.

2. The argument regarding how Luke 17:21 is to be translated hinges upon the Greek preposition "ertos." This preposition can mean either "within" or "among." If the former translation is called for it indicates that Jesus thought of the kingdom as an inner, spiritual reality; if the latter, it is an outer reality of some sort, embodied perhaps in his own person. The difficulty is compounded by the fact that Jesus himself probably spoke Aramaic, so Luke 17:21 is a Greek translation or paraphrase of his actual, original words. The truth is that we have no conclusive way of knowing which way the verse is to be translated.

It is, however, a prejudice of our extroverted, materialistic attitude toward life that the "among" translation is to be preferred to the "within." In English versions of the Bible we find Luke 17:21 is rendered "within" by the KJV, but is rendered "among" by the RSV, the New English Bible, and most other modern translations. Translators claim that it makes more sense this way. The fact is that the "among" translation causes the materialistic bias of our day less confusion, for the "within" translation would throw us into a mystical or psychological sense which would make us uncomfortable. There are exceptions in modern translations, however, to the "among" school. The Jerusalem Bible renders it "among" but in a footnote gives the "within" as an equal alternative. "The Good News for Modern Man" version, by the American Bible Society, uses the "within" directly in the text.

What is interesting is that the early Fathers of the Church consistently used "within" and never "among." In my notes I have instances from twelve of the great doctors of the early Church, all of whom render Luke 17:21: "The kingdom of God is *within* you."

From all this it is apparent that Luke 17:21 can as easily be rendered "within" as "among," which leaves the field open again to the spiritual hypothesis of the kingdom of God. But, more important, it is a false argument that the entire spiritual hypothesis hangs upon this one verse. Not this one verse but the entire tenor of Jesus' sayings points to the spiritual hypothesis, as we shall see.

3. The third objection, that the spiritual hypothesis leaves the interpretation of the Bible open to a hopeless subjectivity, is beside the point as soon as we accept the idea that spiritual reality is as objective as is physical reality. It is true that in the ancient world spiritual reality was plumbed largely by means of speculation, and those who favored a spiritual interpretation of the Scriptures had to adhere to no scientific standards. Today, however, we are in a better position, for spiritual reality is included in the idea of the unconscious, and the unconscious is, at least in part, open to scientific scrutiny. If we take our knowledge of the unconscious as the foundation for a spiritual or psychological understanding of Scripture we have a certain objective basis on which to ground our interpretations, and are not in danger of reducing biblical interpretations to sheer fantasizing.

4. The final objection, that the spiritual hypothesis is unthinkable because modern science has dispelled the spiritual reality of life, is pure prejudice. Science, in its theories of the unconscious, of quantum mechanics, of the elusive nature of matter, and of the mathematical basis we must assume for life and the world makes a spiritual hypothesis more thinkable than ever before. It is not science which tells us that there can be no spiritual reality, but the monistic philosophy of materialism which says all reality must be "out there" and apprehendable through the senses of the body. (We have laid out the foundation of this point of view in the beginning chapters of this book.)

The Kingdom of God as an Inner Reality

The early Christian Fathers of the Church could believe that the kingdom of God was within man because they believed in the objective nature of the invisible world, i.e., of spiritual reality. On the one hand they believed that the world we apprehend through our five senses rested upon an archetypal basis which could be apprehended only through the soul or the enlightened intellect. They also believed that in addition to man's conscious will and his physical body, he was in touch with an inner reality which they called the soul. Because of the soul, man had valid experiences from two sources: he experienced an outer physical order through the five senses, and, on the information arrived at, a knowledge of nature; and he experienced from within, through dreams, visions, inner experiences, and revelations, the non-physical realities of life. The soul of man was in turn in touch with a variety of spiritual powers which worked both for good and ill. Thus the soul of man might fall under the power of demons, or might be inspired or guided by an angel. These spiritual powers, the "principalities and powers of this world," had a great influence upon the course of things in man's life, and if an individual's life was dominated by sin and error, that person could be enslaved to dark spiritual powers.

God, however, acting in Christ, had routed the demons and the powers of evil on the cross. He had established his power in the spiritual realm in which man's soul was immersed, and this power of Christ was available to all men who confessed his name and grounded their lives upon him. For these persons it was possible to become a member of the kingdom of God, to belong to a spiritual order in which man's whole life and being was infused by God, and the kingdom of God was within man in the sense that man found the kingdom through his own soul. The kingdom was a spiritual reality because it was not bounded by space and time as consciousness ordinarily experiences these things, nor was it perceivable through the senses of the body, but could only be known by the soul, or the intellect enlightened by the Love of Christ. But the kingdom was nevertheless an objective reality, as objective to man as the physical world in which man lived, because inner things were as real as outer things, and the world within man was as real as the world outside of him.

Today we no longer use the language of the early Fathers and do not speak of demons, angels, principalities and powers. But we have discovered the reality of the inner world, of the non-physical side to man and to all of life. In the unconscious psyche of man we find very much alive exactly those autonomous powers which the New Testament and the early Christian world described. The discovery of the reality and extent of the unconscious, and particularly of its archetypal, universal quality, is the key to understanding what Jesus meant by the kingdom of God. It is this realization, that man's conscious life is grounded upon a larger unconscious life, which enables us to introduce once more the spiritual hypothesis of the kingdom.

The idea here is that the kingdom of God is a non-physical reality, a personal state of being, an archetypal spiritual realm. When the kingdom emerges into a man's life it brings with it wholeness and creativity. The kingdom, as the spiritual rock on which a man's personality is based, is transcendental because it is of divine, not human origin. God created our lives, not we ourselves. It is transpersonal because this inner reality of the kingdom is not "my" kingdom, but "the" kingdom. The individual who belongs to the kingdom does not follow his own plan of life, but must fashion his life according to the larger reality within himself.

The kingdom is a psychological reality in that it is personally experienced by each individual. It is a mystical reality in that only an *experience* with the kingdom can reveal what it is, and no words, including these, can do more than vaguely adumbrate the kingdom to those who have not been initiated into it. The kingdom is an objective reality because it is not subjectively created by man's experience or wishes, any more than a man who has seen the Himalayas for the first time can say that he has created them. The kingdom is an inner reality in that a man perceives it not out in space and time through the media of the senses of the body, but in the inner dimension of life, via the illumination of his soul.

At the same time the kingdom of God has a great social significance. The one who experiences the kingdom is called upon to translate his relationship with God into social concerns, and to seek to make the outer order and fabric of men's lives conform to the inner archetypal order of the kingdom within. The kingdom thus has a universal significance and is the impelling force calling upon men to establish a social order grounded upon God's will. But it can only be realized socially through individuals, and cannot be established through collective media. The one who enters into the kingdom enters into a personal, individual relationship to God, his neighbors, and himself. He becomes an *individual* man, that is, an undivided person, whose outer personality and inner self are in harmony, and who is distinct as a person from the collective psychology around him.

All of this describes the kingdom as a present spiritual reality, but the kingdom as a spiritual reality also has an eschatological character. It is a present state insofar as it is a reality which already exists within men, and in which those men can participate who are conscious enough and have formed their lives according to its pattern. But the kingdom in another sense is still to come in the future, for it cannot be said to be completely established until all men belong to it. Therefore the kingdom is eschatological in nature insofar as it embodies God's plan for man, a plan not yet completed and so still to come.

D. Outline and Reading for Class on Working with the Dying, Given at the University of Notre Dame

Course: Seminar on Death, Dying and Suffering. Theology 454
Instructor: Morton T. Kelsey

Purpose: This seminar explores—"with no holds barred"—the meaning of death and suffering in our modern culture. Our failure to deal with this problem may be one reason for the inability of so many people to relate adequately to each other. The course is exploratory in nature. The reading list, provided below, is only a small selection from the available studies.

The following preliminary suggestions are offered:

1. This is a group exploration. The class interaction is of great importance and the absence of one person changes the character of the group. If an absence is unavoidable, please advise the instructor in advance. It is hoped that we shall deal with the subject in a more than purely cognitive manner. This is facilitated by the group. Additional groups can also be arranged.

2. If the interaction of the group is to be meaningful, a record or journal of one's personal reactions, feelings and dreams during this period will be helpful.

3. Turn in brief reflections, no more than two pages, on each two books read.

4. In place of a final examination the students will be asked to make a careful, critical evaluation of what they have learned, the value of the seminar, possibilities for its improvement, etc.

Reading list (numbered books are to be read in the order shown):

Periodicals:

(13.) *Psychology Today*, August 1970.

(13.) *Medical World News* (McGraw-Hill publication), May 21, 1971.

(13.) *Psychiatric Opinion*, Vol. 7, No. 2, April 1970; Vol. 7, No. 5, Oct. 1970.

(13.) *Patient Care*, May 31, 1970, "Managing the Dying Process."

(13.) *Bulletin of Suicidology*, National Institute of Mental Health, No. 6, Spring 1970. (Other issues also relevant.)

(13.) "The Dying Patient," *Psychosocial Dimensions of Family Practice*, Roche Laboratories, Nutley, N.J. 07110.

(13.) *Event*, American Lutheran Church magazine, Dec. 1972, issue on Life and Death.

(13.) *The Marriage and Family Counselor's Quarterly*, Vol. 7, No. 2, Winter 1972, "Terminal Illness Counseling—The Death Experience."

(13.) *Notre Dame Lawyer*, Vol. 45, No. 2, Winter 1970, "Undue Influence, Confidential Relationship, and the Psychology of Transference" (Dean Shaffer).

Psychology and Suffering:

    C. G. Jung *et al.*, *Man and His Symbols*, Doubleday, 1964, or Dell pap.— Sections by Jung, Jacobi and von Franz.

(1.) C. G. Jung, *Memories, Dreams, Reflections*, Random House, 1963, also pap.—with particular attention to Chap. 6, Confrontation with the Unconscious.

(8.) ———, *Two Essays on Analytical Psychology*, Collected Works, Vol. 7, or Princeton Univ. pap.

    ———, *Modern Man in Search of a Soul*, Harcourt Brace pap.

(12.) ———, *Answer to Job*, Coll. Works, Vol. 11, pp. 355-470, or Princeton Univ. pap.

    Death Inside Out, ed. by Peter Steinfels and Robert M. Veatch. Harper pap., 1975.

(4.) M. T. Kelsey, *Encounter with God*, Bethany Fellowship, Minneapolis, 1972, pap.

(11.) ———, *Healing and Christianity*, Harper pap. 1973.

    ———, *God, Dreams, and Revelation*, Chapter 9, Augsburg pap. 1973.

    S. Freud, *Beyond the Pleasure Principle*, Compl. Works, Vol. 18, or Norton pap.

    ———, *Civilization and Its Discontents*, Norton pap.

    Jerome Frank, *Persuasion and Healing*, Schocken pap.

(10.) Adolf Guggenbühl-Craig, *Power in the Helping Professions*, Spring Pub.

(6.) Karl Menninger, *Man Against Himself*, Harcourt Brace pap.

General Discussion of Suffering:

    The Book of Job, in a modern translation.

Alan Paton et al., Creative Suffering: The Ripple of Hope, United Church, 1970.

Aldous Huxley, The Devils of Loudun, Harper pap. A study of man's inhumanity to man.

Anne Walters and Jim Marugg, Beyond Endurance, Harper, 1954. What it is like to come through polio and be in an iron lung.

Kurt F. Reinhardt, The Existentialist Revolt. Ungar, 1960 or later ed. Chaps. on Kierkegaard and Nietzsche.

Baron F. von Hügel, Essays and Addresses on the Philosophy of Religion, 1921, Dutton, 1963. 1st Series, pp. 98-116; 2nd Series, pp. 167-213.

Miguel de Unamuno, Tragic Sense of Life. Dover pap.

General Discussion of Death and Dying:

(2.) Elisabeth Kübler-Ross, On Death and Dying, Macmillan, 1969.

_____, Death: The Final Stage of Growth, Prentice-Hall, 1975, pap.

_____, Questions and Answers on Death and Dying, Macmillan, 1974, pap.

(7.) Herman Feifel, ed., The Meaning of Death, McGraw-Hill, 1959, also pap.

Robert Kastenbaum and Ruth Aisenberg, The Psychology of Death, Springer Pub., 1972.

Group for the Advancement of Psychiatry, Death and Dying: Attitudes of Patient and Doctor, Mental Health Center, 1967, pp. 615ff. (Samuel Feder, "Attitudes of Patients with Advanced Malignancy.")

Leo Tolstoy, The Death of Ivan Ilych, New American Library pap.

Plato, Phaedo. On the death of Socrates.

Geoffrey Gorer, Death, Grief, and Mourning, Doubleday pap. On the value of rituals at the time of death.

Alfred Worcester, The Care of the Aged, the Dying and the Dead, Thomas, 1961.

(3.) Ernest Becker, The Denial of Death, Free Press, 1973.

John Hinton, Dying, Penguin pap.

Bernard Schoenberg et al, eds., Loss and Grief: Psychological Management in Medical Practice, Columbia Univ. Press, 1973, also pap.

Marjorie Mitchell, The Child's Attitude to Death, Schocken, 1967.

Kurt R. Eissler, The Psychiatrist and the Dying Patient, Int'l Univ. Pr., 1955.

Notre Dame Journal of Education, Vol. 5, No. 2, Spring 1974, pp. 121ff. (McNeill, "Learning and Teaching Experiential Theology: An Intergenerational Journey.")

Earl Grollman, ed., Explaining Death to Children. Beacon pap.

Dealing with Death, Grief and Life after Death:

Albert Camus, The Plague, Modern Library pap.

Karlis Osis and Erlendur Haraldsson, At the Hour of Death, Avon pap., 1977.

C. S. Lewis, A Grief Observed. Seabury, 1963. Personal discussion of grief.

Alan Paton, *For You Departed*, Scribner, 1969. Personal discussion of grief.

Glen W. Davidson, *Living with Dying*, Augsburg pap., 1975.

Baron F. von Hügel, *Eternal Life*, T. & T. Clark, Edinburgh, 1929.

———, *The Mystical Element of Religion*, Dutton, 1928—Vol. 2, Chap. 12, pp. 182-258.

Bernadine Kreis and Alice Pattie, *Up from Grief: Patterns of Recovery*, Seabury, 1969.

Evelyn Waugh, *The Loved One*, Dell pap. A satire on Forest Lawn mortuary.

Emily Gardiner Neal, *In the Midst of Life*, Morehouse-Barlow, 1963.

Helen Chappell White, *With Wings as Eagles*, Rinehart, 1953. A woman's story of recovering from her son's death.

Edgar Herzog, *Psyche and Death: Archaic Myths and Modern Dreams in Analytical Psychology*, Putnam, 1967.

Dante, *The Divine Comedy*, Sayers translation. Penguin pap., 3 vols.

(14.) Helen Luke, *Dark Wood to White Rose*, Dove, Pecos, New Mex. The meaning in Dante.

(5.) Raymond Moody, *Life After Life*, Bantam pap.

(5.) ———, *Reflections on Life After Life*, Mockingbird Press, 1978.

Arthur Ford (as told to Jerome Ellison), *The Life Beyond Death*, Berkley pap.

Journal for the Scientific Study of Religion, Vol. 12, No. 2, June 1973, pp. 209ff. (R. Kalish and D. Reynolds, on "Post-Death Contact").

Death to Life, papers by biologists, theologians and philosophers, Argus Communications, Chicago, 1968.

The Problem of Evil in General:

(9.) Elie Wiesel, *Night*, Avon pap.

Eldridge Cleaver, *Soul on Ice*, Dell pap. Evil, suffering, and the blacks.

Malcolm X, *Autobiography*. Dell pap. Evil, suffering, and the blacks.

John H. Griffin, *Black Like Me*. New Am. Lib. pap. Evil, suffering, and the blacks.

Herbert Kohl, *36 Children*, New Amer. Lib. pap. Urban evil and suffering.

Jonathan Kozol, *Death at an Early Age*, Bantam pap. Urban evil and suffering.

Kerényi *et al.*, *Evil*, ed. by Curatorium, Jung Institute, Northwestern Univ., 1967.

Charles Williams, *Shadows of Ecstasy, War in Heaven,* and *Descent into Hell.* Eerdmans pap. Three novels depicting the reality of evil.

C. S. Lewis, *Out of the Silent Planet, Perelandra,* and *That Hideous Strength*, Macmillan pap. Trilogy dealing with the roots of evil.

(9.) ———, *The Lion, the Witch and the Wardrobe*, Macmillan pap. An amazing children's allegory of evil.

J. R. R. Tolkien, *The Lord of the Rings*, 3 vols, Houghton Mifflin pap.

Leon Christiani, *Evidences of Satan in the Modern World*, Macmillan, 1962.

Suicide as Ultimate Suffering:

Maurice L. Farber, *The Theory of Suicide*, Funk and Wagnalls, 1968.

N. L. Farberow and E. S. Shneidman, *Cry for Help*, McGraw-Hill pap.

E. S. Shneidman, ed., *Essays on Self-Destruction*, Science House, 1967.

H. L. Resnik, *Suicidal Behaviors: Diagnosis and Management*, Little, Brown, 1968.

H. Peck and A. Schrut, "Suicide Among College Students," *Proceedings of the Fourth International Congress for Suicide Prevention*, Delmar Pub., 1968.

A. Schrut, "Suicidal Adolescents and Children," *Journal of the A.M.A.*, 188: 1103-1107, 1964.

A. Schrut, "Some Typical Patterns in the Behavior and Background of Adolescent Girls Who Attempt Suicide," *American Journal of Psychiatry*, 125:1, 1968.

Louis Dublin, *Suicide: A Sociological and Statistical Study*, Ronald Press, 1963.

Erwin Stengel, *Suicide and Attempted Suicide*, Penguin pap.

E. S. Shneidman and N. L. Farberow, eds., *Clues to Suicide*, McGraw-Hill pap.

James Hillman, *Suicide and the Soul*, Harper, 1965.

James J. Lynch, *The Broken Heart*, Basic Books, 1977.

E. A Near-Death Experience
Reported by C. G. Jung*

I would like to give an example from my own medical experience. A woman patient, whose reliability and truthfulness I have no reason to doubt, told me that her first birth was very difficult. After thirty hours of fruitless labour the doctor considered that a forceps delivery was indicated. This was carried out under light narcosis. She was badly torn and suffered great loss of blood. When the doctor, her mother, and her husband had gone, and everything was cleared up, the nurse wanted to eat, and the patient saw her turn round at the door and ask, "Do you want anything before I go to supper?" She tried to answer, but couldn't. She had the feeling that she was sinking through the bed into a bottomless void. She saw the nurse hurry to the bedside and seize her hand in order to take her pulse. From the way she moved her fingers to and fro the patient thought it must be almost imperceptible. Yet she herself felt quite all right, and was slightly amused at the nurse's alarm. She was not in the least frightened. . . .

The next thing she was aware of was that, without feeling her body and its position, she was *looking down* from a point in the ceiling and could see everything going on in the room below her: she saw herself lying in the bed, deadly pale, with closed eyes. Beside her stood the nurse. The doctor paced up and down the room excitedly, and it seemed to her that he had lost his head and didn't know what to do. Her relatives crowded to the door. Her mother and her husband came in and looked at her with frightened faces. She told herself it was too stupid of them to think she was going to die, for she would certainly come round again. All this time she knew that behind her was a glorious, park-like landscape shining in the brightest colours, and in particular an emerald green meadow with short grass, which sloped gently upwards beyond a wrought-iron gate leading into the park. It

*C. G. Jung, *Collected Works*, Vol. 8 (*The Structure and Dynamics of the Psyche*), 2nd Edition, Princeton, New Jersey, Princeton Univ. Press, 1969, pp. 507ff.

was spring and little gay flowers such as she had never seen before were scattered about in the grass. The whole demesne sparkled in the sunlight, and all the colours were of an indescribable splendour. The sloping meadow was flanked on both sides by dark green trees. It gave her the impression of a clearing in the forest, never yet trodden by the foot of man. "I knew that this was the entrance to another world, and that if I turned round to gaze at the picture directly, I should feel tempted to go in at the gate, and thus step out of life." She did not actually *see* this landscape, as her back was turned to it, but she *knew* it was there. She felt there was nothing to stop her from entering in through the gate. She only knew that she would turn back to her body and would not die. That was why she found the agitation of the doctor and the distress of her relatives stupid and out of place.

The next thing that happened was that she awoke from her coma and saw the nurse bending over her in bed. She was told that she had been unconscious for about half an hour. The next day, some fifteen hours later, when she felt a little stronger, she made a remark to the nurse about the incompetent and "hysterical" behaviour of the doctor during her coma. The nurse energetically denied this criticism in the belief that the patient had been completely unconscious at the time and could therefore have known nothing of the scene. Only when she described in full detail what had happened during the coma was the nurse obliged to admit that the patient had perceived the events exactly as they happened in reality.

. . . [the patient] had suffered a genuine heart collapse followed by syncope due to cerebral anaemia. . . . She really was in a coma and ought to have had a complete psychic black-out and been altogether incapable of clear observation and sound judgment. The remarkable thing was that it was not an immediate perception of the situation through indirect or unconscious observation, but she saw the whole situation from *above*, as though "her eyes were in the ceiling," as she put it.

Notes

Introduction

1. Gordon D. Kaufman, *Systematic Theology: A Historicist Perspective*, New York, Charles Scribner's Sons, 1968, p. 464.
2. Schubert M. Ogden, *The Reality of God*, London, SCM Press Limited, 1977, p. 230.
3. Dag Hammarskjöld, *Markings,* trans. by Leif Sjöberg and W. H. Auden, New York, Alfred A. Knopf, 1964, p. 160.

Chapter I

1. Helen Luke gives an excellent introduction to *The Divine Comedy* in her book *Dark Wood to White Rose* (Pecos, New Mexico, Dove Publications, 1975). In it she sketches out the significance of the poem for people today. A superb translation of *The Divine Comedy* has been provided by Dorothy Sayers and Barbara Reynolds (Baltimóre, Penguin Books, 1949-1962). It is available in three paperback volumes with just the right amount of introduction and interesting notes.
2. The difficulty seems even greater if we must peer into black holes in the universe, or warm holes and white-hot holes, to find the origins of our lives, as the latest physical theories suggest. These ideas are set forth by Bob Toben in conversation with Jack Sarfatti and Fred Wolf in *Space-Time and Beyond: Toward an Explanation of the Unexplainable*, New York, E. P. Dutton & Co., Inc., 1975.
3. The effects of such stress are discussed in detail in Chapters 10 and 11 of my book *Healing and Christianity*, New York, Harper & Row, 1973.

Chapter II

1. Freud's research made him see that psychic realities as well as material ones influence human behavior, but he saw only chaotic and

primitive elements in the psyche. These elements, as Freud saw them, were either so instinctive and unconscious, or so subject to the death wish (the down-drag that tries to take everything back to the non-existence of inorganic matter), that they did nothing but cause problems for human beings. The only part of a person that could be valued differently was human reason, and there seemed to be no evidence that our reason would continue after death.

In fact, Freud considered that the highest human developments, our artistic and intellectual achievements, were merely the result of neurotic repression. As he saw it, men and women grow and make creative strides when civilization puts the lid on instinctual urges and other elements arising from the unconscious psyche. Human consciousness is then only a secondary product, a will-o'-the-wisp that is bound to disintegrate and disappear, slipping back into the original mass of inorganic matter. The only permanent and self-sustaining reality is found in material things. In *The Future of an Illusion* (New York, Doubleday & Company, Inc., 1957), Freud brought these conclusions into focus.

2. There is no question about the importance of the ideas of China and East Asia if we are trying to consider the religious views of all humankind. Yet few of us are well informed about this half of the world. One excellent introduction to these cultures and their religions is found in *Half the World: The History and Culture of China and Japan*, edited by Arnold Toynbee, New York, Holt, Rinehart and Winston, Inc., 1973.

3. The reader who is interested in following the intricacies of philosophical existentialism can find ample material in the book edited by George A. Schrader, *Existential Philosophers: Kierkegaard to Merleau-Ponty*, New York, McGraw-Hill Book Co., 1967. Sam Keen's fascinating interview with Ernest Becker shortly before his death is found in *Psychology Today* for April 1974, pp. 71ff.

4. In the Greek version of the Old Testament *hádēs* was the word generally used for Sheol. It was also used for hell in the New Testament.

Chapter IV

1. The book I have mentioned by Mircea Eliade, *Shamanism* (Princeton, New Jersey, Princeton University Press, 1964), shows how common these visions have been. Anyone who is interested in this subject will find it fascinating reading.

2. *The Comedy of Dante Alighieri, Cantica I: Hell*, trans. by Dorothy L. Sayers, Baltimore, Penguin Books, Inc., 1949, p. 39. A valuable introduction to *The Divine Comedy*, including the principal facts of Dante's life, is found in this volume.

3. *Ibid.*, p. 9. This is the original translation by Dorothy Sayers before her death.

4. These diagrams were drawn by C. W. Scott-Giles especially for the Sayers-Reynolds translation of *The Divine Comedy*. They are found in *The Comedy of Dante Alighieri, Cantica III, Paradise*, trans. by Dorothy L. Sayers and Barbara Reynolds, Baltimore, Penguin Books, Inc. 1962, fold-out at the end; *Cantica I, Hell, op. cit.*, pp. 70 and 138; *Cantica II, Purgatory*, trans. by Dorothy L. Sayers, Baltimore, Penguin Books, Inc., 1955, p. 62.

5. Helen M. Luke, *Dark Wood to White Rose, op. cit.*, p. 37. This is probably the most rewarding study of the meanings in *The Divine Comedy* that has been produced.

6. It may well be that Dante was simply giving in to Church authority in excluding pagans and unbaptized Christians from heaven, no matter how deserving they were.

7. *The Comedy of Dante Alighieri, Cantica III, Paradise, op. cit.*, p. 82 (IV, 35-52).

8. The full story of the effects of the discoveries of Copernicus is told by T. S. Kuhn in his excellent study, *The Copernican Revolution: Planetary Astronomy in the Development of Western Thought*, Cambridge, Harvard University Press, 1957.

9. Church authorities later required the text itself to be amended so that it would be equally ambiguous.

10. These facts are discussed by Ernest R. Hull, S.J., in *Galileo and His Condemnation*, London, Catholic Truth Society, 1913; see particularly p. 125. See also James Broderick, S.J., *Galileo: The Man, His Work, His Misfortunes*, New York, Harper & Row, 1964, pp. 101ff. and 127ff. For a discussion of the continued restriction of Catholic thinking, see *The New Catholic Encyclopedia* (New York, McGraw-Hill Book Company, 1967), particularly the article on the Oath Against Modernism.

11. Rudolf Bultmann first expressed this thinking in 1941 in the essay "The New Testament and Mythology," which is included in *Kerygma and Myth: A Theological Debate*, ed. by Hans-Werner Bartsch, London, S.P.C.K., 1957 (also Harper & Row Torchbooks). *Honest to God* by Bishop John A. T. Robinson (London, SCM Press Limited, 1963) introduced millions of Americans and other English-speaking people to this point of view.

Chapter V

1. Quoted by Alan McGlashan, *Gravity and Levity*, Boston, Houghton Mifflin Co., 1976, p. 33.

2. See Arnold Toynbee, ed., *Half the World: The History and Culture of China and Japan, op. cit.*

3. T. S. Kuhn, *The Structure of Scientific Revolutions*, 2nd edition, Chicago, The University of Chicago Press, 1974, pp. 112ff.

4. The study by Richard A. Kalish and David K. Reynolds is reported in their article "Phenomenological Reality and Post-Death Contact," *Journal for the Scientific Study of Religion*, Vol. 12, No. 2, June 1973, pp. 209-221.

5. Most of this material is dealt with in more detail in Chapter 5 of my book *Encounter with God*, Minneapolis, Bethany Fellowship, Inc., 1972.

6. The *Encyclopedia of Philosophy* (New York, The Macmillan Company and The Free Press, 1967) gives a brief account of Gödel's importance. Since his original proof, nearly a dozen additional examples of his findings have been provided.

7. Quoted in my book *Healing and Christianity, op. cit.*, p. 11.

8. Jerome D. Frank, *Persuasion and Healing*, 1st edition, New York, Schocken Books, Inc., 1969, p. 234.

9. Alan McGlashan, *Gravity and Levity, op. cit.*, pp. 37f.

10. Among them are Charles Panati's *Supersenses* and Adam Smith's *Powers of Mind*, which offer the best summaries of the new discoveries in this field. Lyall Watson's *Supernature* and Lawrence LeShan's *The Medium, the Mystic, and the Physicist* also give summaries of the material. *Space-Time and Beyond* by Bob Toben offers tentative explanations of these phenomena from the point of view of physics. Two of these books were written by highly qualified scientists, and the study by Toben grew out of conversations with two physicists, Jack Sarfatti and Fred Wolf. I know of no book which relates any of these experiences to Christianity and Christian religious experience except for my own book, *The Christian and the Supernatural*.

11. Quoted by Andrew Greeley in *The Sociology of the Paranormal: A Reconnaissance*, Beverly Hills, California, Sage Publications, 1975, p. 4, from a letter written by Freud to Hareward Carrington.

12. Jung described the occasion in Volume 10 of his *Collected Works, Civilization in Transition*, New York, Pantheon Books, 1964, p. 272.

13. Alan McGlashan, *Gravity and Levity, op. cit.*, p. 11.

Chapter VI

1. Plato, *The Republic*, 10.614B ff.

2. *Ibid.*, 7.514 ff.

3. Raymond A. Moody, Jr., *Life After Life*, Atlanta, Mockingbird Books, 1975, p. 48.

4. Dr. Osis described his preliminary study in his monograph *Deathbed Observations by Physicians and Nurses*, New York, Parapsychology Foundation, Inc., 1961 (Parapsychological Monograph No. 3). The entire project is reported by Karlis Osis and Erlendur Haraldsson in *At the Hour of Death*, (New York, Avon Books, 1977), including background material, methods and similar studies by other researchers.

5. *The Reality of the Spiritual World*, Pecos, New Mexico, Dove Publications, 1974, pp. 36f. This material is also published in my book *Discernment: A Study in Ecstasy and Evil*, New York, Paulist Press, 1978, pp. 146f.

6. J. B. Phillips, *Ring of Truth*, New York, The Macmillan Company, 1967, p. 119.

7. Ambrose, *On the Decease of Satyrus*, Book 1, 73.

8. *Letters of Sulpicius Severus*, Letter II, to the Deacon Aurelius.

9. Greeley discusses this survey in *Death and Beyond*, Chicago, The Thomas More Press, 1976, and in *The Sociology of the Paranormal: A Reconnaissance, op. cit.* A similar, nationwide survey in Great Britain in 1976 produced strikingly similar results. This data has been carefully analyzed by David Hay and Ann Morisy in "Reports of Ecstatic, Paranormal or Religious Experience in Great Britain and the United States—A Comparison of Trends," mimeographed paper, School of Education, Nottingham University, October 1977.

10. The study made in Iceland is reported by Haraldsson in his paper "National Survey of Psychical Experiences and Attitudes Towards the Paranormal in Iceland," in *Research in Parapsychology 1976*, edited by W. G. Roll, *et al.*, Metuchen, New Jersey, Scarecrow Press, Inc., 1977.

11. This British research is described by Osis and Haraldsson in *At the Hour of Death, op. cit.*, p. 14.

12. The study by Kalish and Reynolds is reported in their article, "Phenomenological Reality and Post-Death Contact," *Journal for the Scientific Study of Religion, op. cit.*

13. *Ibid.*, pp. 218f.

Chapter VII

1. The *Encyclopedia of the Unexplained*, edited by Richard Cavendish with J. B. Rhine as consultant (New York, McGraw-Hill Book Company, 1974), offers an interesting introduction to occult phenomena and an excellent bibliography. It is simply an attempt to give a view of this vast subject by describing the ideas that have been held in occult circles, as far as possible avoiding value judgments about their reality or lack of it.

2. Lyall Watson, *The Romeo Error: A Matter of Life and Death*, Garden City, New York, Anchor Press/Doubleday, 1975, p. 123.

3. *Ibid.*, p. 112.

4. *Ibid.*, p. 113.

5. *Ibid.*, p. 114.

6. Readers who are interested in finding out more about spiritualism will find further material in Chapter 5 of Andrew Greeley's *Death and Beyond, op. cit.*, Chapters 4 to 6 of *The Life Beyond Death* by Arthur Ford as told to Jerome Ellison (New York, G. P. Putnam's Sons, 1971), and in the articles on Mediums and Spiritualism in the *Encyclopedia of the Unexplained, op. cit.*

7. M. Lamar Keene, as told to Allen Spraggett, *The Psychic Mafia*, New York, St. Martin's Press, Inc., 1976, p. 163.

8. From an unpublished paper by Franz Riklin, "Psychotherapy and Death."

9. Edgar Herzog, *Psyche and Death: Archaic Myths and Modern Dreams in Analytical Psychology*, trans. by David Cox and Eugene Rolfe, New York, G. P. Putnam's Sons for the C. G. Jung Foundation for Analytical Psychology, 1967, pp. 191f.

10. Lawrence LeShan, *The Medium, the Mystic, and the Physicist: Toward a General Theory of the Paranormal*, New York, The Viking Press, 1974, p. 243.

11. Andrew Greeley, *Death and Beyond, op. cit.*, p. 106.

12. Hay and Morisy, "Reports of Ecstatic, Paranormal or Religious Experience in Great Britain and the United States—A Comparison of Trends," *op. cit.*

13. William Blake, *The Poetry and Prose of William Blake*, edited by David V. Erdman, Garden City, New York, Doubleday & Company, Inc., 1970, p. 544.

14. *Loc. cit.*

Chapter VIII

1. In *Guru, Psychotherapist, and Self* (Marina del Rey, California, De Vorss & Co., 1976), Peter Coukoulis discusses the wisdom of Eastern spiritual leaders in guiding people to wholeness. In many of his writings von Hügel referred to the influence of Abbé Huvélin on his life. Huvélin was a good example of the direction that was once available to Christians right in our own churches, but has become so much a lost art that we have to seek it elsewhere.

2. E. J. Fortman, *Everlasting Life After Death*, New York, Alba House, 1977, p. 114.

3. *The Comedy of Dante Alighieri, Cantica III, Paradise, op. cit.*, p. 347 (XXXIII, 142-145).

4. See J. T. Addison, *Life Beyond Death in the Beliefs of Mankind* (Boston, Houghton Mifflin Co., 1932), for a comprehensive study of the range of beliefs about life after death.

5. Baron Friedrich von Hügel in *Eternal Life* (Edinburgh, T. & T. Clark, 1929) provides a review of philosophical ideas about immortality and a future life.

6. Robert L. Wilken, "The Immortality of the Soul and Christian Hope," *Dialog*, Vol. 15, No. 2, Spring 1976, pp. 110-117.

7. *Ibid.*, p. 113.

8. Leonard J. Biallas, "Von Hügel's Contribution to Religious Studies and to Religion," *Horizons,* June 1, 1979, pp. 78f.

Chapter IX

1. Günther Bornkamm, *Jesus of Nazareth*, New York, Harper & Row, 1960, p. 128; see also pp. 64ff.

2. St. Augustine, *The Confessions*, I.1.

3. St. John of the Cross, *Dark Night of the Soul*, trans. by E. Allison Peers, Garden City, New York, Doubleday & Company, Inc., 1959, pp. 33f.

4. Austin Farrer, *A Faith of Our Own*, Cleveland, The World Publishing Company, 1960, p. 68.

5. Thomas Wolfe, *You Can't Go Home Again*, New York, Harper & Brothers, 1940, p. 743.

6. Andrew Greeley, *Death and Beyond, op. cit.*, p. 133.

Chapter X

1. C. S. Lewis, *The Great Divorce*, New York, The Macmillan Company, 1959, pp. 25f.

2. *Ibid*, p. 26.

3. C. G. Jung, *Modern Man in Search of a Soul*, New York, Harcourt Brace Jovanovich, Inc., 1955, p. 235.

4. *Loc. cit.*

5. Soren Kierkegaard, *Fear and Trembling* and *The Sickness unto Death*, trans. by Walter Lowrie, Princeton, New Jersey, Princeton University Press, 1954, p. 56.

6. C. G. Jung, *Memories, Dreams, Reflections*, recorded and edited by Aniela Jaffé, New York, Pantheon Books, 1963, pp. 353f.

7. Laurens van der Post, *The Face Beside the Fire*, New York, William Morrow & Company, Inc., 1953, p. 79.

8. These are the words of the central song of "The Man from La Mancha," which portrays beautifully and imaginatively the quest of Cervantes for meaning beyond this present earthly life.

9. John A. Sanford, *The Kingdom Within: A Study of the Inner Meaning of Jesus' Sayings*, Philadelphia, J. B. Lippincott Co., 1970, p. 101; see also p. 126.

Chapter XI

1. Carl Rogers' books, particularly *Client-Centered Therapy, On Becoming a Person*, and *Person to Person* (co-authored by Barry Stevens), can be helpful. I have also published a leaflet on listening (*Listening*, Pecos, New Mexico, Dove Publications).

2. Both Jung and Freud wrote extensively about the problem of transference, but these are among their most difficult and technical works. *Power in the Helping Professions* by Adolf Güggenbuhl-Craig (New York, Spring

Publications, 1971) is probably the clearest, most useful discussion of the subject for laypeople.

Chapter XII

    1. C. G. Jung, *Memories, Dreams, Reflections, op. cit.*, p. 316.
    2. *Ibid.*, pp. 317f.

Chapter XIII

    1. C. G. Jung, *Collected Works*, Vol. 11, *Psychology and Religion: West and East*, New York, Pantheon Books, 1958, p. 520.
    2. These seven novels by Charles Williams are *All Hallows' Eve, Descent into Hell, The Greater Trumps, Many Dimensions, The Place of the Lion, Shadows of Ecstasy,* and *War in Heaven.* Helen Luke has written an interesting study of these imaginative works, which is available from Apple Farm, Three Rivers, Michigan.
    3. It is not possible in these pages to give the full rationale for the understanding I am suggesting. I have discussed this position in more detail in my book *Discernment: A Study in Ecstasy and Evil*, New York, Paulist Press, 1978. Interested readers are also referred to Gustav Aulén's *Christus Victor: An Historical Study of the Three Main Types of the Idea of the Atonement*, New York, The Macmillan Company, 1951.
    4. C. S. Lewis, *The Problem of Pain*, New York, The Macmillan Company, 1961, pp. 106f.

Chapter XIV

    1. C. G. Jung, *Memories, Dreams, Reflections, op. cit.*, p. 340.
    2. *Ibid.*, p. 302.
    3. C. G. Jung, *Collected Works*, Vol. 8, *The Structure and Dynamics of the Psyche,* Princeton, New Jersey, Princeton University Press, 1969, p. 402.
    4. C. G. Jung, *Memories, Dreams, Reflections, op. cit.*, p. 354.
    5. Karl Jaspers, *Death to Life*, Chicago, Argus Communications, 1968, pp. 37 and 34.
    6. *The Other Side of Silence*, New York, Paulist Press, 1976, pp. 303ff.

Bibliography

Addison, J. T., *Life Beyond Death in the Beliefs of Mankind*. Boston: Houghton Mifflin Co., 1932.

Ante-Nicene Fathers. Grand Rapids, Michigan: Wm. B. Eerdmans Publishing Co., various dates.

Aulén, Gustav, *Christus Victor: An Historical Study of the Three Main Types of the Idea of the Atonement*. New York: The Macmillan Co., 1951.

————, *Dag Hammarskjöld's White Book: An Analysis of Markings*. Philadelphia: Fortress Press, 1969.

Badham, Paul, *Christian Beliefs About Life After Death*. New York: Barnes & Noble Books, 1977.

————, "Recent Thinking on Christian Beliefs: VI. The Future Life," *The Expository Times* 88 (1977), no. 7, 197-202.

Bailey, Kenneth, *The Cross and the Prodigal*. St. Louis: Concordia Publishing House, 1973.

Barnett, Lincoln, *The Universe and Dr. Einstein*. New York: Bantam Books, Inc., 1968.

Barrett, William F., *Death-Bed Visions*. London: Methuen & Co., 1926.

Becker, Ernest, *The Denial of Death*. Chicago: Free Press, 1973.

Bergson, Henri, *Creative Evolution*. Garden City, New York: Doubleday & Company, Inc., 1954.

————, *The Two Sources of Morality and Religion*. New York: Henry Holt and Company, 1935.

Blake, William, *The Poetry and Prose of William Blake*. Edited by David V. Erdman. Garden City, New York: Doubleday & Company, 1970.

Bornkamm, Günther, *Jesus of Nazareth*. New York: Harper & Row, 1960.

Boulding, Kenneth, *There Is a Spirit: The Naylor Sonnets*. Nyack, New York: Fellowship Publications, 1964.

Broad, C. D. *Lectures on Psychical Research*. London: Routledge & Kegan Paul, 1962.

305

————, *Religion, Philosophy and Psychical Research*. New York: Harcourt, Brace & Co., Inc., 1953.

Broderick, James, *Galileo: The Man, His Work, His Misfortunes*. New York: Harper & Row, 1964.

Bultmann, Rudolf, *Jesus Christ and Mythology*. New York: Charles Scribner's Sons, 1958.

————, "The New Testament and Mythology." In *Kerygma and Myth: A Theological Debate*. Edited by Hans-Werner Bartsch, New York: Harper & Row, 1961.

Burr, Harold Saxton, *Blueprint for Immortality: The Electric Patterns of Life*. London: Neville Spearman, 1972.

Campbell, Joseph, *Myths To Live By*. New York: Bantam Books, 1973.

Canale, J. Andrew, *Masters of the Heart*. New York: Paulist Press, 1978.

Carse, James P. and Arlene B. Dallery, *Death and Society: A Book of Readings and Sources*. New York: Harcourt Brace Jovanovich, Inc., 1977.

Castaneda, Carlos, *The Teachings of Don Juan: A Yaqui Way of Knowledge*. Berkeley: University of California Press, 1968.

Cayce, Hugh Lynn, *Venture Inward*. New York: Harper & Row, 1964.

Cerminera, Gina, *Many Mansions*. New York: William Sloane Associates, 1950.

————, *The World Within*. New York: William Sloane Associates, 1957.

Coukoulis, Peter, *Guru, Psychotherapist, and Self: A Comparative Study of the Guru-Disciple Relationship and the Jungian Analytic Process*. Marina del Rey, California: DeVorss & Co., 1977.

Crookall, Robert, *Casebook of Astral Projection*. Secaucus, New Jersey: University Books, 1972.

————, *Supreme Adventure: Analyses of Psychic Communications*. Atlantic Highlands, New Jersey: Humanities Press, Inc., 1975.

Dante (Alighieri), *The Divine Comedy*. Translated by Dorothy L. Sayers and Barbara Reynolds. Baltimore: Penguin Books. Vol. I: *Hell*, 1949. Vol. II: *Purgatory*, 1955. Vol. III: *Paradise*, 1962.

Dempsey, David, *The Way We Die: An Investigation of Death and Dying in America Today*. New York: McGraw-Hill Book Company, 1977.

Dodds, E. R., *The Greeks and the Irrational*. Boston: Beacon Press, 1957.

Dunbar, Flanders, *Emotions and Bodily Changes*. 4th ed. New York: Columbia University Press, 1954.

Eiseley, Loren, *All the Strange Hours*. New York: Charles Scribner's Sons, 1975.

————, *The Immense Journey*. New York: Random House, Inc., 1957.

Eliade, Mircea, *Shamanism: Archaic Techniques of Ecstasy*. Princeton, New Jersey: Princeton University Press, 1970.

Eliot, T. S., *The Cocktail Party*. New York: Harcourt, Brace & World, 1950.

————, *Four Quartets*. New York: Harcourt, Brace & World, 1968.

Encyclopedia of Philosophy. New York: The Macmillan Company and The Free Press, 1967.

Encyclopedia of the Unexplained. Edited by Richard Cavendish. New York: McGraw-Hill Book Co., 1974.

Ettinger, Robert C. W., *The Prospect of Immortality*. Garden City, New York: Doubleday & Company, Inc., 1964.

Farrer, Austin, *A Faith of Our Own*. Cleveland: The World Publishing Company, 1960.

Feifel, Herman, *New Meanings of Death*. New York: McGraw-Hill Book Co., 1977.

————, ed., *The Meaning of Death*. New York: McGraw-Hill Book Co., 1959.

Ferris, Theodore P., *Death and Transfiguration*. Pamphlet. Cincinnati: Forward Movement Publications, 1974.

Ford, Arthur, as told to Jerome Ellison, *The Life Beyond Death*. New York: G. P. Putnam's Sons, 1971.

Fortman, Edmund J., *Everlasting Life After Death*. New York: Alba House, 1977.

Frank, Jerome D., *Persuasion and Healing*. 1st ed. New York: Schocken Books, 1969.

Freud, Sigmund, *Beyond the Pleasure Principle*. Translated by James Strachey. New York: Liveright Publishing Co., 1961.

————, *Civilization and Its Discontents*. Translated by Joan Riviere. Garden City, New York: Doubleday & Company, Inc., n.d.

————, *The Future of an Illusion*. Translated by W. D. Robson-Scott. London: Hogarth Press, 1949.

Fuller, John G., *Arigó: Surgeon of the Rusty Knife*. New York: Thomas Y. Crowell Co., 1974.

Goethe's Faust. An abridged version translated by Louis MacNeice. London: Faber and Faber Limited, 1951.

Graham, Billy, *Angels: God's Secret Agents*. Garden City, New York: Doubleday & Company, Inc., 1975.

Greeley, Andrew M., *Death and Beyond*. Chicago: Thomas More Press, 1976.

————, *The Sociology of the Paranormal: A Reconnaissance*. Beverly Hills, California: Sage Publications, 1975.

Grof, Stanislav, and Joan Halifax, *The Human Encounter with Death*. New York: E. P. Dutton and Co., Inc., 1977.

Guggenbühl-Craig, Adolf, *Power in the Helping Professions*. New York: Spring Publications, 1971.

Guild of Pastoral Psychology, "Resurrection," papers given at the 1975 Summer Conference, 9 Phoenix House, 5 Waverley Road, London N8 9QU.

Hammarskjöld, Dag, *Markings*. New York: Alfred A. Knopf, 1968.

Haraldsson, Erlendur, *et. al.*, "National Survey of Psychical Experiences and Attitudes Towards the Paranormal in Iceland." *Research in Parapsychology*

1976: Abstracts and Papers, Nineteenth Annual Convention of the Parapsychological Association. Edited by W. G. Roll, *et al.* Metuchen, New Jersey: Scarecrow Press, Inc., 1977.

Harding, D. E., *The Hierarchy of Heaven and Earth: A New Diagram of Man in the Universe.* London: Faber and Faber, 1952.

Hay, David, and Ann Morisy, "Reports of Ecstatic, Paranormal or Religious Experience in Great Britain and the United States—A Comparison of Trends." Mimeographed paper. Nottingham, England: School of Education, The University, 1977.

Heisenberg, Werner, *Physics and Philosophy: The Revolution in Modern Science.* New York: Harper and Brothers, 1958.

Herhold, Robert M., "Kübler-Ross and Life After Death," *The Christian Century* 93, no. 13 (April 14, 1976) 363-364.

Herzog, Edgar, *Psyche and Death: Archaic Myths and Modern Dreams in Analytical Psychology.* Trans. by David Cox and Eugene Rolfe. New York: G. P. Putnam's Sons for the C. G. Jung Foundation for Analytical Psychology, 1967.

Heywood, Rosalind, ed. *Man's Concern with Death.* London: Hodder & Stoughton Ltd., 1968.

Hick, John H., *Death and Eternal Life.* New York: Harper & Row, 1977.

Hillman, James, *Suicide and the Soul.* New York: Harper & Row, 1965.

Höffding, Harald, *A History of Modern Philosophy.* Trans. by B. E. Meyer. London: Macmillan and Co., Limited, 1935.

Holzer, Hans, *Beyond This Life.* New York: Pinnacle Books, 1977.

Hull, Ernest R., *Galileo and His Condemnation.* London: Catholic Truth Society, 1913.

Huxley, Aldous, *The Doors of Perception* and *Heaven and Hell.* New York: Harper & Row, 1964.

Ignatius, Loyola, St., *The Spiritual Exercises of St. Ignatius.* Translated by Anthony Mottola. Garden City, New York: Doubleday & Company, Inc., 1964.

James, William, *The Varieties of Religious Experience.* New York: Longmans, Green & Co., 1925.

———, *The Will To Believe* and *Human Immortality.* New York: Dover Publications, Inc., 1959.

———, *William James on Psychical Research.* Edited by Gardner Murphy and Robert O. Ballou. New York: Viking Press, Inc., 1969.

Jaspers, Karl, *Death to Life.* Chicago: Argus Communications, 1968.

John of the Cross, St., *Dark Night of the Soul.* Trans. by E. Allison Peers. Garden City, New York: Doubleday & Company, Inc., 1959.

Jung, C. G., *Collected Works.* New York: Pantheon Books for the Bollingen Foundation. Vol. 8, *The Structure and Dynamics of the Psyche,* 1960. Vol. 10, *Civilization in Transition,* 1964. Vol. 11, *Psychology and Religion: West and East,* 1958.

————, *Memories, Dreams, Reflections*. Recorded and edited by Aniela Jaffé. New York: Pantheon Books, 1963.

————, *Modern Man in Search of a Soul*. New York: Harcourt Brace Jovanovich, Inc., 1955.

Kalish, Richard A., and David K. Reynolds, "Phenomenological Reality and Post-Death Contact," *Journal for the Scientific Study of Religion* 12, no. 2 (June 1973) 209-221.

Kaufman, Gordon D., *Systematic Theology: A Historicist Perspective*. New York: Charles Scribner's Sons, 1968.

Keen, Sam, in conversation with Ernest Becker, "The Heroics of Everyday Life: A Theorist of Death Confronts His Own End," *Psychology Today* 7, no. 11 (April 1974) 71-80.

Keene, M. Lamar, as told to Allen Spraggett, *The Psychic Mafia*. New York: St. Martin's Press, Inc., 1976.

Kelsey, Denys, and Joan Grant, *Many Lifetimes*. Garden City, New York: Doubleday & Company, Inc., 1967.

Kelsey, Morton T., *The Age of Miracles*. Notre Dame, Indiana: Ave Maria Press, 1979.

————, *The Christian and the Supernatural*. Minneapolis: Augsburg Publishing House, 1976.

————, *Discernment: A Study in Ecstasy and Evil*. New York: Paulist Press, 1978.

————, *Dreams, A Way to Listen to God*. New York: Paulist Press, 1978.

————, *Encounter with God*. Minneapolis, Bethany Fellowship, Inc., 1972.

————, "Facing Death and Suffering: A Group Experiment in Affective Learning," *Lumen Vitae* (Brussels) 28 (1973), no. 2, 281-295.

————, *God, Dreams, and Revelation*. Minneapolis, Augsburg Publishing House, 1974.

————, *Healing and Christianity*. New York: Harper & Row, 1973.

————, *The Hinge*. King of Prussia, Pennsylvania: Religious Publishing Co., 1977.

————, *Myth, History and Faith*. New York: Paulist Press, 1974.

————, *The Other Side of Silence: A Guide to Christian Meditation*. New York: Paulist Press, 1976.

————, *The Reality of the Spiritual World* (Pamphlet). Pecos, New Mexico: Dove Publications, 1974.

Kierkegaard, Soren, *The Concept of Dread*. Translated by Walter Lowrie. Princeton, New Jersey: Princeton University Press, 1944.

————, *Fear and Trembling* and *The Sickness Unto Death*. Translated by Walter Lowrie. Princeton, New Jersey: Princeton University Press, 1954.

————, *The Gospel of Suffering* and *The Lilies of the Field*. Trans. by David F. and Lillian Marvin Swenson. Minneapolis: Augsburg Publishing House, 1948.

————, *Purity of Heart Is To Will One Thing: Spiritual Preparation for the Office of Confession*. Translated by Douglas V. Steere. New York: Harper & Row, 1938.

————, *The Stages of Life's Way.* Translated by Walter Lowrie. New York: Schocken Books, 1967.

Kirsch, Hilde, ed., *The Well-Tended Tree: Essays into the Spirit of Our Time.* New York: G. P. Putnam's Sons, 1971.

Kirsch, James, *Shakespeare's Royal Self.* New York: G. P. Putnam's Sons, 1966.

Koestenbaum, Peter, *Is There an Answer to Death?* Englewood Cliffs, New Jersey: Prentice-Hall, Inc., 1976.

Krippner, Stanley, *Song of the Siren: A Parapsychological Odyssey.* New York: Harper & Row, 1975.

Kübler-Ross, Elisabeth, *Death: The Final Stage of Growth.* Englewood Cliffs, New Jersey: Prentice-Hall, Inc., 1975.

————, *Images of Growth and Death.* Englewood Cliffs, New Jersey: Prentice-Hall, Inc., 1976.

————, *On Death and Dying.* New York: Macmillan Publishing Co., Inc., 1969.

————, *Questions and Answers on Death and Dying.* New York: Macmillan Publishing Co., Inc., 1974.

Kuhn, Thomas S., *The Copernican Revolution: Planetary Astronomy in the Development of Western Thought.* Cambridge: Harvard University Press, 1957.

————, *The Structure of Scientific Revolutions.* 2nd ed. Chicago: The University of Chicago Press, 1970.

Langley, Noel, *Edgar Cayce on Reincarnation.* New York: Paperback Library, Inc., 1967.

LeShan, Lawrence, *The Medium, the Mystic, and the Physicist: Toward a General Theory of the Paranormal.* New York: The Viking Press, 1974.

Lewis, C. S., *The Chronicles of Narnia* (especially *The Lion, the Witch and the Wardrobe* and *The Last Battle*). New York: Macmillan Publishing Co., Inc., 1970.

————, *The Great Divorce.* New York: The Macmillan Company, 1959.

————, *The Problem of Pain.* New York: The Macmillan Company, 1961.

————, *The Screwtape Letters.* New York: The Macmillan Company, 1952.

————, *That Hideous Strength.* New York: The Macmillan Company, 1965.

Lindsey, Hal, *The Late Great Planet Earth.* Grand Rapids, Michigan: Zondervan Publishing House, 1973.

————, *Satan Is Alive and Well on Planet Earth.* Grand Rapids, Michigan: Zondervan Publishing House, 1974.

Lings, Martin, *Shakespeare in the Light of Sacred Art.* New York: Humanities Press, Inc., 1966.

Lorenz, Konrad, *On Aggression.* Translated by Marjorie K. Wilson. New York: Harcourt Brace & World, Inc., 1966.

Luke, Helen M., *Dark Wood to White Rose: A Study of Meanings in Dante's Divine Comedy.* Pecos, New Mexico: Dove Publications, 1975.

————, *Through Defeat to Joy: The Novels of Charles Williams in the Light of Jungian Thought.* Privately printed. Three Rivers, Michigan: Apple Farm, n.d.

Lynch, James J., *The Broken Heart: The Medical Consequences of Loneliness*. New York: Basic Books, Inc., 1977.

MacGregor, Geddes, *Reincarnation in Christianity*. Wheaton, Illinois: Theosophical Publishing House, 1978.

Macquarrie, John, "Death and Eternal Life," *The Expository Times* 89, no. 2 (November 1977) 46-48.

_____, *Principles of Christian Theology*. 2nd ed. New York: Charles Scribner's Sons, 1977.

McGlashan, Alan, *Gravity and Levity*. Boston: Houghton Mifflin Co., 1976.

Menninger, Karl A., *Man against Himself*. New York: Harcourt, Brace & Co., 1938.

Milner, Dennis, and Edward Smart, *The Loom of Creation: A Study of the Purpose and the Forces That Weave the Pattern of Existence*. New York: Harper & Row, 1976.

Monroe, Robert A., *Journeys Out of the Body*. Garden City, New York: Doubleday & Company, Inc., 1971.

Moody, Raymond A., Jr., *Life after Life*. Atlanta: Mockingbird Books, 1975.

_____, *Reflections on Life after Life*. Atlanta: Mockingbird Books, 1977.

Murphy, Gardner, *The Challenge of Psychic Research*. New York: Harper & Row, 1961.

Myers, Frederic W., *Human Personality and Its Survival of Bodily Death*. New York: Arno Press, 1975.

Myers, John, compiler. *Voices from the Edge of Eternity*. Old Tappan, New Jersey: Fleming H. Revell Co., 1971.

Netherton, Morris, and Nancy Shiffrin, *Past Lives Therapy*. New York: William Morrow & Co., Inc., 1978.

New Catholic Encyclopedia. New York: McGraw-Hill Book Company, 1967.

Noyes, Russell, "The Experience of Dying," *Psychiatry* 35 (1972): 174-184.

Ogden, Schubert M., *The Reality of God*. London, SCM Press Limited, 1977.

Oppenheimer, Robert, "Analogy in Science," *The American Psychologist* 11 (1956): 127-135.

Ornstein, Robert E., *The Psychology of Consciousness*. New York: The Viking Press, 1973.

Osis, Karlis, *Deathbed Observations by Physicians and Nurses*. (Monograph). New York: Parapsychology Foundation, Inc., 1961.

_____ and Erlendur Haraldsson, *At The Hour of Death*. New York: Avon Books, 1977.

Panati, Charles, *Supersenses: Our Potential for Parasensory Experience*. New York: Quadrangle/The New York Times Book Co., 1974.

Panteleimon, Archimandrite, *Eternal Mysteries Beyond the Grave*. Minneapolis: Light and Life Publishing Co.

Parabola, Myth and the Quest for Meaning 2, no. 1 (Winter 1977), (Tamarack Press).

Paton, Alan, *For You Departed: A Memoir.* New York: Charles Scribner's Sons, 1969.

Phillips, Dorothy, *et al.*, eds., *The Choice Is Always Ours.* Rev. ed. New York: Harper & Row, 1960.

Phillips, J. B., *Ring of Truth.* New York: The Macmillan Company, 1967.

Philokalia: Writings from the Philokalia on Prayer of the Heart. Translated by E. Kadloubovsky and G. E. H. Palmer. London: Faber & Faber Ltd., 1954.

Plato, *The Dialogues of Plato.* Translated by B. Jowett. New York: Random House, 1937.

Rawlings, Maurice, *Beyond Death's Door.* Nashville: Thomas Nelson, Inc., 1978.

Ritchie, George G., Jr. and Elizabeth Sherrill, *Return from Tomorrow.* Lincoln, Virginia: Chosen Books Publishing Co., Ltd., 1978.

Roberts, Jane, *The Seth Material.* Englewood Cliffs, New Jersey: Prentice-Hall, Inc., 1970.

———, *Seth Speaks: The Eternal Validity of the Human Soul.* Englewood Cliffs, New Jersey: Prentice-Hall, Inc., 1972.

Robinson, John A. T., *Honest to God.* Philadelphia: Westminster Press, 1963.

Rogers, Carl R., *Client-Centered Therapy.* Boston: Houghton Mifflin Co., 1951.

———, *On Becoming a Person.* Boston: Houghton Mifflin Co., 1961.

——— and Barry Stevens, *Person to Person: The Problem of Being Human.* Moab, Utah: Real People Press, 1967.

Sanford, John A., *Dreams: God's Forgotten Language.* Philadelphia: J. B. Lippincott Company, 1968.

———, *Healing and Dreams: A Succinct and Lively Interpretation of Dreams.* New York: Paulist Press, 1979.

———, *The Kingdom Within: A Study of the Inner Meaning of Jesus' Sayings.* Philadelphia: J. B. Lippincott Co., 1970.

Schrader, George A., ed., *Existential Philosophers: Kierkegaard to Merleau-Ponty.* New York: McGraw-Hill Book Co., 1967.

Schroeder, Frederick, and Craig Meyers, *The Potential for Spiritual Direction in the New Rite of Penance.* New York: Catholic Book Publishing Co., 1977.

Select Library of the Nicene and Post-Nicene Fathers of the Christian Church. 1st and 2nd Series. Grand Rapids, Michigan: Wm. B. Eerdmans Publishing Co., various dates.

Sexton, Mary Patricia, *The Dante-Jung Correspondence.* Northridge, California: Joyce Motion Picture Co., 1975.

Simonton, O. Carl, Stephanie Matthews-Simonton, and James Creighton, *Getting Well Again: A Step-by-Step Self-Help Guide To Overcoming Cancer for Patients and Their Families.* Los Angeles: J. P. Tarcher, Inc., 1978.

Skinner, B. F., *Science and Human Behavior.* New York: The Macmillan Company, 1953.

———, *Walden Two.* New York: The Macmillan Company, 1960.

Smith, Adam, *Powers of Mind*. New York: Random House, 1976.

Stevenson, Ian, *Cases of the Reincarnation Type*. Charlottesville, Virginia: University Press of Virginia. Vol. 1, *Ten Cases in India*, 1975. Vol. 2, *Ten Cases in Sri Lanka*, 1976.

————, "The Evidence for Survival from Claimed Memories of Former Incarnations," Journal of the American Society for Psychical Research 54, no. 2 (April 1960) 51-71; no. 3 (July 1960) 95-117.

————, *Twenty Cases Suggestive of Reincarnation*. New York: American Society for Psychical Research, 1966.

Sugrue, Thomas, *There Is a River*. New York: Holt, Rinehart and Winston, Inc., 1942.

Swedenborg, Emanuel, *Heaven and Its Wonders and Hell: From Things Heard and Seen*. New York: The American Swedenborg Printing and Publishing Society, 1925.

————, *Spiritual Diary*. 5 vols. New York: Swedenborg Foundation, Inc., 1966.

Tanquerey, Adolphe, *The Spiritual Life*. Westminster, Maryland: Newman Press, 1945.

Teilhard de Chardin, Pierre, *The Appearance of Man*. New York: Harper & Row, 1966.

————, *The Future of Man*. New York: Harper & Row, 1964.

————, *The Phenomenon of Man*. New York: Harper & Brothers, 1959.

Tibetan Book of the Dead. Edited by W. Y. Evans-Wentz. New York: Oxford University Press, 1957.

Tiller, William A., "Consciousness, Radiation, and the Developing Sensory System," *The Dimensions of Healing*. Los Altos, California: The Academy of Parapsychology and Medicine, 1972, 61-85.

Tillich, Paul, *The Courage To Be*. New Haven, Connecticut: Yale University Press, 1952.

Toben, Bob, in conversation with Jack Sarfatti and Fred Wolf, *Space-Time and Beyond: Toward an Explanation of the Unexplainable*. New York: E. P. Dutton & Co., Inc., 1975.

Tolstoy, Leo, *The Death of Ivan Ilych and Other Stories*. Translated by Aylmer Maude. New York: New American Library, 1960.

Toynbee, Arnold, *Life After Death*. New York: McGraw-Hill Book Company, 1976.

————, ed., *Half the World: The History and Culture of China and Japan*. New York: Holt, Rinehart and Winston, Inc., 1973.

Unamuno, Miguel de, *Tragic Sense of Life*. New York: Dover Publications, 1954.

van der Post, Laurens, *The Face Beside the Fire*. William Morrow & Co., Inc., 1953.

von Hügel, Baron Friedrich, *Eternal Life*. Edinburgh: T. & T. Clark, 1929.

————, *The Mystical Element of Religion as Studied in Saint Catherine of Genoa and Her Friends*. 2 vols. London: J. M. Dent & Sons, Limited, 1931.

Watson, Lyall, *The Romeo Error: A Matter of Life and Death*. Garden City, New York: Anchor Press/Doubleday, 1975.

————, *Supernature: A Natural History of the Supernatural*. New York: Bantam Books, Inc.

Watts, Alan, *Behold the Spirit: A Study in the Necessity of Mystical Religion*. New York: Pantheon Books, 1947.

Way of a Pilgrim and the Pilgrim Continues His Way. Translated by R. M. French. London, S.P.C.K., 1954.

Weatherhead, Leslie D., *The Case for Reincarnation*. Tadworth, Surrey: M. C. Peto, 1970.

Weldon, John, and Zola Levitt, *Is There Life After Death?* Irvine, California: Harvest House Publications, Inc., 1977.

White, Helen Chappell, *With Wings as Eagles*. New York: Rinehart and Co., Inc., 1959.

Wilken, Robert L., "The Immortality of the Soul and Christian Hope," *Dialog* 15, no. 2 (Spring 1976), 110-117.

Williams, Charles, *He Came Down From Heaven* and *The Forgiveness of Sins*. London: Faber & Faber Limited, 1946.

————, *Works (All Hallows' Eve, Descent into Hell, Many Dimensions, The Place of the Lion, Shadows of Ecstasy, War in Heaven)*. Grand Rapids, Michigan: Wm. B. Eerdmans Publishing Co., 1965. Also *The Greater Trumps*, 1976.

Williams, Charles W., and C. S. Lewis, *Taliessin Through Logres, Region of the Summer Stars, The Arthurian Torso*. Grand Rapids, Michigan: William B. Eerdmans Publishing Co., 1974.

Winter, David, *Hereafter: What Happens After Death?* London: Hodder and Stoughton Ltd., 1971.

Wolfe, Thomas, *You Can't Go Home Again*. New York: Harper & Brothers, 1940.